Curbside Diagnosis and Some Second Opinions

by

Glenn G. McBride M.D.

*To Sandy & Ron
with Best wishes
Glenn*

DORRANCE PUBLISHING CO., INC.
PITTSBURGH, PENNSYLVANIA 15222

This book is dedicated to our three lovely daughters, Betsy, Barbara, and Molly, and to their wonderful mother, Margaret, who is equally responsible, with the writer, for their existence.

The covers, both front and back, were created by Mary Griffith of the White Dove Gallery, Lakewood, Washington.

All Rights Reserved
Copyright © 2002 by Glenn G. McBride M.D.
No part of this book may be reproduced or transmitted in any form or by any means, electronic or mechanical, including photocopying, recording, or by any information storage and retrieval system without permission in writing from the publisher.

ISBN # 0-8059-5602-6
Printed in the United States of America

First Printing

For information or to order additional books, please write:
Dorrance Publishing Co., Inc.
643 Smithfield Street
Pittsburgh, Pennsylvania 15222
U.S.A.
1-800-788-7654
Or visit our web site and on-line catalog at *www.dorrancepublishing.com*

Contents

Foreword 1
The E.R.A. Era 2
What's in a Name? 5
The Length of the Handle on the Pump 7
"Clogged Pipes" 9
Who's in the Tree? 12
Curbside Diagnosis 14
The Moon and the British Isles 17
The Intruder 21
Who Pushed Me? 24
The All-Time Bestsellers 26
We Told You So! 29
The Wave Maker 33
Standing Ovations? 35
Who's Dead and Who Isn't? 37
Dent De Lion 39
A "No-Win" Situation 40
The Center of Gravity 42
A Tale of Two Brass Knuckles 45
ESP 48
The Wrong Bed 52
Genius or Idiot? 54
Switchbacks and the Hitchhiker 56
Two Dogs 58
How Old is Old? 62
Knights of the Sky 63
Courage—Skin Deep 68
"I Think I'm Going Crazy!" .70
Too Close Ahead 71
Who Is He? 73
A Foot in the Mouth 76
The Wicked Witches 77
Ward 21 80
From Failure to Victory 84
It's "No Emergency" 86

Butch	89
Woof! Woof!	91
Mindy's Heaven	93
Mr. Robin's Wormy Welfare State	95
An Apple from the Teacher	97
Rock'n'Roll Racket	99
A Few Good Tips	101
"But, I Had the Green Light!"	103
Soothing Melodies	105
A Handful of Thorns	106
To Quill or Not to Quill?	108
Have a Good Day	112
What's Yours Is Mine, and Mine Is Yours	114
Split Seconds and Great Moments	116
The Three S's of Death	120
The Turbulent Tutor	123
Computer #2345678	125
There's More Than One Way	126
The Gladiators	128
The Awkward Age?	130
"He Sure Spoiled My Dinner"	133
The Night Shift	136
Have Her Make the Call	138
A Trilogy	140
Life's Totem Poles	144
The Bad News Seismograph	146
Don't Be "Cowed"	148
Aging Gracefully	150
The Other Fellow's Turf	152
Big Men	156
You Can't Please Them All	160
The Age of Paradoxes	163
Trying Triads	166
Our Blind Side	168
Our Fantasies	172
Dr. Jonas Salk	174
Measles!	177
Miles Per Apple	179
"You Get What You Pay For?"	183
What's Par?	186
Second Options	187
They Don't Make 'Em Like They Used To!	190
Gustatory Gambits	192
Grandmother and the Indians	197

What a Way to Go	200
A Soft Answer	204
Medical Practice Hazards	207
Mr. Gray	211
"Inflation Is Under Control?"	214
Anatomies of Notes	217
Speakeritis	220
"Oh, Go Hang Yourself"	224
"If You're in Doubt, Don't!"	226
Collectibles	228
Sounds a Bit Fishy	230
The Causes and Cures of Some Weighty Problems	233
"You Gotta Know the Territory"	235
The Sampler	238
The Pot That Called the Kettle Black	239
Retrospective Vision	242
Life's Phases and Ages	244

Foreword

Just as any cook or chef has to have a recipe in order to create a tasty dish for others to consume, so it is with a writer. In both fields there has to be a plan of procedure in order to obtain the desired end product.

As a result, in the following hodgepodge the recipe consists of mixing a large amount of non-fiction with a smaller portion of fiction. To this is added a sprinkling of humor, some satire, and even a touch of pathos where such is indicated. Of course, the entire mixture is covered with a liberal coating of integrity.

In the end product resulting, all opinions expressed are those of the writer. These may or may not coincide 100 percent with the beliefs of the reader. Wherever there is a conflict of ideas, each individual involved should feel free to retain his or her own opinions.

If such an unlikely situation should arise, it might be wise for the reader to add a small amount of doubt and even a few drops of tincture of dissent to the mixture to make it more palatable and easier to swallow. However keeping an open mind also helps. Even if the differences are quite great, both parties should be willing to thoroughly explore the subject in dispute and if possible be anxious to modify their previously held opinions if they find enough evidence to so do.

It is the writer's hope the reader will enjoy the following missives and will appreciate the fact some are written with a generous amount of "tongue in cheek."

The E.R.A. Era

It has often been said this is a man's world. Much has been written and uttered about the lack of women's rights and the downtrodden state of the so-called "weaker sex." With repetition much of this is believed and accepted as factual. I would like to refute these inaccurate assertions. In so doing, I know I put my life and well-being in great jeopardy. While I will place irrefutable evidence before the reader, I realize that because of bias and prejudice, much of my logic will be ignored or twisted in its interpretation. In spite of these illogical possibilities, let us proceed to examine the evidence.

First of all, we must dispel the "weaker sex" myth. For example, have you ever noticed a married couple shopping together in a department store? The woman strides forth like an Amazon, displaying unlimited and inexhaustible strength. In contrast, the poor man follows along behind with stooped shoulders; a weak-kneed, staggering gait; drawn face; and sunken eyes. These last he casts furtively about, attempting to spy a chair or even a quiet corner of the floor upon which to collapse. It's a wise man who says, "Dear, I just remembered I have an errand at the bank, hardware store, or library. Can I meet you some place after you have finished shopping?"

In spite of this commonplace example of the superiority of female strength, there are those who will say, "This is just a single situation, and in no way convinces me women are stronger physically. Look at the Olympic Games and the weight lifting records of men vs. women. The men are much stronger."

Of course, on close examination, this argument doesn't hold water. Let's concede that men have bigger and even stronger muscles than women. This is largely the result of the mother's overfeeding their sons and constantly telling them if they eat well, they will grow up to be big and strong like their daddies. Then, later on, the girlfriend encourages the boy to do the heavy work by telling him how "big and strong" he is. Naturally, the male muscles will develop with this urging and extra usage. An elephant is stronger than a human, but which one captures, tames, and utilizes the strength of the other?

One need not search far to find other evidence of woman's toughness, both physical and emotional. While it is neither the fault of nor to the credit of either sex, who in this world has the babies? Who suffers the travails of childbirth labor? What is the husband doing while his wife is enduring this ordeal? He is in the waiting room, drinking gallons of coffee, smoking cigarette after cigarette, and generally feeling sorry for himself. And then, when the baby finally arrives, he strides forth bragging and acting like he had accomplished the feat all by himself.

Still further, if more proof of women's superior stamina is required, have you ever watched men and women swimming in cold ocean water? The men jump in, swim rapidly, and then head for shore, cyanotic in color and quaking in every muscle. The women, on the other hand, paddle leisurely about interminably and often pause for prolonged conversations with other female swimmers while still immersed in the frigid liquid.

In addition, tests indicate women tolerate extreme heat better than men. It has been shown that women have better night vision and more acute hearing. These equip them for much more efficient night feeding of their babies, allowing the husband to get his much-needed rest.

Also it is a well-known fact that women outshine men in verbal ability as well as in tasks requiring fine motor coordination and the kind of nimble finger movements necessary for typing, knitting, and piano playing.

In an entirely different field, the world of finance, women also predominate. Here again, some skeptics will argue and point out that men's salaries are greater than women's for the same work. Let us assume this argument is valid. However to get an accurate picture of the true fiscal state, we must progress to the bottom line. Who spends the most money month in and month out? Who controls the exchequer in the average home? Women do, of course.

There are many other examples of the supremacy of women which could be listed, but for the sake of brevity let me mention just one more proof of women's preeminence—the actuarial tables of life insurance companies. Who lives longer? Women do. We all know and accept this truth.

And so, without belaboring this subject further, I think you will have to agree that, on the average, women have been shown to be stronger, wiser, wealthier, and more in control of their environment than men. There may be an occasional exception here and there, but when this does occur, in nine out of ten cases, there is a woman in the background manipulating the actions of the supposedly dominant male.

Why is all this of any importance? In this day of the E.R.A. (Equal Rights Amendment) controversy, no matter what the final outcome of the legislative battle may be, women will still be predominant in this world of ours. Just don't ask me to referee any arguments pertaining to this subject.

P.S. I haven't even mentioned the power of women's tears.

THE SNUGGLERS

As anyone can see,
It takes two to snuggle;
The snuggler, and the snugglee.
Is the snuggler a he,
And the snugglee a she?
It really doesn't matter,
As long as they get free—
E—ven—tu—al—ly.

What's in a Name?

Things just aren't the same anymore. A few months ago, the garbage man left me a note on our garbage can which stated he would not pick up our can in the future if I persisted in putting fireplace ashes into it.

I can understand the logic of his thinking and can appreciate how one hot ember could cause considerable excitement for the garbage crew if that same ember did ignite a truck loaded with flammable material. What did give me reason to wonder, when I reflected on this, was that the present-day garbage can was in the past originally called an "ash can."

The more I thought about this matter, the more I realized that, as the years have rolled along, not only has the term "ash can" disappeared from our lingo, but also many other names and terms have completely changed. At the present time it takes considerable effort to keep alert mentally just to stay abreast of the changing terminology.

For example, an automobile tire is no longer a simple tire, but goes by a variety of names, such as a steel-belted radial, a six-rib polyester, or a 720, just to name a few.

In a different field, airline stewardesses are now flight attendants. Also, the majority of "flagmen" on highway repair crews are, in reality, "flag girls."

In the athletic sports field, the names of football positions and lineups are constantly changing. Today we have the "veer" formations in place of the former "I" or the old "single wing." The ends are no longer just plain ends, but are now called "tight" or "split." The backfield has such strangers as tailbacks or flankers in place of the old familiar halfbacks and fullbacks. In this game of muscle and brawn, the one position which elicits my heartfelt sympathy is the one known as the "weak safety."

In the business world as well as at home, computers and word processors have nearly eliminated typewriters and adding machines. Medically speaking, sedatives are now called "downers" and stimulants are "uppers."

In the political arena, President's Day has taken over for the birthdays of our famous forefathers, Washington and Lincoln. Armistice Day is now called Veteran's Day.

Automobiles are no longer named for the manufacturer, but are identified by one of several completely extraneous titles. Some of the favorites of these are those of the aristocracy (Coronet, Regal, La Baron, and Diplomat). Others are named after natural catastrophes (Tempest and Fury). Wild animals also are favorites (Bobcat, Cougar, Mustang, and Taurus). In this age of space exploration, using the titles of interplanetary phenomenon has become increasingly popular (Meteor, Nova, and Galaxy).

Then there are other unrelated automobile titles which it seems someone just picked out of the air (Volare, Granada, and Cutlass). Of course, none of these has anything to do with the appearance, performance, or as far as can be determined, the manufacturer. In addition, car motors don't seem to have horsepower anymore, but are rated according to their liters or CID, whatever the latter means.

Speaking of liters, it brings to our attention one of the real and major threats to our familiar terminology which lies just ahead of us, namely the metric system of weights and measures. If this is ever officially adopted, the adjustments which will be necessary will boggle our minds. Aside from the speed limits on our streets and highways, which will be listed in kilometers, trying to determine, according to the centigrade thermometer, what to wear each morning as we venture forth to begin the day will be the cause of considerable chaos.

Also, imagine the confusion in other aspects of our lives. For instance, the song "Five Foot Two and Eyes of Blue" would be completely out of rhythm. What can you do with "135 Centimeters" which would sound at all romantic?

In an entirely different field, that of computers, the terminology is so new it hasn't had time to undergo a lot of change, but in itself it is so confusing it complicates our already mixed-up mental processes. The average person, when listening to experts in this realm, is completely at a loss. On occasion, the computer language sounds like a veterinary clinic with such remarks as, "We now have megahertz when browser bytes our modem." It can be so confusing even a saintly person may become a cursor.

I could go on and on with other illustrations of our changing language flow, but suffice it to say that today it requires an alert mind to keep up with these "advances" in our modern nomenclature.

I guess we shouldn't be surprised with all these changes now that the old "ash can" is called a "waste disposal container" as the former "garbage man" himself is now known as a "health department engineer."

The Length of the Handle on the Pump

How many times have we been fooled into buying a book by the graphic and often lurid illustrations on its cover or by the comments of the reviewers on the back? While both of these enticements are commonly used to promote sales of the product by over-emphasizing certain aspects of the contents, they may or may not reflect a true picture of what is inside the covers. The old adage, "Don't judge a book by its cover," was never more true than it is today. This same saying can also apply to human beings. Don't let yourself be fooled into judging another person solely by his or her outward dress and appearance.

This truth was well illustrated to us several years ago in a hotel lobby in Vancouver, B. C. where we were waiting to attend a reception. Sitting across the lobby from us was a distinguished-looking couple. The man was very handsome as he sat erect in a dignified, nearly regal manner. His clothing was immaculate, as was that of his female companion. She was equally impressive in appearance and dress.

As we couldn't help but be impressed by them, we began to speculate about who they were and what their mission might be. Could they be emissaries from the queen of England on an inspection trip from the home land to this distant commonwealth? In our various guesses, we even mentally conferred upon them the rank of duke and duchess, or at least viscount and his lady.

Later that afternoon at the reception, we were surprised to see this same couple. When we talked to them, there was no hint of any typical Englishman's accent. On closer inspection, even their regal manner seemed to be markedly diminished. In spite of this diminution, they were a charming couple. In our conversation with them, he happened to mention they were from California and he was in the pickle exporting business. This, of course, was a far cry from the royal courts and regal titles we had previously mentally conferred upon them.

In an entirely different setting a few years later, when we went to see the movie *The Great Waltz*, then playing in Hawaii, we found ourselves sitting behind a half-clad native Hawaiian. He wore an old t-shirt and a pair of ragged cut-off shorts, plus a pair of beaten-up thongs which only partially covered his dusty and calloused feet. We couldn't help but wonder why a Strauss musical attracted this beach boy type.

We both felt he wouldn't last out the entire performance. This feeling was confirmed as soon as the intermission lights went on. He jumped up and disappeared. We thought this was the last we would see of him. However just as the second half was about to start, he returned to his seat. During the entire performance, he was very attentive, probably more so than we were as we spent considerable time observing his reactions to the musical.

After the show ended and as we waited for our bus, we found this same man standing next to us. When we asked if he had enjoyed the show, we half-expected to hear his reply in the "pidgin talk" so often used by the boys on the beaches. Instead we were surprised to hear his answer in perfect English. He thought the performance was excellent. As we talked, it became apparent he was well-acquainted with many other musical scores. Further discussion revealed he was a music professor at the local university as well as a graduate of an Eastern mainland musical conservatory, having obtained a master's degree. He was at the present time working toward his doctorate. In addition, when he found out we came from the state of Washington, he said, "I have a brother who is the chief of orthopedic surgery in a hospital in Vancouver Washington, and my sister is attending the University of Washington school of nursing."

How wrong we had been in our original snap judgment based solely on his outward appearance!

In reflecting on the above experiences, we decided it is a mistake to make hasty judgments about others based on superficial observations. These for the most part are often inaccurate, unwise, unjust, and prejudicial. There may be such a thing as love at first sight, but it would behoove each of us to take a second, third, and even a fourth look.

Again, the adage, "Never judge a book by its cover," nor a human by his or her external appearance, is still true. To put it another way, and to borrow a line from that musical composition "The Pump Song"—"It's hard to tell the depth of the well by the length of the handle on the pump."

"Clogged Pipes"

There is a common saying in baseball: "A player is as old as his legs." Once these extremities begin to lose their nimbleness and speed, the player had better start looking for some other line of work.

In a similar but slightly different way, the rest of us are as old as the arteries which supply blood to all of our various tissues. If for any reason this flow is slowed or cut off to any of our multiple parts, be it the brain, heart, kidneys, extremities, or any other area of the body, the function of that part will be impaired. As is often the case in this slowing or blocking process, more than one area may be involved at any given time.

A graphic illustration of this multiple involvement took place in the case of an elderly man. Prior to the introduction of the coronary bypass type of surgery, he had an acute coronary obstruction of a moderately severe degree. On a scale of one to ten, it would have been a five or six in its intensity. For several days immediately following the initial attack, he was in stable condition and resting well. His mental state was upbeat and his attitude optimistic. Financially he had no worries since he was nearing his retirement date, and in fact had enough accumulated terminal leave time to cover him until his actual retirement date arrived. All seemed to be well under control. However we were shortly afterwards to find how wrong this positive outlook would prove to be.

As if to add insult to injury, two days after his admission to the hospital he suffered a cerebral stroke with a resulting right-sided paralysis of his body and a complete loss of his ability to speak. And then, in addition, a few days later he developed gangrene of one of his toes. It seemed like the poor man was being attacked in rapid succession from all sides. When compared to a building, his problems were on all floors from the attic to the main floor and even the basement. To the average observer, what appeared to be a series of entirely different afflictions were in reality one disease manifest in widely different locations. In other words, this man was much older physically than his chronological age indicated.

Naturally his family was deeply disturbed, and rightly so. It was difficult for them to understand how a previously healthy man could suddenly, like the old one-horse shay, just seem to fall apart. The main spokesman for the group was the eldest son, a plumbing contractor from Seattle. Understandably he wanted to transfer his father to one of the larger hospitals in that city. While I could understand the son's fears and his desires, I also wanted to try to explain to him what was taking place; to point out that though his father's problems were widely separated in location, they were all part of one anatomical system—his arterial network—and his arteries unfortunately had happened to clog in several locations in a relatively short period of time.

In spite of my explanations, I could tell the son remained skeptical and unconvinced. While trying to find yet another approach in my explanation, I recalled what one of our professors had said in medical school many years before: "Your ability to communicate with your patients will depend largely upon your being able to talk to them in a language they can easily understand. For example, with a carpenter discuss his problems in terms referable to his work. With a plumber, illustrate his symptoms with pipes, gaskets, and other plumbing terminology. The same with auto mechanics and many other occupations."

With this advice in mind, and recalling that the son was a plumbing contractor, I said, "Come with me. I want to show you something that may help to explain your father's multiple problems."

It so happened that just prior to this time, several of the return pipes from the hospital steam radiators had become partially blocked within a relatively short period of time. The coincidence of these pipes and my patient's illness proved to be fortuitous. Taking the son, we headed for the hospital maintenance shop. Once there, I asked the head man, "Do you still have those return pipes from the steam registers?"

In answer to this he brought out all three of the partially clogged pipes. These were all similar in appearance, and each one was nearly completely plugged with sediment which had been accumulating over a period of many years. Without too much imagination, this sediment could be considered comparable to deposits of cholesterol in a human artery. I then asked the maintenance man, "Can you tell us which of the pipes came from the main floor, and which came from the other floors?"

His answer was, "There's no way to tell that. The pipes are all the same. We didn't see any need to label them as to which floor they came from."

The son of the patient added, "I agree with the maintenance man. Unless there was a good reason for marking the pipes, it would serve no purpose and would be impossible to tell which came from which floor."

He then looked at me and said, "Now I understand what you have been trying to tell me about my father's problems. From now on, please keep it up and use whatever treatments you feel are indicated."

Of course, these were the very words I wanted to hear. From then on, we were able to concentrate on treating the father's illness. As a result, his heart responded rather rapidly. In the following weeks his paralysis gradually lessened, and after several months his speech returned to a nearly normal level. We did have to amputate the gangrenous toe, but he didn't seem to miss it since he still had nine others remaining.

Just as the song about every cloud having a silver lining and the old saying that it is an ill wind that doesn't blow some good, so it is that even "clogged pipes" can on occasion be used with beneficial effect.

Who's in the Tree?

At this stage in time, we happen to live in a culture preoccupied with its roots; a culture with a curiosity about its ancestors and its family trees. As individuals a certain amount of interest in our ancestry is commendable, and it is only natural that, as we age, this inquisitiveness should and does intensify. In a way, it's similar to a salmon returning to the stream of its birth after several years on the high seas. While there is no real harm in this search for our past, a bit of caution is required. We must be on guard against those numerous and nefarious characters who attempt to exploit this inborn natural characteristic.

Genealogists, true and false, can be divided into three separate categories: The Bona Fide, The Inaccurate, and The Fraudulent. In this discussion, there is no need to be concerned with the first group since they are interested only with the truth and are anxious to be of assistance to those seeking true information. However beware of the second and third groups. To them, accuracy is only a secondary factor. This is especially true of group three. One easy way to identify either of the two is by their ever-present request for large advance fee payments prior to their release of their supposedly authentic information.

A case in point occurred recently. In the mail we received a very impressive and authoritative appearing certificate. This was accompanied by a letter explaining the certificate was an accurate reproduction of our family crest which they, the writers of the letter, had been able to obtain only after diligent research and much labor. The letter then went on to ask for a considerable sum of money, on receipt of which the writers would then send a complete genealogical study of our tribal tree.

The family crest illustrated was quite an elaborate-looking document. Prominently positioned across the face were three rather large black birds. It was not possible to ascertain whether they were plain blackbirds or just common black crows. Our name, having an Irish ring to it, probably prompted the makers of the crest to assume we were all heavy imbibers of alcoholic spirits and, therefore, the three old crows pictured would seem to be very appropriate. In all fairness to the makers, how were they to know they were dealing with a bunch of teetotalers?

In addition to the birds, also on the crest were the other accouterments usually found on regal emblems, such as shields, spears, maces, and guns. The whole document was quite overwhelming in appearance, especially since our family name, in large black letters, was positioned in a tangential manner running from the lower left to the upper right.

Of course our first reaction to this quasi-official document was a feeling of pride, followed by a blush of importance. Next came the problem of how to raise the necessary funds to pay for this study. It took considerable fortitude to resist the temptation to immediately send off for the promised complete family records. However on further consideration, doubts began to surface. Several questions arose. Was the record worth the money asked? Was all this really authentic? Finally, on more sober consideration, the answer was NO.

It would be interesting to know how many other families of our same name in the United States had received a similar mailing. How many of these families had sent the requested monies? If only 10 percent had responded, the makers of the crest would have been well paid for their efforts. We were happy we had skipped the offer.

We found later our family was not alone in this type of scam. A friend who owned a small boat docking facility located on a narrow body of water, appropriately named "The Narrows Marina," received a letter addressed to Miss Marina Narrows. The letter stated there were only a few "Narrows" families in the United States, and for a fee (a substantial one) they would be pleased to forward a complete family tree and genealogical study of her ancestors.

The marina owner, an ardent fisherman, and one who had heard many a tall tale from his fishermen customers, didn't bite at the extended bait. The whole proposition sounded mighty fishy to him, so he confined the letter to his wastebasket.

While he couldn't be blamed for tossing out the request, perhaps it would have been worth the asking price to find out what sort of genetic fabrication these authors could produce. In other words, to learn "who's in Marina's tree?"

Curbside Diagnosis

Personal toothbrushes and individualized dental plates may be necessities, but the use of customized automobile license plates is something else.

Whatever the etiology of this new fad—be it the need for personal recognition, or because of some hidden frustration, or perhaps even a touch of rebellion, or maybe just a bit of good old American humor—these plates do serve a definite useful function. With their advent, long gone is the need for such antiquated and often inaccurate methods of personality studies, such as the standard behavioral psychology tests, palmistry, astrology, and the use of the once popular ouija board. No longer is it necessary to spend hours waiting for your favorite psychologist to tell you about your fellow man and his foibles.

These personalized licenses supply all of us with a much more open and dependable approach for psychological observations of our daily contacts with our neighboring motorists. They are available for all to use in evaluating other drivers. Without much effort on our part, these plates furnish a rather quick method of analyzing a car owner's mental makeup and often reveal excellent clues as to who and what is behind the steering wheel of the other vehicles. These clues, in turn, allow us a bit of time in which to maneuver and to decide on how wide a berth to give the driver in question.

It should be noted that all motorists can be placed in one of several different categories. The majority are conservative and are the ones who feel the old-fashioned state-issued license plates are adequate. The second group are those who use the customized plates merely to state their manes: **GREEN, WHITE,** or **BROWN**. Still others employ the licenses as a means of advertising their occupations or businesses: **BIG MAC; EAT PIE; TYPIST; CPA; STORK** (obstetrician); **2TH AKR; CUT UP, SO N SO,** or **SUIT UR** (all of the last three are surgeons); **ABC** and **ABC XYZ** (school teachers); **SUE U** and **DIS BAR** (lawyers); **SWT 2TH** (candy maker); and **FEET** (podiatrist). While the meanings of most of the above are clear and quite harmless, they do hint at the presence of an extroverted personality.

On the other hand, the nature of some plates do send a signal to other drivers about the owner of the nearby car and allow him to take precautions. For instance, is the owner a music lover, and if so, what type of music is his favorite? **T42 24T, BLUE MOON, KNEED U**, would indicate a musical comedy fan. A lover of classical music would likely have: **OPERA, SONATA, ALLEGRO**, or **BACH**. A music teacher might use **ETUDE** or perhaps **DO RE ME**. Still others could choose **JAZZ, SWING**, or **DXY LND**. Those interested in dancing might use **2 STP** or **SQR DNC**. Of course at the bottom of the list would be **HRD ROC**.

Flower growers and gardeners could have **SUITE P, PANZE**, or **2 LPS**. Athletic buffs—**JOGGER, SKI BUM, 10 IS, PADLIN**, or **QTR BAK**. Some plates could have double or triple meanings. **PEDDLE** could refer to either a bicyclist or to a door to door salesman. **DRY DOC** might be a ship repairman, a boring college professor, or a teetotalling MD.

Some licenses denote a bragger or some other unfavorable personality characteristic. These are illustrated by **SPOILT, MACHO, 4U2NV** (for you to envy), **MR. BOSS, OH YEAH**, and **ELITE**. Some are more for owner identification: **ALL MYN, PA, MA, HIS**, and **HERZ**. One all-inclusive matrimonial plate was **MR MRS, EVE** and **EDDY**. These last two could be combined to form one word, **EVEDDY**. Others express desires, such as: **ITS FUN** and **B MYN**. Still others admit making an error: **MIZTAK** or having a troublesome car, **LEMON**. Some even compliment other drivers: **URAQT**.

A degree of wanderlust is illustrated by **NVR HOM**. Frustration is expressed by **O NURTZ** and **NO KIDS**. Some express fatigue **AWL IN** or other bodily conditions, **FRZZIN**.

Some plates carry subtle messages. These often are so vague they tend to divert the attention of the other motorists to an extreme degree as the latter attempts to decipher their hidden meanings. **KID NK9** took a while to solve and caused enough driver distraction a collision nearly resulted before the answer (child and dog) became apparent.

Then there is that group of plates which make no sense to anyone except the owner, his immediate family, or his close friends. **GETWJT** is an example. Some even attempt to include all of the family initials in one plate: **IMZASA, MARGLE**, and **GLEMAR** for example. These are quite diverting and even at times downright dangerous.

It hasn't been mentioned previously that one of the unwritten rules of the game in formulating a customized plate is, if possible, to spell incorrectly the word being used. We have already seen examples of this above, but to reiterate, **TENNIS** contains only six letters and would fit on the plate quite well. However it seems to be more fun to use **10 IS**. Likewise, **SUSIE** is modified to **SOOZ E** or **SUZZI**. Of course these variations, in turn, reveal moderate aberrations of the owner's personality.

In summary, it is fun to look for these unusual licenses as they often brighten a somewhat routine or boring trip. It is also possible that someday even you might want such a set of these personalized plates for your car. If so, you may be surprised to find what you choice will reveal about your own character traits.

The Moon and the British Isles

It was a summer to remember. It was the time of the first manned moon landing. The world was agog with amazement that such a feat could be accomplished; that mere mortals could conquer all of the hazards of outer space; the dangers of the first touchdown; the doubts about how far they would sink on their first steps on the moon's surface; the uncertainty of their chances for a successful return to earth; and all of the other unknowns of this historical event.

Coincidentally, at this same time, Margaret and I had a journey of our own. Without meaning to detract from the accomplishments of the astronauts, we had, in a lesser degree, some moments of apprehension, as well as some doubts about the outcome of our own adventure. We had just arrived in England and were confronted by a few unknowns and fears. If you have ever ridden in a London taxi you will understand our feelings. In the first place, these cabs travel on the wrong side of the road. This, in itself, is somewhat nerve-wracking for someone from the "colonies" who is used to the other side. The situation becomes even more hazardous when the driver, an affable fellow, happens to be so excited about the moon landing he insists on discussing all the details with us as we zip along. In addition, he had a disconcerting habit of turning to face us in the back seat while we were barreling along at top speed. This, of course, raised the hackles on the back of our necks. While the astronauts had their problems, they at least had a trained support team in addition to a well-thought-out plan of action for their safe return. In contrast, we had our problems, but no definite plans for our safe return.

The London taxies, when compared with our cabs, are quite unique. First of all, they are all exactly alike: black, spotless, shiny, and driven by neatly dressed, uniformed drivers. In addition, the cabs present an imposing sight as they wait, several abreast, for the traffic signal to turn green. Once this occurs, their charge, reminiscent of that of a stampede of wild buffalo, begins. Woe be to any unsuspecting pedestrian who is not really nimble of foot.

One other problem confronting a visitor to the isles is the proper precautions to take when crossing a street. At home, he or she looks first to the left and then to the right. In the British Isles, exactly the opposite procedure must be used. This adjustment requires a few days. During this period, the dangers are compounded by the onrush of the aforementioned taxi horde.

As strange as it seems to us, the origin of the use of the left side of the road, according to one belief, came about in the following manner. During the golden days of knighthood, as most of the knights were right-handed, they carried their swords on their left side. When riding their steeds on the narrow trails, and when meeting an oncoming horse and rider, they would each automatically veer to the left so that their swords would not clang together. As the trails widened into streets and wagons became common, this action of staying to the left persisted.

How we in America, and many other parts of the world, took the opposite side of the road is not entirely clear. One theory is as follows: As time passed, the revolver gradually replaced the sword. It must be presumed that most of the rides were right-handed and kept their weapon on their right side. As a result, they veered to the right when meeting oncoming riders. One other theory is the rebellious settlers in America just didn't want to do anything in the same manner as those in the home country. It is interesting to speculate about the exact origin of this custom.

But I digress. On our arrival in England, we were amazed to find out how excited the English and the Scots were about the lunar landing. When they learned we were from the United States, and especially from Washington (many thought this was Washington, D.C.) they plied us with question after question. All of this was quite flattering, but I'm afraid our answers didn't live up to their expectations.

The primary purpose of our trip was to try to locate the site of Margaret's ancestor's castle in Kent. Margaret had read a good deal about the history of the Weyburn family (Margaret's mother's side of the tree) so we have some specific information regarding the castle's original site. Without too much difficulty, we located what was left of the ruins, and while there learned many of the building blocks had been carted away and used for the nearby town's city hall and library. This experience was quite a thrill, to find she was in a way part of the history of the area.

Getting used to the British currency was a little tricky. The pences, shillings, and pounds were a bit beyond my abilities to decipher. On one occasion, when buying a newspaper, and not knowing one coin from another, I held out the largest I had. The paper man said, "That's a bit big, isn't it, guv?" I then held out a handful of coins and let him take his pick. On another day, while riding in a two-decker bus next to the entrance, the conductor (a woman) told me to collect from any new passengers. Before I could object, she left for the second level. While it's one thing to be confused by the local currency, it's another to collect this same money for an unknown amount of fare. As a result, when a new arrival boarded, I would hold out my hand and he or she would drop some coins into my palm. Fortunately, each passenger seemed to know how much was owed. By the time the conductor returned, I had quite a bit of loot for her. I never did understand how she kept track of the passengers and when they were supposed to debark. I hope she was able to balance her accounts at the end of the day. Later on, between our first and second visits to the isles, some of the confusion in the coins was eliminated when the currency was changed to one hundred pence per pound. This made a lot of sense, but even so it wouldn't have helped me in collecting the fares on the bus.

Riding in a bus or taxi on the wrong side of the road was hazardous enough, but driving in our own car was even more so. Because of my apprehension about having to contend with sitting on the right side of the car and trying to shift with my left hand, we had reserved an automatic shift vehicle. However on arrival at the rental agency in Glasgow, we were told that there were no automatic shift cars available. As a result, off we went in a stick shift model trying to get used to the rearview mirror located in its upper left-sided position. Fortunately, the clutch pedal was in the right place for the left foot, just like at home.

After being honked at and cursed, we learned early to stay in the far left-hand lane of the carriageways (similar to our freeways) except when passing. Motorists are somewhat the same the world over. In contrast, the Scottish people were very cordial and charming when personally contacted. They seemed to be more than happy to give us directions, plus other assistance. One man from whom we bought some postcards in Edinburgh insisted on putting the stamps on the cards. One policeman, when Margaret asked him if he could direct us to one of the castles, said, "Of course I can, lass." In another situation, a garage mechanic took the time and effort to crawl out from under the car he was repairing and, with a smile, directed us to our destination.

We had reservations for approximately every other night. On the intervening days we were on our own. This arrangement gave us a bit of leeway in our travels and seeing Edinburgh, the Highlands, Lock Lomond, and Abbotsford (the home of Sir Walter Scott) were a few of the highlights of Scotland. In England, the Lakes country, Portsmouth, Dover, Kent, Canterbury, Stratford on Avon, Windsor, and London were major stops. We were surprised to see so much open countryside. In all our travels, we drove one thousand seven hundred miles.

As we approached London, we tried to arrive at what we thought would be a quiet time—vehicularly speaking. Later we found that no such time existed. Having studied the maps carefully, we were sure we knew when and where to make the proper turns, only to find that on arriving at the right turn corner, a large sign proclaimed NO RIGHT TURN. The next corner greeted us with NO LEFT TURN. We finally ended up in Piccadilly Circus, which is aptly named as it is a large traffic circle as busy as one of the three rings of a Barnum and Bailey Circus. Somehow, largely by good fortune, we did find our hotel, only to learn it didn't have a reservation for us. With some difficulty, we were able to remedy this oversight.

Having experienced a sample of London's traffic, we couldn't turn in our rental car fast enough. From then on, taxies, subways, buses, and walking formed our means of locomotion. London is a fascinating place historically; Westminster Abbey, the National Museum, London Bridge, the Thames River, St. Paul's Cathedral, Buckingham Palace, the Tower of London, the farmer's market, the Soho District, the theater district, and the parks were all worthwhile.

Prior to arriving in London, we had spent a couple of days in Stratford on Avon, the site of the William Shakespeare Theater. This was an extremely interesting and somewhat quaint little town. For both of us, it proved to be the site of a rather weird adventure in the form of "The Intruder," of which more will be told in subsequent pages.

The Intruder

The crisp crunch of footsteps on the crushed cinder pathway which led to our cabin door awakened us from our sound sleep at 4:00 A.M. In the dim light of the room, we could see the interior door knob turn slowly, first clockwise, then counter-clockwise. We could even sense the pressure being applied to the other side of the door in the intruder's attempt to force it open. After failing on his first try, our visitor slowly retreated. Again there were the crunching footsteps on the pathway. To add to the suspense, his shadowy form passed by the opaque bathroom window as he sought an alternate entry route. After a few minutes of silence, the shadow once again appeared, and again the footsteps approached the front door.

Our small cottage, surrounded by trees and bushes, was in an isolated area of the grounds located about a hundred and fifty feet from the entrance to the main mansion. There was no telephone nor any other means of communication with the outside world. Lacking anything better, I grabbed the only weapon I could find, a heavy candlestick, and with considerable trepidation, awaited the next move of our unwanted visitor. This was not long in coming.

We had arrived in Stratford on Avon late the preceding afternoon and had been directed by the tourist bureau to this bed and breakfast hostelry. The main house was an imposing mansion surrounded by extensive grounds and gardens. The whole area was enclosed by a high brick wall. This estate was conveniently located in a section of the town near the Shakespearean Theater, the restaurants, and the shops. On first glance, we felt we were indeed fortunate to find such a glamorous place in which to stay. We had no idea of what was to transpire within the next sixteen hours.

As the Shakespearean festival was in full swing, the town was filled to overflowing with visitors. Because of this, the main mansion was completely filled. The woman in charge said we could occupy the guest chalet. This, before we saw it, sounded mighty glamorous, but in reality, it was no more than a made-over tool house with curtains. It was remotely located in the garden area behind the main house.

After moving in, I asked for the key to the door but was told this would not be necessary since no one ever locked up in this neighborhood. I thought this seemed odd, but decided to go along with the local ground rules.

In Stratford, at festival time, the big event each evening was the Shakespearean play. This attracted tourists from all over the world, as well as many local English people from the neighboring areas. Tickets were hard to get since each performance was usually a sellout.

Being tired from a long day of driving, we decided to skip the play, relax, and go to bed early. Before turning in, I did locate a fragile door lock of sorts which could be loosely fastened once we were inside the cottage. The windows were at ground level. Their catches were rather old and somewhat flimsy. None of these facts caused us any apprehension, and in a short time we were both sleeping soundly. However once we heard the crunching footsteps on the walkway, all sleepiness vanished. Our minds went on full alert our adrenalin production increased, and our entire self-survival apparatus automatically clicked into high gear. As I stood by the door, still grasping the candlestick, several thoughts raced through my mind. Was this some common thief intent on robbery? Was Jack the Ripper on the prowl once again? Or was this someone who had seen too many Shakespearean tragedies and was now acting out the part of **MACBETH, HAMLET**, or some other violent character? Which ever part he was enacting, I decided to give the bloke a tussle before giving in. I meant to mete out **MEASURE FOR MEASURE**.

My chest felt like **THE TEMPEST** raged within. My mind was somewhat confused, but I was reasonably certain this rascal was not **THE MERCHANT OF VENICE**, nor even the friendly Avon representative coming to call. One thing was certain—this whole experience was no **MIDSUMMER NIGHT'S DREAM**. I'm sure that most of you readers would agree the situation was not **AS YOU LIKE IT**. Of course, we at that moment had no idea as to what the final outcome would be.

The stranger again tried to force entry at the door. By this time, I had partially recovered the use of my vocal cords, so I asked him, "What are you trying to do?"

His reply, in beautiful standard English, was, "I'm looking for my room."

There is something about the dignified way the English people enunciate their words which tends to put a listener at ease. Their manner of speaking can be reassuring even as they plunge in the rusty blade and, to use the slang expression, "do you in." I'm sure our intruder wanted me to open the door. This was not my intention, so I told him, "This is not your room, so be off."

Finally after several tense minutes, he realized he was not welcome, so he took his leave. As he departed, we did get a brief glimpse of his face just before he disappeared into the garden bushes. Needless to say, there was no more sleep for us the rest of the night. Margaret said, "I won't stay another night in this place."

I didn't need any persuading and immediately concurred. With the coming of full daylight, we started to pack and then locked all of our luggage in our car.

Later, at breakfast, this same blighter was sitting at a nearby table. He was a mean-looking character. From the moment we entered the dining room, he kept watching us. As soon as our breakfast was served, and he knew we would be occupied for a few minutes, he left the room. On his return, he had a somewhat disappointed look on his face. We both felt he had gone to our unlocked chalet to pick us clean. Be that as it may, he had been thwarted in his attempt to rob us.

I guess that the moral to this story, if there is one, can be summarized in that old saying, "When in Rome, do as the Romans do," but when in Stratford on Avon, be sure to choose a room with a stout lock on the door.

As we left this beautiful and quaint little town, we felt perhaps our experience had been a **COMEDY OF ERRORS** and possibly **MUCH ADO ABOUT NOTHING,** but we were very happy to know that in the final analysis, **ALL'S WELL THAT ENDS WELL.**

Who Pushed Me?

Without a moment's hesitation, and without thought, he plunged into the swirling, turbulent river in an attempt to rescue a frantic victim who thrashed wildly about in the muddy waters. Later, on shore, when the hero was asked how he had managed to have the courage to leap into the icy waters, he replied, "It all happened so fast, and there was so much confusion, I didn't have time to think. However, there is one thing I'd like to know, and that is, WHO PUSHED ME?"

Heroic acts of courage, like Christmas presents, come in different-sized packages to each of us. Some individuals have large amounts. Some, small. Some display theirs ostentatiously. Others keep theirs hidden. Some share theirs. Others, not. Just as muscular strength can be increased by repeated exercise and usage, so also can courage be developed and strengthened by practice and repetition.

Frequently we read about an act of heroism and self-sacrifice performed at the risk of the hero's life for some complete stranger, such as running into a burning building to bring out those trapped inside. Many times these heroic deeds are done on impulse, without any thought of the possible consequences to the one performing the act.

As heroic as many of these acts are, and without meaning to discount what these individuals have accomplished, there is another form of heroism which is even greater. This is the kind of courage which requires much thought, effort, and perseverance. These are acts which are not done on a sudden impulse, but are done over and over on a prolonged basis by an individual who regularly performs some arduous or distasteful task for the benefit of others without asking or expecting any reward in return.

A case in point was Hilda, an elderly woman who worked nights year in and year out cleaning suites in an office building. She was a small, wiry person who moved rapidly at her work, but always took time to smile, call others by name, and ask some question about them or theirs. In contrast, she rarely volunteered any information about herself. She never complained, although it was obvious that often she did not feel well. Her work required much bending, stooping, and lifting, all of which was difficult for her because of her chronic arthritis. Each evening, as the last of the daytime office workers departed, she faithfully and regularly appeared to begin her lonely tasks which would occupy her until early the next morning.

One evening a few days before Christmas, as she was busily working and humming to herself, a late office worker asked her if she was going to be with her children during Christmas Day. She had three grown sons and daughters whom she had supported all through their high school and college years following the death of her husband, many years prior. With a broad smile, which seemed sincere and showed no evidence of reproach, she replied in the negative. "They all have their own families and friends and are so busy they sometimes forget to ask me to come for Christmas or for other holidays."

In retrospect, she had worked night after night, year after year, doing lonely, hard, and dirty work in order to feed, clothe, house, and educate these three children without expecting any reward in return. This dedication to her family portrayed a degree of heroism in its ultimate form.

Some critics might say she was too self-sacrificing and did not demand enough; that she should have trained her ungrateful offspring to be more generous and appreciative. Possibly these critics are correct, possibly not.

On the other hand, perhaps in a small way this lady was simply reflecting some of the light which emanated from the Cross of Calvary two thousand years ago by the one who sacrificed everything for us without expecting any reward in return.

At least one thing is certain—the cleaning lady need never ask, "WHO PUSHED ME?"

The All-Time Bestsellers

If asked, how many of us could correctly name the three all-time bestselling books, the same three which year after year head the list? While the names on the current bestseller lists are constantly changing and their titles come and go, the all-time champions consistently, year in and year out, remain at the top of the list.

In choosing these first three, most of us would be able to name the number one, the Holy Bible, as the premier bestseller. However we might stumble in our choices of numbers two and three. We would probably feel that works of Dickens or Shakespeare or some other famous author would come next. We, undoubtedly, would be surprised to find the next two on the list are the English language dictionary and the modern American telephone directories. Unexpectedly, we would find both of these two make for interesting reading. While the subject matter does change rapidly in each, there is much to be learned as well as considerable amusement to be derived from their pages.

Because the Bible is changeless and should be read daily, and because the dictionaries make additions or alterations only in a somewhat grudging and unyielding manner, most of the remainder of this missive will be confined to the study of the ever-changing telephone directories.

The reader may have serious doubts about any interesting subjects, or any amusement these ubiquitous volumes may have to offer, but let me mention a few names which can be found in their pages. To list a few, for starters there are: Running Boys, Do, Stray, Tripp, and Fall. In addition are those names of the anatomical and pathological varieties such as: Head, Lipp, Hart, Foot, Toews, Spinale, and Colon; plus Lipoma and Emndometritis, to say nothing of Burpee and Belcher.

Without meaning to make fun of anyone because of his or her name, a serious perusal of the phone book will reveal some interesting information and tell us a good deal about our past and about the occupations of our ancestors. A few well-known examples are such names as Carpenter, Baker, Archer, Carver,

Houseman, Porter, Butler, and Miller.

While it is true that some of our ancestor's names were derived from their occupations, it is also possible a person's name may, in turn, subconsciously influence him or her in their choice of their life's work. A few years ago, two college students decided they would do a little light and frivolous research on this subject. They discovered some interesting facts. In their studies they found a doctor named Doctor; a veterinarian named Barker; a physiologist who worked with dogs named Purp; a tree farmer, Alder; a trumpeter, Hornblower; and a surgeon named Cutter. In addition, a restaurateur, Aita; a horse raiser, Filley; and autobody repairman, A Dent; a mountain climber, Peak; a logger named Stump; a labor crew boss, Foreman; a dermatologist, "Red" Rash; a cucumber farmer, Pickles; and a skeet shooter named Ames, just to mention a few.

We all know it is not possible for us to pick our names at the time of our birth, but we do have the privilege of changing or modifying them in later years. However these changes may give rise to some problems as far as family relationships are concerned. In addition to the familial upsets, there are also the inconveniences of having to change all of our personal records (birth, postal, bank, etc.) as well as having to redo the initials on our handkerchiefs, silverware, and stationery.

Because of these problems, it is often easier for us to change our life's goals and enter an occupation which would not be in conflict with our original name. For instance, an Aker or a Hertz would be better off skipping dental school; a Dye or an Ails should get out of premedical training. Mr. Ash should give up his life-long desire to be a fireman. Mr. Steal and Mr. Crook should both abandon their courses in law school and law enforcement.

Often combinations of two or more names can cause unfortunate connotations when aligned with a particular vocation. An accounting firm of Hit and Miss would not tend to inspire confidence, especially if their secretary was a Miss Stake. Al Said and Dunn wouldn't sit well in the publishing business.

Conversely, names may be either accidentally or purposely joined in combinations which are advantageous to the partnership. A few examples are: The Aqua-Sprinkler, well diggers; the pickle company of Dill and Sweet; the legal firm of Judge and Jury; the golf course owners of Driver and Putts; and the target range operators, Bow and Archer. In addition, the brew makers, Still, Hopps, and Stein; plus the stockbrokers, Bull and Bear.

Some individual's names inadvertently become attached to occupations or life styles with resulting unfortunate connotations, like: the interior decorator named Askew; the druggist, Pill; the secret service operator, Messinger; the mattress maker, Pillow; and the recluse named Loveless. Depending on one's attitude about gambling, there is a question as to whether or nor Jack Potts should ever visit or live in Las Vegas or Reno.

In this day of equal rights for the sexes, there is an increasing tendency for girls intent on matrimony to want to retain their last name and combine it with that of their husband-to-be. While most combinations, like Black-Smith are innocuous, there are dangers present if this same tendency is allowed to go unchecked. It doesn't take much imagination to project into the future a few years to find the telephone book filled with the likes of: Stern-Wheeler, Stear-Roper, Ice-Cream, Waffle-Irons, Cole-Shooter, Alotta-Noyes, Strong-Mann, Cowan-Bull, Moon-Shoot, Carr-Hopp, Ball-Chaney, Phon-Booth, Burger-Bunn, Rice-Paddie, Peach-Pitt, Curtain-Draper, Leake-Fawcett, and Knott-Able.

As upsetting as the above examples might be, there are even more hazardous possibilities confronting some women. This group consists of those young ladies with certain given names. These girls should flee in terror, never acknowledging the presence of a suitor or potential mate if his name is not appropriate. For instance, a girl whose given name is Paige should ignore all advances by males surnamed Turner; and April should stay away from Mr. Showers; as should May or Misty avoid Mr. Day. Of course, Peach and Pitt should never consider marriage to each other. Some other potential combinations to be avoided are: Doris Oppen, Sandy Beach, Rose Budd, Penny Pinch, Nina Ten, June Bugg, and Anna Toomey to name a few. A mixed racial marriage between a Swiss girl and a Vietnamese man could result, heaven forbid, in a Heide Ho.

While the above dissertation has barely scratched the surface of information available in the telephone books, it has brought to the fore a few up until now ignored facts. Much more research has been left for the reader in his or her frequent references to these volumes. This study is especially fruitful when visiting a new locale or large metropolitan areas.

When considering all of this world's literature, it is easy to understand why these books remain at the top of the bestselling lists year in and year out. All three have much to offer. For wisdom, inspiration, and salvation, the Holy Bible, read on a daily basis, is supreme. For pure knowledge and mental advancement, the dictionary is tops, but for light diversion and pleasure an occasional perusal of the telephone directories is hard to beat![*]

[*] All of the above proper names are bona fide, and are listed in one or more of the many telephone books.

We Told You So!

Just as we have begun to make progress in the field of racial integration, a new problem of divisiveness has appeared to plague us. This is not based on political ties nor on the differences of the sexes, but on something even more fundamental. Already the battle lines are drawn. Only one question remains: Just exactly who will be the adversaries and who will be the allies? Whatever the alliances, it is only a matter of time until the firing begins. Because of the fanatical nature and beliefs of some of the combatants, we, the noncombatants, are in grave danger of being cut to ribbons in the crossfire as we huddle in no-man's land.

You may feel we are overreacting and this crisis is not important. Don't be deluded by the apparent calm which exists now. The emotions of the opposing forces are at a fever pitch and will not be held in check for long. These divergent beliefs of the various factions are very real and in many cases so firmly held that they are, in essence, engraved in stone. The ironical aspect of this entire threatening tempest, and what makes it seem so improbable in this land of plenty, is these new schisms are based on a few differences of opinion regarding what elements in our diets are good or not good for each of us.

What has caused this ruckus to occur? It seems all of a sudden we have become a society of nutritional experts. Approximately every third person has become an authority on the various components in our foods. The end result is a host of widely divergent schools of thought regarding the current dietary requirements necessary for our well being.

The membership of each particular clique is largely influenced by one or more of the following factors:

1. The latest dietary article in a newspaper, magazine, or booklet.
2. The most recent advice given by a clerk in a health food store or at the vitamin counter in the local drug emporium.
3. The last word on dietary matters given by a persuasive and domineering friend.

4. The utterances or writings of some prominent personage who has gained a reputation in some entirely unrelated field of endeavor, such as law, politics, acting, or science. This type usually feels his or her knowledge in his chosen work qualifies him as an expert in all other phases of life and especially in the field of nutrition.
5. A miscellaneous collection of other factors such as family traditions, racial customs, religious beliefs, or personal idiosyncrasies.

It is not surprising to find very few members of the above groupings have made an in-depth study of human physiology, of our actual nutritional requirements, or of the real chemical composition of their favorite foods. Much of their attentions has been localized on one particular food element such as salt, sugar, or fat. For the most part, they have developed a negative approach to these foods, and put a "black hat" on one or more of them. Unfortunately, just often enough to furnish credence to their misconceptions, someone who could be classified as learned in dietary matters goes off on a tangent in his or her beliefs. Occasionally this tangential track is sincere, but often it is based largely on pecuniary return. Evidence of this is to be found on the paperback shelves in many stores (note the number of books on diet which are prominently featured there). In one recent display there were two books written by the same M.D. One was based on an all-protein diet. The other was on a non-protein diet. A woman who had purchased both books was asked which one she was following. Her reply, "A little of each."

Generally speaking, the food faddists can be divided into several primary categories. The "no salters" should probably head the list. For them, table salt is a "NO-NO." Sodium is the villain here. Not all of these sodium abstainers are completely consistent, however, as they will eat ham, flavor their food with catsup, and drink carbonated beverages with gusto. Of course, all of these are rich in sodium. Recently one of the cola companies bowed to public pressure and is now labeling their carbonated drinks as "salt free."

The "no white sugarers" come next. Ordinary white sugar is very bad with this group. "Natural" sugars are best, with honey and fruit sugars heading their approved list. Where these advocates place cane and beet sugars in nature's scheme of things is somewhat vague.

Next, come the "anticholesterols." This group will meticulously cut off all surface fat, but in an inconsistent manner, eat prime ribs and steaks with all their attendant intramural fat. It is doubtful that, given their full choice, they would pick really fat-free dried beef or "jerked venison."

The number of "vitamin addicts" probably exceeds the total of all of the above categories, but they are usually not quite as vocal. They often take large overdoses of their favorites, which are at the present time vitamins C and E. However the vitamins of choice do change from year to year. Aside from the "spilling" of the overage and the waste of money, relatively little harm results. Occasionally one of this group may develop a vitamin intoxication from an overdose of fat-soluble vitamins, such as vitamin A.

Another classification in our list is of a somewhat variegated variety. This group consists of several diverse types such as the "alfalfa sprouters," the "wheat germ advocates," and the "granola chewers," to name a few. These folks are, by and large, quite innocuous.

The rest of us fit in what, for want of a better name, will be called the "ordinary ones."

You may ask, "Why are any of the above-mentioned classifications alarming or significant? What is there about these groups that presents any threat to the welfare of our nation?"

The answer to these questions is simple. These various dietary splinter groups are becoming more vehement and militant with each passing month. In some instances, near violent encounters have occurred when a "salter" sat next to a "no salter," or when an "ordinary one" was placed near a "no white sugarer."

As there is no really accurate method of detecting a food faddist by his outward appearance, these mismatches do occur frequently. In contrast, it is easy to separate alcoholics and smokers from those who do not indulge because of the tell-tale signs which each of these habits exhibit. The lack of similar clues by the food faddists can result in near mayhem at otherwise happy gatherings. Unless the faddist makes an open declaration of his beliefs or in the rare instances of a "carrot gobbler's" yellowish scleral tint, very little can be done to prevent the close encounters of the various dietary extremists.

As bad as these encounters are with complete strangers or even with close friends, the real tragedy occurs when there is a split within a family group. There was recently an example of this where a "no salter" was married to a "no white sugarer." Cooking a meal in this household was nearly impossible. In another case, a young girl was farsighted. She told her boy friend, "Our engagement will never work. I'm a granola skimmed milk type, and you're a coke and Twinkie fan." As stormy as the past has been in the clashes between dietary groups and subgroups, the future is even more threatening. As the militancy of these factions increases, it is easy to imagine the chaos which might arise in public eating places or on common public carriers. Riots and fights could erupt at anytime. Complete anarchy might not be far behind.

Perhaps the only solution to this problem is to return to segregation once again—this time based on dietary factors. While complete separation in buses, trains, and planes might not be feasible, perhaps in larger auditoriums this could be accomplished. For instance, the "no sugarers" could be located on the right side, and the "no salters" on the left. The right balcony could be reserved for the "anticholesterols" and the left balcony used by the "vitamin advocates." All other aberrations from the average could use the rear balcony. The main floor center could then be occupied by the "ordinary ones."

While these divisions might cause a separation of friends or even of families, this system could assure each person of being in a compatible dietary group. Less arguments would ensue, and the threat of violence would be decreased. Even more importantly, this segregation might be a blessing in disguise. By identifying all of the "ordinary ones," it might be a means of helping to unify all of the various splinter groups. As a result, whenever an "ordinary one" who, incidentally, thinks a well-rounded diet is all that is required for good nutrition becomes ill or dies, all of the others could, with unanimity, arise, point their fingers, and shout, "WE TOLD YOU SO!

The Wave Maker

Do you have a skeleton in your closet? Do you have a hidden secret of some previous trespass of which you are ashamed, which you guard well and which you hardly recall even to yourself? Most of us do.

I carried one of these with me for many years. My wife, Margaret, was the only one who knew of its existence. She told me it wasn't important and certainly not world shaking. I didn't see it in that light.

The episode which caused my mental trauma started over sixty years ago. It came about quite innocently one day when I was applying for membership in a Chicago YMCA. My main interest, at the time, was in the swimming facilities available. The young man showing me around the entire building was very polite, attentive, and anxious to please. He seemed to be trying hard to get me to take out a membership.

When we finally did arrive at the area housing the lockers, showers, and the large swimming pool, I was really excited. The building was quite new and everything was very modern and immaculately clean. The pool was Olympic sized and very alluring. There were no swimmers present when we entered the spectator's gallery overlooking the pool. I was to find out later that two swimmers had just vacated the pool seconds before our arrival. The water was crystal clear and sparkled like a thousand twinkling lights as the waves bounced off the pool sides and each other. All in all, it was a beautiful sight, especially for one who was used to much less sumptuous swimming accommodations.

My guide was chattering away about all the advantages of a "Y" membership, pointing out the finer features of the pool and its accouterments. I was thoroughly impressed by all I saw and a bit nervous at such glamorous surroundings. Looking at the waves and wanting to appear interested, as well as uphold my part of the conversation, I asked, "Do you have a wave maker, too?"

As soon as I had opened my mouth, I knew I had made a big mistake, but the words tumbled out beyond my ability to recall. Following my question, my guide turned to me with a look of complete amazement, and asked, "What did you ask?"

By now, near panic had seized me, and I was completely powerless to hold back the words, "Do you have a wave maker, too?"

"That's what I thought you asked."

His look of incredulity now changed to one of disdain. I don't recall what his parting remarks were, but it was apparent he had lost all interest in me and hoped I would seek some other swimming facility. In spite of his lack of enthusiasm, I did join the "Y" and had many enjoyable swims there in the next four years. During this period, I told no one of my faux pas and tried to put the entire event out of my mind. In this, I was partially successful only because of my preoccupation with a heavy scholastic schedule. Three years later, just prior to our wedding, I did confess to Margaret this misstep, along with a few other of my past behavioral aberrations. However for many years, this one misspoken question remained a smudge on my mental blackboard. Whoever heard of a "swimming pool wave maker?" How ridiculous could a person be?

Finally, some forty years later, while on a trip to Scotland, we were sightseeing in Edinburgh. As the day was sunny and warm, we gravitated to the nearby seashore. There we found a large outdoor natatorium filled with, literally, hundreds of people. Above the pool, on a large billboard, all the positives of the pool were advertised. Prominently featured, in large letters, was one of its outstanding attractions. The pool had a LARGE WAVE MAKER.

At last, to be finally vindicated and have this burden removed from my back after so many years brought a smile to my face and lightened my step. What a relief it was to dust off this old skeleton which for so long had resided in my mental closet and send it on its way.

This may all seem ridiculous to anyone who has read this far and, in a way, it really is. However, before you pass judgment, go back into your own past and recall how many emotional waves you may have created in your own life by some silly "wave maker" episode.

Standing Ovations?

Have you ever wondered where the custom of "standing ovations" at public performances originated?

Most of us have attended a concert, speech, or play where we were so fascinated we didn't want it to end. In contrast we have also, on other occasions, witnessed an event from which we wished we could quietly escape without causing a commotion.

In many productions, the active participants seem to be having all the fun. By all that is fair, they ought to be the ones who should have to pay to be admitted. A case in point occurred years ago when I was in an amateur (emphasis on the amateur) play promoted by a small community church group. For our dress rehearsal, we visited the local tuberculosis sanatorium, supposedly to entertain the patients. Our production was so bad we all began to feel sorry for the audience. The poor people couldn't escape. When the final curtain closed, they all silently and thankfully filed out to return to the safety of their rooms. The whole production was a disaster. This catastrophe occurred in the pre-standing ovation era.

Now everything is different and there has been a rather sudden and marked increase in the frequency of standing ovations given, regardless of the caliber of the performers. While some of these ovations may have been well earned, many have not. One recent stage production was abominable and interminable and yet it was given a standing ovation.

That these standing ovations have reached near-epidemic proportions has puzzled me. Searching for a reason for this increase in frequency has lead me to what I believe is the logical answer. As is true in many epidemiological studies, the real answer to a problem is often quite simple—so simple, in fact, that it is strange it was not discovered much sooner. In my study of this ovation phenomenon, I found the answer is not to be found in any sudden upgrading of the quality of the performers nor in any additional merits of the entire program. Nor is it due to any expanded magnanimity of the audiences.

The answer is much more obvious.

In studying the seating arrangements of the average audience, one fact becomes quite apparent. By looking closely, it becomes apparent that usually the most expensive seats are front and center. Often, sprinkled throughout this choice section are a rather high percentage of the affluent older age group. Unfortunately, many of these same elderly individuals have a common, nearly universal trait—they do not tolerate prolonged sitting in one spot for very long. They often become, to use the slang expression, "rump sprung" quite quickly.

Of course, the obvious remedy for this ailment is to remove the pressure on the affected part as soon as possible. Thus, with the first wave of applause, those so afflicted with this malady see an opportunity for relief. Up they jump with a smile and a happy sigh, and occasionally even with a cry of "Bravo." Being near the front of the auditorium, their action initiates a general uprising. Even those who are quite comfortable or those who may have been dozing during the performance are forced to stand up in order to see the stage or to get their heads elevated to where there is enough oxygen to sustain consciousness. The end result of this mass uprising, as reported in the following day's newspaper, is that, "The performance was given a standing ovation."

What can the rest of us learn from this somewhat common phenomenon? From the view point of the audience, let them be aware that from an anatomical and physiological standpoint, the human brain can take in and absorb external stimuli only as long as the other parts can withstand the pressures put upon them. One more word of caution: Remember also, at the end of any performance, don't be stampeded the next time someone jumps to his feet in front of you. Hold steady in your seat, conserve your strength, breath easily, and don't panic.

From the perspective of the performer, if you desire a standing ovation, there are two possible answers. Number one, be sure to get your act together and do your best to make it a superior production. Number two, if you lack talent of inherent ability, be sure to prolong your presentation past the endurance point of the pressure areas of at least some of the audience.

Whichever method you use, it always helps to have at least a few of those so afflicted with a low sensory threshold sitting near the front and center.

Who's Dead and Who Isn't?

A visitor from outer space would be completely confused and have reason to wonder who is running the show here on earth. He or she would have reason to be completely mystified by the apparent paradoxes present. For example, on the one hand we willy-nilly terminate lives via the abortion route and then, on the other hand, go to extraordinary means to preserve individuals who have lived a long and useful life but who now are in a semi-vegetation state. Our world is no longer a "cradle to the grave," but instead is rapidly becoming a "test tube to the repair shop" habitation. In place of saying, "I'm off to see my doctor," it's "I'm going to see my General Electric repair man."

One of the dilemmas which has confronted mankind for many generations and is now becoming more and more of a problem with each advance in medical science is the question of how hard should we try to preserve life in every individual no matter how dire his or her situation may be. After all, there is such a thing as allowing a person to die with dignity.

A prominent ophthalmologist tells the story of a patient who was involved in a one-car automobile accident. The car he was driving ran into a telephone pole. It seems the driver, the patient, had markedly impaired vision and was legally blind. His wife, who could see, but who didn't drive, coached him by telling him when and how much to turn the car right or left, etc. The cause of the accident? The driver's hearing aid momentarily failed to function. Incidentally, his cardiac pacemaker kept right on working during and after the crash. Sounds a bit weird, but is it?

Then, there was another case in which the patient had a massive cerebral hemorrhage and ordinarily would have died. However his cardiac pacemaker was in perfect running condition and kept his heart functioning. Was he alive or dead, and if the latter, who would ultimately have the authority to disconnect the pacemaker?

While the goal of the medical profession is to prolong life by using as many aids as possible, including someone else's heart, lungs, liver, or kidneys, how long should these and other procedures be employed—for a reasonable time, or for as long as there is any sign of life? At what point should the use of these substitute organs be discontinued in an individual case?

In other words, who will make the final decision as to WHO'S DEAD AND WHO ISN'T?

Dent De Lion

Have you ever been unjustly maligned, unfairly derided, cursed, treated as a pest, and banished to the scrap heap? If such has been your lot, you can appreciate the plight of the poor dandelion.

Beautiful and decorative in its youth, graceful and fragile in its old age when its head becomes a white ball of fluff; a source of food in salads, cooked greens, and tea, this creation of nature is truly multifaceted.

Named "Dent De Lion" by the French because of the deep tooth-like notches on its leaves, it is a ubiquitous and wild inhabitant of the world which soon withers and wilts when put in captivity.

Because of its many attributes, let us no longer continue to treat this native asset in such a shabby manner as we have in the past. Let us give it the respect it deserves, especially when it grows in our neighbor's yard.

A "No-Win" Situation

Most formal debates end with a winner and a loser. A few may conclude in a draw or a win-win. In contrast, there is one debate which always ends as a "no winner." This is the age-old, futile, and unproductive discussion between husband and wife about which one works harder. No matter how well one of them presents the most logical answer, the opposite member will not admit defeat.

If these arguments were ever to come to arbitration, no rational outsider should be foolish enough to volunteer as a referee. If in a moment of reckless abandonment he did so, he would discover, to his dismay, that both of the combatants would turn upon him with marked vigor. To illustrate, one day a friend of mine came upon a couple arguing vociferously. In addition, the husband was physically assaulting his wife. My friend realized this was not as it should be, so he intervened. The next thing he knew the wife was hitting him over the head and back with her umbrella. Naturally he beat a hasty retreat.

Several years ago, we had neighbors who used to spend considerable time and effort arguing about how hard each of them worked and how easy their partner's life happened to be. She would say, "You just go down to your office, sit around, talk to your co-workers, drink coffee, and make a few phone calls."

He, in turn, would answer, "All you do is a little cooking, sweeping, dusting, play with the four children, and spend the rest of the time chatting with the neighbors.

Of course, for us it was a bit embarrassing to have to sit and listen to them harangue at each other, especially when we realized no good would come from their debates. Luckily, neither of us took sides in these skirmishes. We both felt that in spite of their differences they probably were in love with each other. At least we assumed this to be true since they had four young children.

After several years of these arguments, the final resolution of their battles occurred in the following manner. One Thursday the woman received a telephone call telling her that her father was critically ill and she had better hurry to his bedside, which was located several hundred miles away. She immediately departed, leaving her mate to care for the children for the next few days. Following her departure, we didn't see him for the next three days. Finally late on Sunday evening, the wife returned home.

In the past, prior to this fateful weekend, it had been the husband's habit to pass our house on his way to work each morning. On these journeys, he would trudge up the street in a slumped-over gait looking like he was going to his doom. We used to feel sorry for him, not that he had such an arduous job, but because he acted like he believed it was such. We could understand how he may have thought his wife had the better lot in life when all she had to do was to stay home, grocery shop, clean, cook, and supervise the house, plus dress, bathe, and ride herd on four small wildly active children. Of course, in addition she had numerous volunteer jobs with various charities, the church, the community, and the children's school. Then there was considerable time spent in chauffeuring the children to their ever-present lessons in ballet, swimming, soccer, baseball, and preschool.

However on the Monday morning after his wife's return, and after he had spent three and a half days caring for these same wild little ones, he strode forth to work. His appearance was completely altered from his previous work days. He looked like a liberated man. Instead of his usual caved-in appearance, his head was held high, his chest expanded, and his stride was like that of a soldier on parade. No longer was there the look of a man condemned to a life of hard labor.

She, in turn, having just returned from several days of strenuous duty taking care of a somewhat difficult patient, her father, was delighted to be back home once again in the bosom of her family. She immediately pitched in and tackled her multiple duties with a renewed vim and vigor, even humming a lively tune as she worked.

Never again did we hear any mention of how hard either of them worked nor how easy was the life of the other partner. Once more all became serene and happy in their home.

I guess the lesson for all of us to learn from the above is to never, never feel sorry for ourselves and to never compare our lot in life with that of others, especially with that of our spouse. If, per chance, we do on occasion think such thoughts, we must be sure to quickly erase them from our minds immediately and never be foolish enough to give voice to them, for no matter how we might express these ideas, they will always result in a "NO-WIN" situation.

The Center of Gravity

With a resounding thud they both landed on the floor. He, a three hundred pounder on top, and she, a one hundred ten pounder on the bottom. They both, and she in particular, had ignored one of the basic fundamentals of the science of physics—namely, the importance of the center of gravity.

Speaking of physics, many of us consider this a dull subject; one reserved for the egghead type of student and not of much practical value for the average person. Part of this lack of enchantment for the subject may stem from our early classroom experiences. One high school teacher, when asked to explain a physics problem, would reply, "Luk in de booook." Similarly, when questioned, a college professor's standard reply was, "It's either square or it isn't square." The students never did figure out what this answer had to do with anything. It was a noncommittal reply, about the same as the veterinarian's statement, "Most horses are four-legged, but not all four-legged animals are horses." Neither statement made much sense.

In spite of our prejudices regarding the study of physics, it is a subject of great practical value. For example, grasping a live electrical wire while standing in a puddle or turning on a radio while sitting in the bathtub may prove to be a person's last mistake. In the same vein, ignoring the principle of gravity while leaning out of an eighth-story window may prove to be one's downfall (no pun intended). In a less spectacular way, the use of the principle of leverage with a fulcrum and lever is something we all use frequently, such as in the changing of an automobile tire or lifting a heavy load. These activities, plus such mundane acts as boiling an egg and many other daily activities, are all basic tenets of physics.

We often hear the expression, "The bare floor is so much colder than standing on the rug." If the floor and rug are in the same room, they are both the same temperature. The difference in our perception is explained by the fact the bare floor conducts the heat from our feet at a faster rate than does the rug. Again, applied physics.

But let us return to the couple mentioned above who landed on the floor in such a spectacular way, illustrating how catastrophic the ignoring of a basic physical principle can be. This debacle occurred in one of the larger hospitals where a petite nurse was trying to change the sheets of a bed-confined patient. For those unfamiliar with hospital procedures, a few words of explanation about this task are appropriate. In order to accomplish the sheet exchange without removing the patient from the bed, it is necessary to roll the patient onto one side near the edge of the bed. The lower sheet on the other side can then be folded up and a fresh sheet applied. Then the patient is rolled onto his or her other side and the process repeated. It is a fairly simple chore, but does require a sense of leverage and balance.

In the case in question, the patient was a very, very large man. He was not only large physically, but also large in his influence as a member of the board of trustees of the hospital. In addition, he was a big contributor of money to this same institution. In other words, he was a man of much weight in more ways than one.

By way of contrast, the little nurse was very small. In the process of changing the sheets, it was necessary for her to reach around the rotund man in order to fold the old linen and replace it with new. In so doing, she failed to notice that in rolling him onto his side, she arrived at the point of no return as far as the center of gravity was concerned. During this maneuver, the patient, usually an astute and knowledgeable person, was also unaware this critical stage had been reached.

Perhaps if the weights of the two had been reversed or even if they had been equal, the end result might have been different. However such was not the case. With a feeling akin to terror, the small nurse was the first to become aware things were getting out of hand. A split second later, this same feeling came to the attention of the patient. Try as she did with all of her strength, she was unable to stem the inevitable flow of his massive weight pushing against her. This problem was similar to the relentless movement of a mighty glacier in its migration down a mountain side. Except for the difference in their respective speeds, the end result was the same as each completed its journey with a mighty crash. Fortunately for him, and unfortunately for her, she served as a shock absorber and bumper for his large frame as they both hit the floor.

Of course, the noise which ensued initiated an immediate response from the nearby staff. With much effort and a great deal of huffing and puffing, several husky male orderlies were able to hoist the patient back into bed. Having had such a nice cushion upon which to land, the patient was not injured. However he received the best care the hospital had to offer.

In contrast, the little nurse, who was nearly suffocated during the ordeal and who now was beginning to be covered with numerous bruises, was left to her own devices. She received very little attention until later on when she was given a reprimand by her superiors. She had learned the hard way the dual importance of gravity. First, the gravity of her error, and second, the importance of the center of gravity in accomplishing her nursing duties.

It may be purely coincidental, but from that time on there were very few small nurses to be found in this same hospital. In fact, most of the crew looked more like candidates for linebacker positions on a professional football team.

While hiring a stouter crew was one way of avoiding a repetition of the above mentioned catastrophe, possibly a simpler solution might have been for the instructors of the staff to have paid more attention to and give more training in one of the basic principals of physics, namely the importance of THE CENTER OF GRAVITY.

A Tale of Two Brass Knuckles

While it wasn't the best of times and it wasn't the worst of times, it was a time of considerable tension world wide. The Gulf War was at it peak. Terrorist attacks, real and threatened, were ever present, and airplane hijackers were in full swing. At the airports, the guards were in a state of maximum alert. Even the most blasé and experienced travelers jumped when the metal detectors gave off their eerie howls.

It was at this same time Karin ran to catch her plane. She was late and in a terrible hurry. As she rushed through the alarm gate, it reacted violently. Karin immediately stopped, thought for a moment, and then said, "Oh, it must be my brass knuckles!" With this, she pulled out a set of brightly painted knuckles; tossed them into the box provided for keys, coins, etc.; and ran back through the gate—which now remained mute.

Karin was a registered nurse working the night shift at one of the local hospitals. Some of her fellow workers, partly as a joke and partly for her protection during the nighttime hours, had painted a set of knuckles and given them to her. She had then put them in her coat pocket and promptly dismissed them from her mind.

What made this gift so incongruous was she was one of the last people who would think of using physical force in any but the most extreme situations. Her entire nature and her big heart were dedicated to helping others. It is doubtful she would harm any living creature, much less another human. While these characteristics were exemplary, they did make her somewhat vulnerable to others who were less charitable. Of course, none of these good qualities were apparent or known to the guards at the airport.

The words "brass knuckles" alerted the entire airport security force. Guards literally came out of the cracks, some with guns drawn. Karin, still in a hurry, naively said, "Oh, go ahead and keep them. I've got to catch my plane."

"You bet your life we'll keep them, young lady. In the first place brass knuckles are illegal anywhere and certainly are not allowed in airplanes."

The inquisition which followed was thorough and extensive. Poor Karin, by now bewildered and embarrassed by the furor she had caused, tried to explain how she had happened to possess the knuckles. Finally, after much interrogation, the guards realized they were dealing with a nice, sweet young lady and not with a potential plane hijacker. She was then released and allowed to proceed to her long since departed plane, a shaken but wiser girl—minus her brass knuckles.

Karin's experience brought to mind another time and place during the 1940s when brass knuckles were legal. In those days, house calls were an integral part of medical practice. On these calls, the doctors often had to visit the rooms and apartments in the less desirable parts of town. During these calls, several different methods of self-protection were employed. Many of the medics simply swung their house call bags in a pendulum-like manner, figuring that they had a fifty-fifty chance on it being on the up-swing in case they were accosted. Others carried tear gas revolvers, and an occasional one had a real gun within easy reach. For one doctor, a good set of brass knuckles was always handy in a side pocket, ready for instant use.

On one occasion, in the middle of the night, the brass-knuckled M.D. was called to see a supposedly sick woman who complained of abdominal pain. The apartment building was in a very unsavory area, and the patient's apartment was even more so. When the doctor started to examine the patient, a man burst into the room and yelled, "Get your hands off my wife!" (It's questionable about the wife part.) This obviously was a cooked-up attempt at extortion or, even worse, at blackmail. As the so-called husband charged the doctor, who was not a milque-toast type, the doctor slipped on his brass knuckles and with a deft sweep of his hand, hit the man in the mouth. The blow ripped open a large gash in one corner of the lower lip and from there up his cheek. With a tremendous howl of pain, the man covered his face and rapidly retreated across the room.

In turn, the doctor made a hasty exit into the hall and down the stairs. On arriving at the street level, he nearly ran down a policeman who was making his rounds. The officer called, "You're sure up late tonight, Doctor. What's that noise upstairs? Sounds like someone is in pain."

"Probably just some drunk who is waking up with a good hangover."

"Sounds more like someone in pain. You'd better come with me, Doctor, and check on what's going on."

In spite of the doctor's attempts to be on his way, the officer insisted they go up together. On arriving at the room (there was no difficulty in locating it since the bellowing was at a high decibel level) and as they opened the door, the injured man took one look at the doctor and dove for cover behind the bed.

It took a good deal of persuading by the policeman to get him to come out from his hiding place and to get his consent to be taken to a hospital emergency room where the same doctor was then able to repair the wound—free of charge, of course.

While the doctor and Karin were the antithesis of each other in many of their individual characteristics, their respective brass knuckles were essentially the same. However it is ironic that, largely because of the passage of time and changes in government regulations, it was the naive, sweet, and innocent one who had broken the law.

At least, her fate wasn't as severe as that of the hero in "A Tale of Two Cities," where the innocent one had to go to the guillotine.

ESP

Is there such a thing as Extra Sensory Perception (ESP)? Many skeptics say, "No, it's just coincidental," but others take the opposite view. What do you think? In all fairness, let us examine briefly a few examples of this somewhat questionable phenomenon.

One such occurred when a retired doctor was suddenly and completely awakened from a sound sleep at 2:00 A.M. by a soft rustling sound and the feeling of a gentle rush of cool air on his face. In addition, he then heard a quiet voice distinctly call his name, followed by a "goodbye." The voice he recognized as definitely that of his former office nurse. The experience was so vivid and even eerie, he couldn't go back to sleep. As he lay quietly contemplating what had occurred, the telephone rang. It was a call from the nurse's husband telling him she had just died a half-hour earlier. What added to the apparent mystery was the doctor had not been aware of her illness nor even that she had been hospitalized.

In another instance few years earlier, this same doctor had been dreaming about one of his patients, a woman. In the dream her symptoms were very graphic and consistent with an acute bowel infection. The dream was interrupted by the jangle of the telephone. The caller was this same woman's husband, who started to describe his wife's problem. The doctor listened, but didn't have to ask many questions because the woman's symptoms were the same as those in his dream. After instructing the husband regarding what should be done, the doctor then returned to sleep.

The next morning as he drove to work, puzzled by the similarity of the dream and the telephone call, he tried to recall how long it had been since he had seen any member of this same family. At the office when he checked his records, he found it had been over three years since he had had any contact with them. He couldn't help but wonder why the dream had been so vivid and so accurate.

That same day at lunch time after recounting this event to some of his colleagues, several of them told of similar experiences they had had. One told of a night during World War II when he and several of his fellow soldiers were in a jeep driving through a heavy rainstorm in California. After they arrived at their destination, because of the storm they decided to spend the night there. The story teller then decided to telephone his father, who lived in the Midwest in a two hour earlier time zone. When his father answered the call, he immediately said, "Son, I was just dreaming about you. In the dream you were driving in a jeep with several of your fellow soldiers through a heavy rainstorm." Was this purely coincidence or was it a form of ESP?

Twins seem to have a greater potential for ESP than do ordinary siblings. There are many stories about identical twins who were separated at birth but who, when reunited years later, found they had had very similar life styles and habits during their years of separation. A true example of the close relationship of twins occurred one stormy night when one twin developed an acute kidney colic due to a renal stone. Her twin brother, who lived over one thousand miles distant, developed an acute pain at the same moment and on the same side as his sister's colic. The second twin's pain was intense and came in waves similar to those of his sister. By morning, the renal stone had passed and the patient's pain subsided. Likewise, the distant twin's pain disappeared. At the time, neither of the twins was aware of the other's symptoms until several days later when they compared their experiences.

Is there a true pattern emerges from these events and other incidents many of us have experienced? Scoffers will say these are purely coincidental. Still others feel there is really such a thing as ESP. At the present time, much research is being done in this field.

I, for one, had an experience I still find difficult to explain when I attended a lecture given by a professor of a large Eastern university where intensive studies in ESP were being conducted. In his early remarks he told of experiments where the tester and the subject being tested were placed in different rooms. The tester would then concentrate on a given object in his room and ask the one being tested to identify the object. The end results were much better than could be expected by the law of averages. At the lecture, after his opening remarks, the speaker asked for a volunteer to assist him in putting on a blindfold. I was drafted for this task. The blindfold consisted of eight layers of heavy cloth which, when applied, extended from well down his nose to above his eyebrows. Once these layers were in place, I then sealed them with several layers of heavy, opaque, adhesive tape. There was absolutely no way he could peek through or around this mask. As I was about to depart the stage, the speaker asked me if I had a dollar bill in my wallet. While I held this bill well away from the speaker, he asked me to concentrate on the bill's serial number one letter or number at a time. As I slowly perused the numbers there was no verbal communication between us. He then excused me, and I returned to my seat with the dollar bill once again safely tucked into my wallet. The speaker then, still masked, spent considerable time identifying various objects held by others in the audience. The only requirement for each subject was that he or she concentrate their thoughts on the object held and also answer "Yes" or "No" to a few simple questions.

One man held a small pearl-handled pocketknife, which the speaker was able to identify. After so doing, the speaker then said, "You didn't buy the knife and it doesn't belong to you." At first, the man was about to object, but on second thought, recanted and said, "You're right. My wife's uncle gave it to her, but I'm the one who uses it." Identifying the knife was quite an accomplishment in itself, but his question about ownership amazed everyone present.

Nearing the end of his lecture, he removed his mask, looked at me, and said, "Oh, I forgot to give you the serial number of the bill. Do you still have it in your wallet?" He then recited the entire number correctly. By this time, it was approximately one hour after he had first made mental note of it on the stage. There was a tendency for those present to say this was merely some sort of trick. Many in the audience thought the speaker and I were in cahoots. This was not the case. Even if true, it would have been no small accomplishment for him to have been able to repeat the number after an hour's time. Most of us couldn't do so even after just a few minutes' delay. As evidence of such a lack in the average person's ability, let me recount another experience I had. One time, while swimming in the waves at Waikiki, I found a twenty dollar bill floating near the surface. Believe it or not, of the several hundred bathers on the beach, not one of them could recite the serial number of that bill.

Many of us have had an experience during which we have been thinking about a particular person, and then a short time later, have met or received a telephone call from that same individual. While many of these happenings may be simply coincidental, still some may be due to ESP. We humans tend to be skeptical of the existence of anything which might be construed to be a sixth sense, and therefore often discount such happenings. Perhaps our doubts are based mainly on our own limitations in the sensory fields. Even amongst the so-called experts, only about 10 percent believe ESP is a reality. Eighty percent are in doubt but willing to wait for more final evidence. The remaining 10 percent are definitely skeptical.

In contrast to our human limitations in these same fields, much has been written and studied regarding the sensitivity of certain animals and birds prior to and during natural catastrophes such as earthquakes, tornadoes, and hurricanes. It has been postulated that their strange behavior may be due to the fact these creatures have extra sensory perceptions which are much more developed than those possessed by humans.

For example, recently for no apparent reason our canary began to act in a somewhat wild manner. He stopped singing and flew rapidly around his cage like he was very disturbed or very frightened. This behavior lasted for one entire day. We learned later that during this same period of time, there had been a mild earthquake, not noticeable to us, but recorded on the local university seismograph. This may well have been noticed by our bird.

Until more research is done, the existence of ESP is open to some question. However regardless of your personal feelings about this subject, the next time your dog, cat, bird, or any other animal in your immediate vicinity begins to act in an untoward manner, it would be prudent for you, without delay, to start removing and packing, in well-insulated cartons, all of your valuable and fragile glassware, porcelains, Hummel's, table settings, and any other breakables.

At least it won't hurt to play it safe.

The Wrong Bed

Cornered like a wild animal, he crouched on his haunches in the corner of the hospital room. He looked like a madman. In fact, in his present state he *was* a madman. His gray-streaked blond hair was wildly disheveled. All of his muscles were tense, rigid, and bulged like steel cables under his ashen-hued skin. No sound came from his lips, and yet he seemed about to growl as he glared across the room toward the semicircle of frightened nurses facing him. His eyes had a savage, untamed look. They shifted from side to side as though searching for a potential enemy. Paradoxically, however, these same eyes seemed not to focus upon nor really see anyone or any specific thing in the room. While his physical size was only average, his general manner and appearance made him seem gargantuan.

My entrance and participation in this tense scene had been initiated when I had literally been grabbed and pushed down the hall by a nurse's aide who had cried, "Come quickly, doctor! There's a terrible emergency!"

Without any more explanation of the forthcoming problem than this, I hurried to the designated room. One glance at the confrontation between this wild man and the nurses told me this was not the time or place for the usual formal history and physical examination.

The tension in the room was so marked, I feared any untoward noise, even the spoken word, or any sudden movement, would cause this unstable creature to spring forth with uncontrolled fury.

Being the only male aside from the patient in the room, and being the only M.D. present, I realized I must assume a leadership role. In order to demonstrate for those present how to calm a savage beast, and with an outward calmness which I did not feel internally, I slowly advanced toward the brute. In a soft voice I said, "Why don't you climb into bed so we can help you?"

His eyes, now directed only at me, were filled with a look of hate and anger. They never wavered. No sound escaped his lips. The silence in the room was eerie and yet it was electrifying. As I slowly advanced to within approximately six feet from him, I began to feel I had mastered this crisis and had once again displayed the merits of a calm and reasonable approach.

Just as these thoughts were crossing my mind, he, with startling rapidity, leaped from his crouched position like a catapulted projectile, directly at me. I was so surprised that, involuntarily, I jumped aside and reached out with my right hand and arm to shield myself. Somehow, and to this day I don't know how, I was able to grasp his right wrist. I am not adept in the martial arts, and it was by pure accident that in the confusion of the moment, we ended up with my having him under my control by means of a good solid hammerlock on his right arm. With this hold, I now felt much more confident and, with more authority in my voice, again said, "Let's climb into bed, fella."

There was no response to this request until I exerted a bit more pressure on the hammerlock. He then dutifully climbed into the bed. I then called to the nurses, "Who's his doctor? Call him and ask him what he wants us to do, and what this patient needs."

With this, the first words came forth from the patient. "I know what I need!"

"What's that?"

"I need sugar. I'm a diabetic and haven't had enough food to cover my insulin."

Within a short time, this deficiency was corrected, the patient's physician arrived, and I departed.

The next morning, as I made rounds, I was surprised to find my "hammerlock wrestler" of the previous day in a room far removed from our prior area of combat. What a change! Gone were the maniacal facies, the rumpled hair, and the wild demonical creature of the day before. All of these less desirable characteristics had been transformed into a well-groomed, calm, pleasant-looking gentleman.

"I hope I wasn't too rough and I didn't hurt your arm last evening."

"The arm twisting didn't bother me much, Doctor. What did upset me a bit though, at the time, was that you made me get into the wrong bed. In fact, I wasn't even in the right room."

Genius or Idiot?

The highly touted modern computer—is it a genius or is it an idiot? Whichever, it is often paradoxical. One moment it displays astounding capabilities, and the next moment the utmost stupidity. While on the one hand it has no emotions, it can, with ease, recall all sorts of sentimental occasions such as anniversaries, birthdays, and other happy events. On the other hand, it can be completely insensitive to situations which even the unlearned or the most naive individual could solve.

Most of us have at one time or another been either completely amazed or conversely, frustrated by these complex machines. Recently when I called an airline to confirm our reservations for a flight which was to take place within the next few days, the clerk asked me my telephone number. Within seconds the computer not only located the reservation, but also recalled our first and last names, the flight number, the date of the flight, and our destination. Considering the number of flights for this airline each day and for every day of the year, plus the multiple reservations for each flight, this rapid recall portrayed a true magical genie in action.

In contrast, these genies can be awfully dumb. Last year I received and was billed for two books I had not ordered. I returned the books with a note that I did not wish to keep them. In spite of this, for the next few months I received regular billings. Each time, I returned the statement with an attached note stating I had already returned the books. At the end of three months, another statement arrived with the original billing plus the addition of several dollars of interest due on the so-called unpaid balance. Again, a polite reply was forwarded and completely ignored by the company.

Finally, at the end of six months, I did become a mite irked, and having heard of one way to get the computer's attention, I poked several holes in the statement and enclosed another note asking it to let me speak to some human being, just anyone. This did the trick. Shortly thereafter a note arrived with an apology for any inconvenience the improper billing may have caused, plus a promise the error would be corrected. The next month, another statement arrived giving us credit for the returned books and showing a zero balance due. However, the computer was not to be denied. Accompanying this last statement was an advertisement for the same two books which had started the whole problem in the first place.

This event leads us to the subject of the difference between knowledge and wisdom. The dictionary defines knowledge as "the state of knowing or the accumulation of a body of facts." No one can argue that computers can be knowledgeable to the ultimate degree. However how a computer uses this knowledge can, in many instances, be open to question.

Wisdom, on the other hand, is defined as "the quality of being wise or the use of good judgment." These two definitions mark the difference between a machine and a human brain. The former can be programmed to react in a specific manner to any given set of circumstances, but cannot be asked to use any judgment or to vary its behavior from its original programming.

The well-balanced human mind, while somewhat lacking in its total knowledge and even at times fallible, has the advantage of judgment. Therefore it can adjust to unforeseen or unusual situations. It can manifest wisdom and more importantly, compassion.

One of the astronauts was asked what would be his preference if he had to choose between a human or a computer in the handling of a space vehicle. He smiled and replied, "Considering all the factors, I would have to choose the human for several reasons. Where else but in a human can you find a binary computer with a billion connections in line that only weighs between 150 and 170 pounds and that can be mass-produced for so little cost by unskilled labor?"

While we may never decide completely whether computers are geniuses or idiots, it will behoove all of us not only to take advantage of what these mechanical marvels have to offer, but also to use our God-given powers of evaluation and insight. As is written in Proverbs 8:11: "For all wisdom is better than rubies; and all things that are to be desired are not to be compared to it."

Switchbacks and the Hitchhiker

After having spent several years learning the three "Rs" in school, it took the fifteen-year-old hitchhiker only a few minutes to learn the three "Ps," namely: patience, persistence, and proficiency.

Historical records are replete with stories of others who have learned these same truths. King Robert Bruce in Scotland learned them from a spider. According to legend, in 1315 while holed up in a run-down hut after fleeing from his enemies, discouraged and ready to admit defeat, the king noticed a spider attempting to spin a web between two ceiling beams. After many failures, the spider finally spanned the difficult expanse with the web's main support. From then on, the building of the rest of the web was easily accomplished. The king, taking heart from his observations of the spider, was then able to free himself from his fears, leave the hut, mobilize his followers, reunite his country, and reestablish his kingdom.

In a far different setting, Africa, where survival often depends on an individual's attention to minor irregularities such as a torn leaf, a paw print, a rustling bush, or other slight variation in the environment, patience, persistence, and proficiency are essential. For generations, the tribal elders have taught their sons these values by repeating over and over, "Be patient, don't hurry, be careful, and try again and again."

The above-mentioned hitchhiker's first lesson in the three "Ps" occurred one summer evening as he walked alone an Eastern Washington highway. He had spent the entire day looking for a job in the apple orchards. Having been rebuffed several times in the Wenatchee area, he decided to try to find work near Lake Chelan several miles to the north. Again he received all negative answers to his requests for work. It was early evening when he started to hitchhike back to Wenatchee; there were only a few cars on the road, and none stopped to give him a ride. The countryside was barren of houses, and with darkness rapidly approaching, he could picture himself being stranded on this lonely road all night long. Not being familiar with the area, he could imagine all sorts of predatory beasts lurking in the shadows behind each bush and shrub. His feelings rapidly ran the gamut from discouragement and loneliness to fear, desperation, and finally, near panic.

At that time the road leaving the small town of Chelan had a series of switchbacks as it ascended the steep hill leading to Wenatchee. The hiker was about midway on the first of these switchbacks when a car, the first he had seen in nearly an hour, approached at high speed. The driver sped by, ignoring his by then nearly frantic signaling for a ride. As the car's tail lights faded into the evening's rapidly diminishing light, the hiker's fears and frustrations were replaced by anger and resolve.

With all the energy he could summon, he started to scramble up the bank to the next level of the switchback and was able to reach this just in time to hail the same car as it ascended to this leve1. Again the driver ignored his hand signals and sped on. With a second effort, the hiker once more struggled up the next steep bank, using any small scrubby brush or bush he could grasp in his efforts to reach the third level. For the third time, he arrived to meet the same car. This time, the driver, with a look of astonishment on his face, did stop and offer the boy a ride.

As the hiker climbed into the car, the driver said, "I'm a traveling salesman and usually do not pick up hitchhikers. However in all my years of travel, I have never before, within a matter of minutes, had to pass the same hiker twice, much less the same one three times. In my work as a salesman, I appreciate the value of persistence and effort. This evening you have demonstrated to me that you have perseverance and stick-to-itiveness. Either that or perhaps you are desperate. The only other possibility is that you are one third of a set of triplets."

With these remarks, he then drove on, and not just to Wenatchee, but he even went out of his way to deposit the boy at the entrance of the YMCA where the boy had a room.

That day, the hiker had learned a valuable lesson. Like the African tribal elders and their sons, and like King Bruce in Scotland, he had learned the value of patience, persistence, and proficiency.

Two Dogs

An old Indian once said, "Each of us has within us a black dog and a white dog. These two are constantly fighting each other. Our outward actions show which dog is winning."

This battle is well illustrated by the actions of a young man as he prepared to back into a vacant parking place. Just as he was going to reverse his car, a young woman in a small red sports car made a rapid approach from the rear and slipped into this same space. His first impulse was to back up his truck rapidly and splash into the little bug of a car. Squelching this feeling, his second thought was to find another space, wait until the young woman had left her car, and then let the air out of her car's left front tire. Fortunately, he was able to resist this second thought also. His white dog had won that battle.

Almost everyone likes and even loves small babies and little children. It is hard for us to imagine that a black dog could reside inside such an adorable creature, but it is there, nevertheless. When looked at, realistically, babies—ourselves included—are all born as uncivilized, completely selfish creatures. In order to become desirable and useful as we grow, a marked modification of these basic primitive traits is required. This change or training is not sporadic, but requires consistency and, to be successful, goes on from birth until death.

Once, a new mother asked, "When do I start disciplining my baby?" The answer: "From the moment the hospital nurse puts the child in your arms as you are leaving for home. Of course, this training should be positive and loving with the emphasis on the good behavioral patterns more than on the bad."

With proper training some individuals win the battle early, some later, and some never do. Even devoted Christians have to struggle to achieve success in the conflict between the good and the bad, or as the Indian so aptly said, "between the white and the black dogs."

One of our strongest emotions is anger. In order to defuse this basic trait there is a frequently held belief by some that we should give vent to our frustrations, that to keep our hostilities bottled up is harmful. Those who hold this view seem to ignore what might happen to the ones upon whom the barbs and frustrations are thrust. Free expression of these undesirable emotions can be extremely harmful not only to the recipient but also to the donor; often more so to the latter.

A case in point occurred one beautiful Fourth of July day as I stopped at a self-service gas station. In the next lane was another car all packed and ready for what appeared to be a joyous family picnic. The driver of this car was having a heated argument with the station attendant. He was livid, ranting and raving. When he finally jumped into his car, he was practically frothing at the mouth. With his car wheels spinning and gravel flying in all directions, he rushed off to take his family on what promised to be a completely spoiled outing. According to the attendant, he was upset over a few cents difference in the charge for the services received. While he had given vent to his feelings and had certainly released his hostilities, he had also ruined the day for everyone else as well as for himself. The black dog had won the day.

In another situation, when a driver became upset with another driver, he made an obscene gesture and cursed the other man, who in turn promptly got out of his car and beat the first man over the head with a heavy metal chain. On arriving home, the beaten man complained of a severe headache. Shortly thereafter, he lapsed into a coma and within a few hours was in surgery to have a large blood clot evacuated from his brain. Following his return home, he became very moody and was never able to return to his usual routine. A few weeks later, in his depressed state he shot himself in the head. Again, an example of venting of hostile feelings, but with tragic consequences.

One other aspect of anger that is likely to take place is the loss of equanimity and the decrease of efficiency of response which occurs when we "lose our cool." This loss, in turn, results in a compounding of our frustrations and a further aggravation of an already disturbed mental state. It is a well-known fact in courtroom trials that if one adversary can make the other angry, the battle is half won.

On the other hand, as stated in proverbs in the Holy Bible, "A soft answer turneth away wrath." Suppression of anger conserves energy and increases strength. If a cool head prevails, actions and words become more logical and the whole situation becomes much easier to handle. With this comes an increased efficiency. The opposition becomes more vulnerable, and the chance of winning becomes greater. This more logical approach may even convince the other side to modify its views, and instead of destroying may preserve a friendship or even win a new one. Abraham Lincoln, when asked how he treated his enemies, replied, "I try to make them my friends."

While anger is bad enough, there are other "black dog" characteristics which must be modified and eliminated if possible, namely jealousy, selfishness, covetousness, conceit, and animosity. These should be replaced by love, patience, joy, meekness, faith, goodness, gentleness, and other desirable traits. Of course, these must be taught and learned by Christian teaching and example.

There are those who feel discipline is a negative and punishing procedure. Actually, it is just the opposite. To be most effective, it should be done in a positive, loving, kindly manner and done primarily by our own example rather than by our words alone. A good rule to follow is never to discipline when in an angry mood. It is wise to learn to evaluate each situation and give it its proper emphasis. For instance, when a child leaves a pair of shoes in the middle of the front room, while not desired, it is not a capital offense and not to be compared to a major error. In most situations, a bit of humor can solve trying situations.

Frequently parents say, "He never does what I say." This, of course, sends a message to the child that he or she is always wrong, so why try. The opposite approach would be, "He always tries to do his best." This gives the child an incentive to keep up the good work.

One mother, who was quite knowledgeable in most things, brought her four-year-old daughter to the doctor's office. In front of the girl, she said, "She must have something wrong with her feet. We have bought seven different pairs of shoes, but she won't wear any of them. Also, she won't eat her meals and sometimes throws her food on the dining room rug. She never does anything I tell her. When my husband comes home from work, I tell him, 'You take her, I've had it.'" On examination, the girl's feet were normal. She was cooperative during the entire visit. As soon as the doctor could, he asked the nurse to take the girl out of the room while he talked to the mother. He then told the mother, "Try the positive approach. Tell her how much you love her, and what a sweet little girl she is. When your husband comes home, and in front of the child, tell him how good she has been all day." Within a few days, the child not only was wearing her shoes, but also was eating well.

Most of us are willing to live by rules if they are fair, consistent, and for our own good. If we know the speed limit, we are willing to obey if it stays consistent. However, if it is changed from time to time, we become confused and even rebellious. Some parents act in a capricious manner and change their rules willy-nilly. They become very upset over an infraction at one time, and then at other times completely ignore the same situation. This inconsistency causes the child to become somewhat baffled. A neighbor who had recently planted a new lawn would spank his sons severely if they ran over the new blades of grass on a day when he was tired, and then at other times, laugh at them when they did the same thing. As a result, the boys were very confused.

Of course, even the best of us may fail to follow the rules in all situations. There is the story of the minister who had spent his entire free day putting in a new concrete driveway. After he had washed up and was feeling mighty satisfied with his work, he looked out and saw a small boy making large foot prints in the newly laid concrete. Rushing out, he grabbed the boy and started to spank him. Just then a neighbor walked by and said, "Reverend, I'm surprised to see what you are doing. I wouldn't expect that reaction from a minister of the Gospel. I thought that you loved children."

"Oh I do—in the abstract, but not in the concrete."

One rule of thumb to use in disciplining a child or even an adult is to consider what is best for the individual. You don't have to be judgmental. Just use common sense. Put the other person first, allow your love to flow, and place your decision in the hands of the Lord. If you do these things, you will find that the "white dog" will always win.

How Old Is Old?

What is old age? The answer is to be found largely in the mind and eyes of the beholder. When I was a first grader, the fourth graders seemed old. As an eight grader, I felt sorry for the college freshmen. They seemed to be so old. When the book *Life Begins at Forty* was published, I thought, *Who's kidding whom?*

In my middle years, I used to occasionally wonder, *How will I know when I become old?* Only recently has the answer to this question been partially revealed. Only partially, as there are too many variables which must be considered.

While the limits of middle age have been fairly well defined chronologically, even here there has been some hedging. It is generally accepted that the end of youth and the beginning of the middle years is thirty-five. However the upper limits are still somewhat fuzzy and have been vaguely demarcated as being ten years older than the age of the person setting the standards happens to be at that particular time. Perhaps more accurate boundaries are those definitions which are not limited by chronology, but are of a more practical nature, such as: that morning-after feeling without the night before; or when all your joints ache before you get out of bed.

There was a time when, in the normal course of events, gray hair provided a sign of aging. No longer. Grecian formula and the modern beauty parlor have pretty well wiped out this clue. Lacking gray hair as an easy answer to old age, we must resort to more subtle signs, of which there are many.

One of the first hints I had, personally, came a few years ago when having heard about the Golden Age Pass for our national parks and having passed the required age for same, I asked the nice park ranger at the park entrance about these. She (the ranger) told me to stop at the park headquarters a mile or so away and they would take care of this matter for me. At the headquarters, the clerk was pleasant, He said, "Just sign here," and handed me my pass. What really hurt was the fact that no one asked me for any proof of my age.

Some time later on, at the Elks club, I decided to apply for a locker in the gymnasium. The attendant told me to put my name and lodge number in the registration book. This book contained page after page of those on the waiting list. I could visualize waiting for years for a locker. After the attendant looked at my name and lodge number, he turned to his fellow worker and said, "This is a 9000." It so happens that we are given our numbers in the order of our joining the organization. I was to learn that a "9000" was really an oldie. Most of the younger members were in the 30,000 range. The attendants both looked at me like I was some sort of an archaeological find. One said to the other, "We'd better give him a locker soon." I felt as if they thought I wouldn't last very long, and they'd better hurry up before it is too late.

Each of us have had or will have our own experiences, but in a more general way there are several tell-tale signs of aging which are common to most everyone. Here is a partial list of things for which to watch:

—When you look at your newly shingled roof which has a twenty-five year warranty and realize it will probably outlast you.
—When it becomes common practice for your friends to greet each other with hugs and kisses—and no one seems to mind (unless the friend happens to be a divorcee).
—When you have shortness of breath on stairs and hills when you are *descending* same.
—When the barber no longer has to use his thinning shears.
—When mature adults end their remarks to you with "sir" or "ma'am."
—When you find the articles in the newspapers about elderly persons are referring to someone who is eight to ten years younger than you are.
—When policemen and school teachers look like kids to you.
—When your apparel, especially your shoes, are chosen primarily for comfort.
—When vague and not so vague generalized achings occur both before and after you get up in the morning.
—When Boy Scouts want to help you cross the street even when you don't want to go.
—When you have not only completely adjusted to your bifocals, but also feel lost without them.
—When at least half your friends have had coronary bypass surgery.
—When you find that your colleagues, whom you have considered your contemporaries, weren't even born during the Great Depression and to whom the Pearl Harbor bombing is ancient history.
—When you can't remember the names of your good friends you want to introduce to some other friend whose name you can't recall either.
—When you get a request by mail to buy life insurance and then find you've passed, by several years, the maximum eligible age listed.
—When you don't worry about the outcome of a football game because

you've seen too many other games in years gone by.

—When, by the time you've found your glasses, you've forgotten why you wanted them in the first place.

I could go on and on as there myriad other signs of aging too numerous to enumerate here.

It has been said that one sign of the passage of years is the person's ability to remember the names of everyone in his or her second grade class but not what he had for breakfast that same day. With this in mind, there is still hope for some of us. I can recall only three of my second grade class members, and I do know what I had for breakfast today. It's the same thing every morning.

What will really worry me is that period in the future when I not only won't be able to recall what I had for breakfast, but whether or not I really did have breakfast in the first place. Perhaps, by then I either won't care about such things, or, on the other hand, perhaps I will at last really understand the meaning of HOW OLD IS OLD?

Knights of the Sky

In 1913, with very little effort on my part, I arrived on this earth a few years after the Wright brothers, with a great deal of effort on their part, had succeeded in leaving it in their first flying machine. Whether or not the timing of these two facts played any part in subsequent events is hard to determine, but one thing is certain—I have had more than a passing interest in airplanes ever since.

Most small boys dream of being cowboys, firemen, bus drivers, or some other supposedly glamorous occupation. My dream was to someday fly a mechanical bird. In my early youth, I used to bicycle to the nearest airfield just to see the planes, hoping that occasionally one would take off or land. These planes, for the most part, were open-cockpit, two-winged, two-passenger models. While they were a far cry from the modern jets, they were, in my eyes, marvels of creation. When flying in one, they did give any excited and scared neophytes a real thrill as the wind blew through their hair and by their faces. My first flight was in one of these early birds. It lasted fifteen minutes, for which I paid five dollars of my hard-earned paper route money. This first taste of the upper atmosphere was not only exciting but also whetted my appetite for more of the same.

While these small planes were fun to ride in, they were also accompanied by considerable risk. One of my friends, a medical doctor, walked with a decided limp. It seems that before he became interested in a medical career, he was a pilot of small aircraft. In order to eat, he used to take up passengers for short hops. Most planes had two cockpits, each with separate controls. When a non-pilot passenger was to occupy one of the cockpits, the control lever, or "joy stick" was removed from that cockpit. All that remained was a small open space in the floor board surrounding the socket for the joy stick. On one of his flights the passenger was a woman who happened to be wearing high-heeled shoes. After their flight was about over and as they were in their descend for their landing, the doctor-to-be pulled back on the stick in his cockpit to level off before touching down. His efforts met with considerable resistance. The harder he pulled, the more resistance he encountered. In his struggles, the last thing he remembers was the sight of green trees flashing by in his peripheral vision just before the plane plowed into the ground at an approximately thirty-degree angle.

Fortunately, both he and the passenger survived. He did sustain several injuries, the most serious of which was a nasty fracture of the shaft of his right femur. This, of course, required prolonged hospital treatment during which time he became interested in a medical career.

The cause of the crash: The woman's high heel had inadvertently slipped into the opening in the floor board surrounding the joy stick socket, blocking the movement of the sockets in both cockpits. When the pilot pulled back on his stick, the heel became more tightly impacted. This, of course, prevented any leveling off of the plane as it approached ground level.

Years later, with the development of larger planes, and especially with the advent of the "jets," for me the magnetism of airplanes intensified. In spite of my four years in the US Army Air Force during World War II, there was no let up in this allurement. In addition to the attraction of the giant silver birds, I must have unconsciously transferred some of this same feeling to the fliers themselves. There was a tendency on my part to clothe the fliers in the same shining armor, similar to that of the planes in which they flew—like "Knights in the Sky."

This attitude persisted until a few years ago. At that time, we were enjoying a flight over the beautiful blue Pacific Ocean 39,000 feet below. The outside temperature was seventy-nine degrees below zero. Inside it was a comfortable seventy degrees. All was proceeding smoothly except for one thing. Since shortly after take off, there had been a strange banging or slapping noise above our heads. In the many previous flights we had taken, we had never heard anything similar to this. We weren't alarmed and had decided the noise couldn't be anything too serious since the plane was still flying smoothly.

It so happened that on this trip, the captain of the aircraft came to the passenger section of the plane, probably on a public relations visit. Looking very official yet relaxed and competent in appearance, he stopped next to our seats and asked, "How's everything going?"

"Just fine, but we have been wondering about the slapping noise in the ceiling. We've never heard anything like it on any previous flight."

When the pilot listened for a moment, we expected a knowledgeable answer like, "It's just the flutter valve stuck in the open or closed position," or his even saying it was nothing of any consequence. Instead he resorted to the age-old remedy so often used by the mechanically illiterate who try to remedy balky machinery by striking or kicking the same. He reached over us and struck the offending noisy area twice with his hand. The noise continued unabated. Then, without another word, he shrugged his shoulders in a manner of resignation suggesting, "It beats me." Whatever the cause of the noise, it was not a major one because we landed safely a few hours later.

While this experience did not completely destroy my image of pilots per se, it did reveal the fact they were not completely infallible and they were mortal after all. It could be interpreted as evidence of a small crack in their previously intact and untarnished armor, that perhaps there was a bit of rust on the glamour of these Knights of the Sky.

In retrospect, perhaps I had given too much credit to the pilots, and more emphasis and praise should have been given to the scientists, engineers, machinists, airport personnel, maintenance crews, controllers, ticket agents, stewardesses, flight engineers, and the many others who make these luxurious flying carpets a reality.

Looking at the above in another way and putting it in its proper perspective by bringing it closer to our daily routines, it's true that almost anyone can drive an automobile. A few can pilot an airplane. Still fewer can understand all the operating parts and keep them in good running condition. However only a very, very few can successfully design, build, and merchandise an acceptable model of these marvelous flying machines. In fact, all of these aforementioned are, in reality, the true KNIGHTS OF THE SKY.

Courage—Skin Deep

As he was ushered into the small bare room, he couldn't help but wonder what lay ahead. Without any formality, he was told to wait. Once the door was closed behind him, he had a chance to survey his surroundings. The walls of the room were windowless, glaringly white, and otherwise completely bare. The only furniture present consisted of one plain wooden chair and a small flat white table with its restraining straps hanging loosely from its sides. An overhead spotlight which projected from the ceiling resembled an ominous cycloptic eye which seemed to be looking directly at him.

This confinement was not his first, but at the present time it seemed to be especially threatening. He couldn't help but recall his first incarceration many years before when he had been a prisoner of war during World War II. Then, as a lieutenant, he had been captured by the Germans during the Battle of the Bulge. At that time, in prison he had suffered many privations and endured extreme cold and hunger without complaining. However, this situation was completely different.

Paradoxically, he wasn't so much afraid of the possible pain which he was sure would come as he was of the suspense of waiting. He had endured pain before when as a captain at the invasion of Inchon, Korea, he had been hit in the thigh by shrapnel, but hadn't realized he was wounded until hours later, once the excitement of the battle was over.

Later on, in Vietnam, he had been wounded again, but had shrugged this off as nothing serious. After two tours of duty there as a colonel, he had been awarded the Silver Star for gallantry in action.

He had always taken pride in being called a "soldier's soldier" and never openly displaying fear in front of his troops. However he had to admit to himself that in the past there had been moments of anxiety and, on occasion, he had been really frightened, but he felt quite sure he had been able to conceal these feelings from those around him. But now, this present situation was something else.

Here he was confronted with an entirely new crisis.

Some said this group was made up of a bunch of sadists. He didn't feel that way and realized that while there might be an occasional weirdo in the outfit, the majority were simply following orders issued from higher up. In spite of his understanding attitude, this waiting for some action was getting on his nerves.

His present situation all started two weeks ago when he received orders to go to Africa. At first, he had looked forward to the assignment with pleasure. Of course, he had not contemplated the occurrence of anything like his present predicament.

And now, this waiting was beginning to take its toll. How long were they going to keep him dangling? This bunch were masters at the art of keeping a person in suspense. As he sat in this stark room, he noted his pulse was racing, his breathing had become labored and rapid, and he began to feel like he couldn't get enough oxygen. A cold sweat broke out on his forehead, and he began to feel panic stricken. He thought he would surely faint.

Finally, after what seemed like an eternity, he heard footsteps in the hall outside the door. When it finally opened, in strode his captor carrying all the instruments of torture he had always dreaded so much. Why hadn't he long ago had enough foresight to look ahead and take the necessary precautions to avoid this present confrontation?

At last his adversary spoke, "Good afternoon, General. Do you feel all right? You look a little pale. I'm sorry to have to do this to you, but you did bring it on yourself, you know. I just don't understand why you high-ranking officers are so careful to see that your troops are protected but don't do the same thing for yourselves by keeping your immunizations up to date. Oh well, it won't be too bad. You'll only need four shots today, and three more tomorrow."

"I Think I'm Going Crazy!"

The first words she uttered as she entered the doctor's consultation room were, "I think I'm going crazy!"

"Why do you think that?"

"It's because I'm wild about rolled oats."

"Many people like rolled oats."

"Not the way I like them. My idea of a good time is to go to the grocery store and buy a carton of rolled oats. Then to the theater for a matinee, and while watching the show, eat the oats—raw. I often do the same thing after dinner while reading the newspaper. Occasionally, I even take the carton to bed with me. I must be out of my tree."

A complete physical examination plus several laboratory tests failed to reveal any obvious abnormality. In addition, her mental capacity seemed normal, aside from her statements otherwise. With this in mind, the doctor decided the patient might have a vitamin deficiency, especially the vitamin B factors. As a result, he started her on daily B complex tablets as well as a few injections of the same. Within a few weeks, the patient's craving for rolled oats disappeared.

With this regime, her problems seemed to be resolved for the next several months. Then one day she called the doctor again and said, "You'd better get out the B complex once more. I'm back on the rolled oats and the matinees again."

Too Close Ahead?

Have you ever noticed how nearly everyone involved in an auto accident is the innocent victim and never the one at fault? Insurance companies advise us not to admit anything at the time of a collision, so it is only on a rare occasion that a driver will admit his or her guilt. An example of this admission occurred in one accident when the woman driver said, "It was all my fault."

The driver of the other car replied, "No lady, it was my fault. I saw you coming for three blocks, and I had plenty of chance to dodge up a side street."

Another exceptional case is illustrated in an accident where two cars side-swiped each other at a busy corner. When the police officer asked what had happened, the older, more mature-looking driver said it was nobody's fault; each car had arrived at the intersection at the same time. Neither of them was speeding, and each driver had tried to avoid the other. The driver of the second car was a young man who happened to be on his way to a costume party. He was dressed as Robin Hood or maybe as one of his merry men. He was standing in the rain, which was rapidly soaking his ridiculous-looking uniform and causing his peaked cap and feather to droop in an unseemly fashion. On his appearance alone, the poor guy didn't have a chance with the police officer. Fortunately the older driver was able to convince the officer to let each one share the blame in an equal manner.

In spite of these examples, and possibly a few other exceptions, the usual accident situation is the exact opposite. W.C. Fields once gave a classic excuse after he had run into a statue in the city park. To the officer he said, "He jumped right in front of me."

Most of the various versions of what actually happened in an accident are completely biased and influenced by each driver's pride, as well as by his desire to avoid an unfavorable report to his insurance company. Also, to avoid a lawsuit. From a selfish standpoint, it is only natural that these factors would, even unconsciously, play a big part in influencing the driver's opinions.

One of the most unlikely excuses was given by a motorist who had just rear-ended the car in front of him, when he said, "He was driving too close ahead."

Without being aware of so doing, he had illustrated a basic truth for all of us, which is the driver to watch most closely is the one in the car right behind the car directly in front of the one in which you are riding.

In other words, the cause of most auto accidents is a failure of the nut holding the car's steering wheel.

Who Is He?

Who is this man? What is his story? How many secrets lie locked inside his brain? In his past had he been a professional person: a banker, musician, lawyer, teacher, or even a minister? Or had he been a white collar executive in a large corporation? Possibly he was an ex-athlete or maybe he had been a common, hard-working, unskilled laborer. Whatever his previous occupation, had he influenced others for good or for bad during his productive years?

The true answer to these questions is a mystery because no one seems to know much about his past history, which is somewhat sketchy at best. A bank trust fund pays all his bills, and the trustees either are not aware of his story or else they are not talking. There are no apparent known relatives. At least, no one ever comes to visit him.

He doesn't communicate with his fellow nursing home mates and will sit for hours inside the entry door of the home, staring either into space or at the floor. His face is a complete blank, and his eyes are lifeless and seem not to see anyone or anything in his surroundings.

I first noticed him as I made my daily rounds of the nursing home. His sad, vacant, and yet somewhat sweet countenance attracted my attention and brought out my sympathies for this lonely man. Each day as I passed him, I would greet him with an "hello" or a "good morning." For the first several weeks, there was no response. Then one day, as if in answer, he moved one hand ever so slightly. As the days passed, his hand movements gradually became more and more pronounced. However as he kept staring at the floor or into space, his facial expression remained completely blank.

The day finally arrived when as I was leaving the nursing home, we made eye contact. This was done without any change of his facial expression. Then as the weeks passed, I noticed what seemed to be a slight smile appear, just momentarily. Still no spoken word accompanied these gradual changes.

His usual location at the home during the daytime hours was in a chair near the full-length window next to the entry door. This window was covered by a thin curtain. One day, as I approached the door, I saw him peeking through a small opening in the curtain as if he was looking for my arrival. When I greeted him, I heard what could have been interpreted as "hello" in response. I believe this was probably the first word he had uttered in many months. And then, as the weeks passed, his words became more varied and distinct. His facial expression became more animated, and his eyes developed a bit of sparkle.

While he never did regain full speech, he became a much more complete person. At first, he began to ambulate. Then he gradually started pushing some of the wheelchair-confined patients around the halls. Each morning, he waited for me. Finally the day arrived when he extended his hand to shake mine. All in all, he became a relatively happy individual. Even when my visits to the home became less frequent, he continued to improve. I'd like to be able to say he became completely restored to his prime, but that would be too much to expect. However he did become a happier, more useful person and seemed to have an increased self-esteem.

We all have seen examples of those previously useful individuals who have had a partial shut down of their cerebral functions. While the exact cause of these conditions may be one of a number of different factors, the increased longevity of the population as a whole is paramount. In other words, we are all living too long. Of course, most of us feel this increase is an advantage, but it does have its negative side. Because of this increase, those who have once been prominent business executives, judges, doctors, educators, or housewives may be changed into people who are totally out of contact with their environment.

In addition to the changes due to aging, there are those mental aberrations which occur early in life; for example, catatonic states. In these patients, trying to reach into their brains can be very difficult or even impossible. One such case was that of a former skilled cabinet maker who was completely withdrawn from reality. All attempts to get him to respond had failed. Then one day his doctor decided on a novel approach. The doctor took a beautiful piece of mahogany wood and placed it in front of the patient. The doctor then took two saws, one an old, rusty, rip handsaw and the other a new, fine-toothed cross-cut type. Taking the rusty blade, the doctor approached the fine piece of wood and was about to assault it. At this same moment the patient, who had not spoken or voluntarily moved for weeks, jumped up, pushed the doctor away, and with the fine new saw cut the wood in a professional manner. This was the first breakthrough in the case and allowed the doctor to then proceed with further therapy.

While the brain and its many components is largely an unexplored frontier, gradually more and more of its mysteries are being solved by researchers. It has long been felt that once cells of the central nervous system (the brain, medulla oblongata, and spinal cord) were destroyed, they could not be restored. However recently experiments have shown that increased mental and physical activity may stimulate a regrowth of some of the synapses and nerve fibers in the CNS. It has been graphically demonstrated that giving mentally deficient patients a new interest in life such as gardening, care of pets, painting, music, or other stimulating activities can restore many of the previously lost functions. One man who had to be isolated because of his maniacal spells began to respond when allowed to care for some flowers. He improved enough so that he could be removed from his confined quarters, and eventually he became one of the gardeners for the hospital.

In mental activity, one other factor to consider is most of us do not use our brains to their full potential even when we are considered to be normal. One father, a hard-working mechanic, had a son who was a brilliant student and even considered to be a genius. When the father was asked how he accounted for his son's brilliance, he replied, "I tried to teach him to use his brain to its entire capacity."

In spite of our failure to use our brains to their full potential when we are normal, perhaps there is a cerebral reservoir waiting to be used if we begin to show signs of mental deterioration as we age. At least this does seem to be a possibility. This might account for the improvement in the man mentioned above who sat at the entrance of the nursing home day after day. At least it is encouraging to think we may have this potential brain power waiting to be utilized if we need it and if we are willing to make the necessary effort. Of course, in this situation a bit of tender loving care also helps a great deal.

A Foot in the Mouth

While most of the old familiar sayings like, "A bird in the hand is worth two in the bush," "A penny saved is a penny earned," and "Early to bed and early to rise makes a man healthy, wealthy, and wise," are generally true and are wise paths to follow, there may be some situations where an exception may occur.

For example, it is a commonly held belief that when a person speaks, "putting your foot in your mouth" is always a bad maneuver. This is not necessarily true and on occasion may even be beneficial.

Judy graphically illustrated one variation of this general rule. Arriving home from work a bit late one evening, she found all three of her young children, the eldest a two-and-a-half-year-old and the nine-month-old twins, all in dire need of a mother's love and attention. Tired as she was, her maternal instincts came to the fore. Picking up the eldest, who was complaining the loudest, she hugged her tightly. This, of course, brought loud howls of protest from each of the twins. Then, trying to pacify all three at the same time, she ran to get bottles for each one, but having only two hands she wasn't able to hold all three simultaneously. As the little male twin seemed to be a mite less disturbed than the other two, she put him on the floor at her feet. When he started to howl loudly at this apparent rejection, she slipped off one shoe and sock and lacking anything better, put her big toe in the little boy's mouth. Immediately quietness and peace ensued, and all became serene.

A few minutes later, her husband arrived home, gave the by now quiet domestic scene a casual glance, and said, "All seems under control here. I'll go check the TV news and read the paper until it's time for dinner."

That did it. While the "foot in the mouth" for the twin had been beneficial and was the right answer at the moment, it was an exception to the general rule. On the other hand, the husband's remarks were the exact opposite. They had once again proved the truth of that old saying, "putting one's foot in your mouth" is a big, big mistake.

The Wicked Witches

Have you ever wondered when and where Halloween's "trick or treat" custom originated? If so, I'd like to tell you how it all started. You see, I was there when it was born. Perhaps not on a world-wide basis, but at least when it first began in our little village of Richmond Highlands.

Prior to the mid 1920s, Halloween night was a quasi-legal time of devilment and mischief. A time for all sorts of bizarre and mean tricks, such as turning over outhouses, ripping up wooden sidewalks, and pulling a building's main electric switch, thus plunging the entire house into total darkness. Also such stunts as waxing widows, hoisting a full-sized wagon to the top of the school building, and performing many other "cute" little stunts which in other situations or times would be reason enough for a spell in the "pokey." Strange as it may seem to most normal adults, usually the participants of these so called "harmless pranks" felt really proud of their accomplishments.

The night "trick or treat" was born started like any other Halloween. Several of us ten-year-olds were roving the main road of the our small community looking for mischief. In our search most of the area was fair game, but as is true in most closely knit neighborhoods, there was one exception. This was the house we certainly didn't want to haunt or with which to have any connection of any kind. It was the home of two spinster sisters who we all considered quite sinister, sort of like the wicked witch in the fairy tale "Hansel and Gretel." These ladies were quite aloof with their dress and their demeanor quite severe. Most of the time they stayed by themselves and didn't participate in the various community activities. In addition, there was considerable gossip about their comings and goings. At our tender ages, we believed most of the rumors which circulated. As a result we tried our best to avoid any contact with these ladies.

On the particular Halloween in question, it so happened we were so busy uprooting the board sidewalk next to the spinster's property we failed to notice we had reached the section which ran in front of their house. Incidentally, moving these timbers was quite a task for ten-year-olds, and in any other situation would certainly have elicited howls of anguish from us if we had been forced to do so.

Just as we were about to raise the first board running next to this forbidden property, we heard a soft scraping of feet above our heads. When we looked up, we were confronted by one of the dreaded sisters. She stood on her front porch glaring down at us. Ordinarily, we would have all fled into the darkness to escape, but in our confused mental state we were transfixed to the spot. While immobilized, it was easy for us to imagine her eyes repeatedly emitted lightning-like flashes. With her sharp facial features and her gray hair tied in a tight bun on the back of her head, she really looked quite fierce. In addition to her awesome and imposing manner, she wore a dark-colored dress which topped heavy brown cotton stockings and plain, dark, low-heeled, blunt-toed, thick-soled shoes. Her entire somber costume all added together to give her a really ominous appearance. We all thought our end had come and our doom was sealed.

"You boys come in here this instant!" she shouted.

Any ideas of escape were completely erased from our minds. Our legs would not move and our addled brains held no thought except to obey her command. The whole situation was similar to that which occurs in a nightmare, except this was no dream. It was for real. At her command, we meekly climbed the porch stairs and were literally pushed into the front room. As we entered, I had fleeting thoughts of what horrible fate might be in store for all of us.

Once inside the house, the spinster's appearance underwent a rapid and complete metamorphosis. She, as well her sister, both with broad smiles, led us into the dining room where we found the dining table piled high with all sorts of cookies, cakes, fruits, and juices. We were soon joined by many other would-be pranksters. A grand time was had by all, including the hostesses.

In our childhood eyes, the two spinsters had instantaneously and magically been transformed from wicked witches into fairy godmothers. As far as we were concerned, this was the birthplace of the present day Halloween "trick or treat."

While Halloween was first started in the seventh century in Europe, it seems certain that "trick or treat" didn't originate there. Also it is fairly certain it did not first appear in the British Isles. The following true story seems to confirm this fact. It is told of a British World War II bride who was confronted by several "trick or treaters" on her first Halloween in this country. Being unfamiliar with this custom, at first she looked at the children and then at their sacks full of goodies. Finally, not knowing what was the next step, she very carefully reached into each sack and took out a prize. She then thanked the young ones, and carefully closed the door. Can you imagine the looks on the faces of the children following this complete reversal of the usual procedure?

Returning to the events of our neighborhood, you can rest assured from that time on we not only didn't play any Halloween tricks on the spinsters, but instead made sure no one else did either. The spinsters, in turn, began to participate in the activities of the community, became good neighbors, and seemed to be much happier.

There may have been other "trick or treat" customs in other places at an earlier date, but for us that evening was a first.

Ward 21

The other night I dreamed I was imprisoned in a dingy cell. It was a terrifying experience and seemed so unfair because I was innocent of any crime. On awakening, I found myself perspiring profusely, but was thankful to discover it was only a dream. This experience, even though short lived, made me wonder about those who have been imprisoned unfairly because of mistaken identity or false testimony.

Frequently we read about some innocent person who has been incarcerated for a prolonged period of time for a crime he or she did not commit and who later on was exonerated when the true criminal was discovered. Can you imagine how that falsely charged person felt at the time he was pronounced guilty, when he was led away and the cell doors slammed shut, even as he kept declaring his innocence?

In a somewhat lesser way, I have experienced the eerie feeling which accompanies the clanging of metal prison doors after passing through them. It so happened that early one Sunday morning I was called by a very distraught mother. "My son is in the county jail and is accused of murdering one of his friends. He is hurt and needs medical attention."

The son was one of my good patients and one who would be considered the least likely to commit a violent crime. Thunderstruck by the news, I hurriedly dressed and made my way to the jail. As I entered the jail house proper, the early morning was bright and sunny. This only made the dark interior even more foreboding. No sunshine penetrated the dimly lit corridors. There was nothing charming or decorative to be seen, especially as the jailer and I made our way into the deeper and most secure areas. While it was not to be compared with the dungeons of the Dark Ages, the entire atmosphere was not one which gave comfort or reassurance to a first-time visitor.

To this day I can still feel some of my apprehensions as the first heavy metal door slammed closed with a loud clang behind me. This same feeling was intensified when the second door closed and locked as we progressed into the bowels of the prison. By the time the third door's ringing reverberations had ceased and the jailor had left me alone with the prisoner, I felt completely abandoned. My one hope against hope was that the prison's routine included keeping track of all visitors who, at any given moment, happen to be incarcerated with the real inmates.

In the cell, once my eyes had adjusted to the lack of lighting, I spied the prisoner huddled in one corner. He sat forlornly with his head down, staring at the floor. In what seemed a stuperous state, he gave no sign of recognition when I approached him, and as he was usually well groomed, it was a shock to see his completely disheveled appearance. With rumpled, dirt?filled hair; multiple bruises; and abrasions over most of his upper body, extremities, and face, he was a completely different?looking person than the one I had known before. However in his present predicament, it was understandable he would feel depressed as he sat in his lonely cell looking completely cowed, friendless, and alone.

When questioned, he claimed the previous night was a complete blank, that he did not remember anything that had happened, and that he had no information regarding his present predicament, or how he had sustained his injuries. While I realized amnesia is often a mental mechanism used to obliterate unpleasant experiences, I could not determine whether my patient's loss of recall was conscious or subconscious.

An examination failed to reveal any serious injuries. After treating his superficial abrasions and after trying to give him some consolation, I was somewhat anxious to escape from this undesirable confinement and atmosphere. It was a welcome sound to finally hear the steps of the jailor as he came to escort me back to the real world. What a relief to finally reach the main prison door. I felt sorry for the prisoner and others like him, but couldn't help being thankful for my release. At the time, I wondered how well I would tolerate the confinement similar to the one facing my patient. The details of how he had come to be in such a terrible predicament is another complete story in itself and will have to be told at a later time.

Personally never having been confronted with anything like a jail sentence, I once did have an experience which, on reflection, gave me a bit of a chill. One Christmas season, Margaret was asked to play her violin in a program for the inmates of a nearby hospital which housed a rather large number of the mentally ill. These ranged from the mildly disturbed to the more violent types. As the program took place on my half?day out of the office, I volunteered to drive her and wait in the car. I was dressed rather lightly in my relaxing clothes. As time passed the cold December weather penetrated into the car and into my bones. In addition to my discomfort, I was worried about Margaret's welfare and so decided to check on what was happening at the hospital program.

When I entered the hospital auditorium, it was crowded with patients as well as their numerous attendants. Some of the groups had multiple guards. Others were practically on their own. Not finding any vacant seats, I stood at the back of the hall. As Margaret was scheduled to play near the end of the program, I knew I was in for a prolonged wait.

During the program's progress, there was a constant parade of patients to and from the auditorium. Some had to be escorted by attendants. Most were dressed in their hospital garb. Others wore slacks and sport shirts similar to what I had on. This latter group apparently were allowed to move about without any supervision. All during the program, everyone seemed to act like the hubbub of all the traffic was just the normal routine.

As I stood watching the various performers, who incidentally for the most part were very talented, I noticed one of the attendants who kept glancing back in my direction. At first, I thought nothing of this and felt he was probably concerned I didn't have a chair on which to sit. Finally, when the seat next to him was vacated, he promptly motioned for me to come and sit down. By this time my legs were in need of a change so happily I accepted his invitation. He was a pleasant?appearing person and welcomed me. There was no chance for conversation until the present performer finished. At the pause between numbers, he leaned toward me and in a whisper asked, "Are you from Ward 21?"

Even though I had no idea what "Ward 21" was or where it was located, I did have a momentary chilling feeling run down my spine. It did occur to me it might be where the less disturbed inmates were housed. However, regardless of the degree of supervision required in "21," I had no desire to be classified as one of the patients. With an emphatic answer, I was able to assure him I was just the chauffeur for the next to the last performer.

Fortunately, my answer satisfied him and he didn't pursue the subject further. However, I couldn't help but wonder what it would have been like had I been escorted, while protesting loudly, to Ward 21 and once there incarcerated in spite of my strenuous objections.

If such a situation had occurred, I can well imagine the conversation of the attendants at their coffee break as they discussed my protestations. Their remarks would probably be something like this. "There's a fellow in Ward 21 who keeps yelling he doesn't belong there. He even keeps insisting he is a medical doctor from Tacoma. It's really sad how confused some of these patients can get. If he doesn't calm down soon we may have to give him a hypo or even resort to a straight jacket."

ADDENDUM:
To return to the patient/prisoner story, the following occurred. After a trial, he was convicted of second degree murder. While the exact circumstances of the crime are a bit vague and the entire true story will never be known, many of the witnesses felt the real criminal was the murdered man; that he was the one responsible for what did occur. In addition, it was felt he was a reprehensible character and had been taunting the prisoner about having an affair with the prisoner's wife. Also, he was the one who had given the prisoner the hypo which caused him to "blank out" and later on, in a confused state, go

home and get a gun which he used to commit the crime. It was also established that the prisoner's disheveled state during his original confinement was due to his struggles while trying to resist getting that injection.

In jail, the prisoner was a model inmate and was put in charge of the prison library. He also took computer courses and after his early release, on the recommendation of the prison warden, was able to secure an excellent position with a large American corporation.

From Failure to Victory

There are only two kinds of people who never fail or never make a mistake. First, there are those who never do anything or who never take a chance. The second type are the liars, those who do not accept responsibility and who blame others for any bad results.

A true story is told of a famous doctor who discovered a treatment for syphilis many many years ago, long before the advent of penicillin. During his experiments, his first 605 medications were failures. Finally, the 606th proved to be successful. From that time on the treatment was appropriately called "606." It is apparent this dedicated man was not easily discouraged, was a real pioneer, and became a benefactor of mankind. Without his persistence and willingness to work to overcome his early failures, the world would have been deprived of the benefits of his dedication, and he, in turn, of the fruits of his ultimate success. A truly classic example of a conversion of failures into a victory.

Many of us can recall experiences in our past which at first we thought were failures, only to later on realize they were exactly the opposite. Personally, I can think of one of my failures which subsequently became a victory. It occurred in the following manner. One of my obstetrical patients was about to have her third child. Previously she had had the other two via Caesarian sections. On this third occasion, she and her husband felt three children were enough and did request having a tubal ligation at the time of the Caesarian. This seemed to be a very logical decision.

The technique of tubal ligations is fairly standard and is not too complex. To avoid failure in so doing, it is customary to take a few extra precautions in order to assure success. As a result, in addition to clamping and cutting the tubes, each cut end is doubly ligated with a non-absorbable suture. The ends of the tubes on the uterine side are doubled over and retied before they are buried into the uterine wall. Comparatively speaking, it would be like putting valuables into a safe, locking it, and then burying the safe in a large container of wet cement. In past cases using this technique, the procedure had been 100 percent successful. Consequently, with complete confidence I performed it as described.

Following the Caesarian section and the delivery of a chubby little girl, the post-operative recovery was uneventful and all went well for the next several months. Then, one day, the patient came to my office in a very distraught state. An examination revealed she was once again pregnant; a condition I found hard to believe.

Fortunately the patient, while a bit shaken, did not lose confidence in me and decided to stay on in spite of my apparent failure. I, in turn, had mixed emotions. In addition to my chagrin, I had difficulty understanding how a previously trustworthy procedure could have failed. Also, I wanted to get a chance at the time of the next Caesarian to see what the underlying problem might be. When the time for the delivery arrived, both my assistant, a competent surgeon in his own right, and I were anxious to solve the apparent mystery. During the Caesarian, after the baby had been successfully delivered and the uterus sutured together, we inspected the sites of the tubal ligations. Here all seemed to be in order and both of us were at a loss to explain how an ovum could have managed to pass through the surgical barriers which had been established at the previous Caesarian section. In order for an egg to navigate these barricades it would be somewhat like a train trying to pass through a collapsed tunnel. However, to be sure, we placed some additional non-absorbable sutures at both sites. This accomplished the desired results for as the years passed there were no subsequent pregnancies. While our mission had been accomplished, the mystery of the previous failure remained.

You may ask the question, "How did this failure turn out to be a victory?" The answer was given to me several months later when the mother and the new baby came to my office for routine check-ups. Both were in excellent condition, especially the mother, who was in high spirits and who spontaneously exclaimed, "This child is such a blessing! Both my husband and I keep saying to each other, 'We don't know what we would do without her."

And so, while it wasn't necessary to have 605 failures, like the doctor mentioned above, in order to win a victory, here a victory resulted from one apparent failure. This same lesson may also apply to all of us and to many of our other apparently less than favorable experiences.

It's "No" Emergency

Emergencies, especially medical ones, come in many different guises—some serious, some not so. In fact, in some cases the rescuer may be more at risk than the rescued and may be led into some awkward situations.

I'm not much of a singer, but on one occasion after treating one of the choir members who had collapsed, I had to remain in place until the choir finished its number. While so confined, I decided I didn't want to sit idly by so I sang along with them. This was an exciting experience for me, if not for them. Later on, there surfaced some untoward consequences when a few of the congregation made some derogatory remarks about the choir's renditions on that particular Sunday. Some of the parishioners even wondered if perhaps the church organ's reeds should be checked. Of course, no one in the choir revealed the true cause of the discordant notes. All of which just goes to prove how charitable true Christians can be.

This experience was just one of many "emergency" calls I had to make during the church services over a period of years. Usually in these situations the victim would be found with a marked pallor, fast pulse, and cool and sweaty skin, plus varying degrees of apprehension. Most of them would be found lying quietly on the pew when I arrived. In some instances they would manifest marked anxiety and even a fear of impending death.

In cases of this kind, there are several physical conditions which may be contributing factors. The most common one is what is known as orthostatic hypertension, which is characterized by a marked drop in blood pressure due to prolonged standing in one position, especially if the atmosphere is warm. This type of reaction is often seen in healthy young people such as military personnel who may collapse while standing in parade formation prior to starting to march. It may also occur in some individuals who are taking medications for high blood pressure or in others who have an underlying cardiac weakness or some other debilitating condition. I suspect some cases might even be triggered by a portion of a church sermon which happened to hit home in a telling way.

Because of the many possible causative factors, each situation had to be individually evaluated. None could be summarily dismissed as unimportant until so proven.

Because of the frequency of these occurrences during the church services, we had developed a routine for handling them. In addition to stretchers, bandages, tape, and splints for the trauma cases, we also had oxygen bottles and masks ready for instant use. One of the office workers, who was a competent and efficient type, was always at the ready as my assistant for any and all situations. She would invariably be present with the right equipment, including the walk-around oxygen bottle, for each situation.

In each of these "emergencies" there were several problems which had to be overcome. First of all, most occurred during the main church service when all was quiet and serene. As the pews were crowded, in many instances the person involved was usually somewhat centrally located. Trying to be quiet as we scrambled across the intervening bodies was a bit of a challenge. Questioning the patient, if he or she was conscious, had to be done in whispers. As very few of the victims were patients from my practice, I usually had to start from scratch. It was difficult to get much of a history from them in this subdued environment. Of course, because of the close quarters involved, there were many kibitzers who stared and listened to all that was taking place.

Fortunately, practically all of the individuals rapidly responded physically and with a little reassurance, were able to continue their worship. Some had to be removed to an adjoining room where they could have time to recover. All were cautioned to see their own doctor at an early date for further evaluation. In some rare instances, a serious underlying condition would be found which needed immediate attention. In one case, the person had a cardiac arrest and required cardio pulmonary resuscitation followed by a 911 call. She subsequently recovered and lived for another ten years.

In another case, I found a chronic heart condition which, while important, was not emergent. Learning the name of the patient's doctor, I whispered to my assistant, "Call an ambulance, but it's no emergency."

Apparently the word "no" was not heard as a few minutes later sirens were heard and came wailing to a baleful stop in front of the church. Seconds later, the doors at the rear of the sanctuary burst open and in rushed several firemen. Of course, this was somewhat distracting for the minister who was giving the sermon. I tried to signal to the firemen that all was under control only to hear the wail of another siren. Again the doors opened with a crash and in charged two policemen. With considerable arm waving on my part, I was able to convey the "all's well" message. However within minutes, a third siren followed. This time, the paramedics rushed in. This last group, a smoothly operating team used to taking charge in emergencies, were not to be waved off. As they approached us they simultaneously snapped open their four-wheeled stretcher with loud clicking noises. Then, with considerable speed and actions as smooth as fine silk, they whisked the patient onto their carriage and made a hasty exit.

In addition to the somewhat chaotic state occurring, one other factor added to the noise and confusion. All of the assorted aid men, by now eight in number, had his individual walkie-talkie. Each of these emitted not only various squeals and squawks but also numerous vocal calls from their separate headquarters.

While all of this was taking place, the minister was valiantly trying to deliver his message to his by now understandably less than attentive flock. I, in turn, was perspiring profusely mainly because of my internal tensions as well as the external disturbances taking place, and the part I had had to play in the front and center spotlight.

After the church service finally ended, I awaited, with some apprehension, the reaction of the minister, a forceful preacher, who ordinarily ran everything with clock-like precision. Usually he would not tolerate interference of any kind during his services. When at last he and I did meet in the foyer of the church after most of the parishioners had departed, he approached me with a stern countenance. I expected a strong reprimand and was completely surprised when he extended his hand and, with a smile said, "This morning you certainly gave me some tough competition."

Competition or not, there is one thing the minister could be thankful for on that particular Sunday—at least he didn't have to hear me sing in the choir.

Butch

It sure pays to listen to your elders, especially to your mother. If I'd had enough sense to do so, I'd be a lot better off today and wouldn't have to wonder how I ever got saddled with a guy like Butch.

Mother told me I was making a big mistake to marry him, and she was right. She said, "You're in love with the guy 'cause he's tall, handsome, has curly hair, and likes to dance. Once you're married, he'll stop dancing, lose most of his hair, and probably get fat and dowdy looking."

Well after fifteen years of marriage, and four kids later, most of what mother said has come true. He's sure lost his desire to go dancing, and his hair is getting thinner. He isn't fat, through no fault of his own. He sure eats plenty, but I guess working two jobs a day uses up the calories he takes in. He's plenty dowdy looking all right. Of course, driving an oil truck during the day and moonlighting in a gas station doesn't do much to help keep his clothes stay very neat.

He never complains out loud, but I get tired of the sort of sad look he gives me when he starts off to work in the morning while I'm still in bed. You'd think his getting breakfast for the kids and getting them off to school was some kind of a big deal.

I'll have to admit he does keep enough food on our table, but sometimes he forgets to keep the fridge stocked with beer. I don't know how he expects me to enjoy the morning soap operas and the afternoon shows on TV without something to quench my thirst once in a while. Right now, I could stand another beer as this movie isn't any better the fourth time than it was on the first showing.

Even the kids get tired of TV and sometimes want me to play with or read to them. I can't be bothered. At least on weekends, when Butch takes them to Sunday School and to the park, he gets them off my hands.

Oh well, it's 4:00 P.M. so I guess I'd better get out of this old comfortable bathrobe and put on a dress before he gets home for dinner. He's always in a hurry since he has to start out for his second job right afterwards.

One other thing—he sure has some goofy ideas about a woman dressing up a bit, and combing her hair for dinner. You'd think we were going out to some fancy restaurant or having some ritzy company in.

Putting on a dress is bad enough, but I draw the line when it comes to wearing a girdle. Mine must be shrinking. At least it seems to get tighter and tighter whenever I do try to put it on. Like a lot of modern things, I guess they just don't make them like they used to. Anyhow, girdles are a real pain in the neck, or maybe I should say in some other parts of my anatomy.

I guess everyone is entitled to a few mistakes in his or her life, some big and some little. I've made my share, but I sure pulled a first-class boner fifteen years ago when I married Butch. If I had it to do over again, I'd sure pay more attention to what my mother had to say. Oh well, it's too late now, and besides I'm not sure how I'd get along without his regular paychecks.

When I think about it, I sure wonder how a girl like me ever got saddled with a fellow like Butch.

Woof! Woof!

Henry was an animal lover, especially of dogs—with one irritating exception. This was the mutt who lived next door, a big, shaggy, mean mongrel. During the daylight hours, this beast guarded his home territory in an overbearing and frightening manner, scaring any and all who dared approach the property lines. The dog's size alone was awe inspiring. His massiveness, when combined with his deep rumbling bark and his sharp, bared fangs, was completely intimidating to all but the most foolhardy.

Henry had tried to overlook all of these undesirable characteristics and had made every attempt to be friendly with this brute—all to no avail. As if the dog understood Henry's frustrations and wished to add further stress to their already strained relationship, he, with canine cunning, adopted one additional unpleasant behavioral pattern. Each evening, about bedtime, he would station himself on the side of his house near Henry's bedroom window and every few minutes, with clock-like regularity, give forth with an horrendous "WOOF! WOOF!" These renditions would continue throughout most of the so-called sleeping hours.

After several nights of this nocturnal baying, Henry, in a state of near exhaustion, appealed to the dog's owner. "Could you please take the dog indoors after eleven o'clock? I'm completely done in from lack of sleep."

The answer, in the negative, was, "The dog is on his own property and he can bark whenever and however long he wants to."

With this rebuff, it was apparent the neighbor didn't know Henry very well, nor did he realize the extent of Henry's ingenuity, tenacity, and inventiveness. Second to his love of animals was Henry's fascination and adeptness with electronic gadgets. Following the rude rebuke by his neighbor and realizing the dog needed some form of training and disciplining, Henry went to work to develop a device designed to put a stop to this nighttime yelping.

It took several weeks to perfect an electronic receptor which would be activated by the dog's "WOOF! WOOF!" This instrument, in response to the "woofs," would initiate a high-frequency beam unheard by human ears, but very painful to a dog's more acute auditory mechanism. This beam could be pointed in any direction, and its intensity could be varied in strength from mild to strong. The assembly of this device and its final satisfactory testing came none to soon, as Henry was completely exhausted by lack of sleep.

Mounting his invention on the open windowsill, he aimed it at the spot where the dog usually stationed himself. As expected, that evening the mutt appeared and started his usual barking. With the first "WOOF! WOOF!" the electronic mechanism switched on and the high-frequency beam sped with lightning like speed to the dog's ears. A startled look flashed across the cur's face. He shook his head in an attempt to rid himself of this noxious sensation he had just experienced. The second "WOOF! WOOF!" elicited a similar response. In addition, his ears drooped. He peered over his shoulder as he attempted to see from whence his invisible attacker was striking. With the third "WOOF! WOOF!" both his tail and his head dropped low, and he ran pellmell into the house.

The dog did not appear for three days. When finally he did show his face once more, he crept slowly out onto the lawn, all arrogance and bluff completely absent from his demeanor. Then, with what was apparently nervousness and trepidation, he slowly looked, first to the right, and then to the left. Finally with much hesitation, he gave forth with the faintest of faint "Woof! Woof!"

Henry had long since turned off his electronic dog discipliner, but had it mounted at the ready for instant use in case of any repetition of the dog's previous behavior. This never did occur.

And now once more Henry likes dogs—all of them all of the time.

Mindy's Heaven

I'm not very old and am really kind of ragged looking. My black curly hair goes every which way on my body and even covers my eyes. People say I'm a cute little mutt, whatever that means.

However, what I really want to tell you is I think that I may have found "Dog Heaven." If not, it's something that will do very well as a substitute until the real thing comes along.

My new friends here in "Heaven" are sure varied. Three of them are beautiful big collie dogs with long hair and gorgeous white muffs around their necks. They are so regal they make me feel a bit scruffy in comparison. They don't mean for this to happen and it's not their fault. One of them, Meika, is my special pal. She plays with me, and we have much fun with our mock fighting. In addition to those three, there are three cats, two geese, many ducks, chickens, rabbits, and one big pig named Sam Sam. They, all together, form a constant source of company and amusement. The black lamb next door is fun to tease. His wool is so thick I can't even get my teeth through it to reach his skin as I pretend to bite him when we run through the pasture.

I really like the people who live here. They are: Jim, the father, who was the one who found me and rescued me; Molly, the mother, who feeds me and loves me; and Greg and Brian, the two boys who wrestle me and hug me. Marc, the youngest, hasn't appeared yet, and won't come down from cloud nine for a few more years.

I don't remember very much of my past history. My first conscious thoughts were those of flying through the air after being hit by a big black automobile wheel. When I landed in the grass by the roadside, my left leg hurt terribly. I don't know how long I lay in the field, but when I did awaken, I could hear running water. I was very thirsty and also very hungry. Slowly, I hobbled on my three good legs toward the stream. There on the bank I found a couple of old fishheads. I did nibble at them, but they weren't very tasty. In contrast, the water was clear, cool, and sparkling and did a lot to quench my thirst.

Time means little to me, but I do know I lay in the grass at the water's edge for quite a spell. Later on, someone said I must have been there at least for two or three days. I do know my left leg hurt a great deal during this period, and I was very hungry. It seemed to me it would have been easier just to close my eyes and go to sleep, forever.

About the time I was ready to give up, I heard footsteps approaching through the grass. When I opened my eyes I looked into a man's face. It was a kind face and expressed concern. Immediately I knew a friend had arrived. I guess he knew I was hungry, because he gave me what was left of his hamburger. After carefully examining me, he gently picked me up and carried me to his car, then to the doctor.

My leg was really in pretty bad shape. It was broken in three places and had to have a metal rod placed down the inside for the entire length of the bone to hold it together. I'm sure it was an expensive procedure. Later on, someone said something about one hundred eighty-five dollars. The only reason the sum was mentioned was because the people really didn't have that much to spend on a little mutt like me. Anyhow, I think I know a bit about what they had to sacrifice to bring me back to where I am today.

The above partially explains why I feel I have found a piece of Heaven here on earth. It's not just the rolling hills and the deep grass; it's not just the other animals; it's not just the people, or even the fun I have here. What is really important is the one quality I have discovered in this paradise. It's the love that is expressed by all and for all, including me.

Mr. Robin's Wormy Welfare State

'Tis often said the early bird gets the worm, but Mr. Robin found an easier solution in his search for food—he broke a wing.

This tale all started one bright spring morning when Dave's springer spaniel came trotting home proudly and carefully carrying a wounded bird in his mouth. This he gently deposited at his master's feet. Dave, an ardent animal lover, didn't take long to diagnose the bird's problem—a broken wing. This he splinted with two Popsicle sticks. Then he started looking for worms with which to feed his new patient.

At first, finding enough worms to satisfy the robin's voracious appetite was fairly easy, but as time passed the supply diminished and digging up one hundred worms a day became a fatiguing chore. Soon it became necessary to enlist the help of the neighborhood children who had taken an avid interest in the bird. Later on, the efforts of the young pupils in a nearby school were called upon.

As a result of all the good care and plentiful supply of succulent worms, within a few weeks the wing healed and Mr. Robin was able to start flying once again, at first just around the yard. Later on, he made more distant trips. However he made no attempt to leave his newly found food supply and regularly returned to his perch on the back porch railing, especially at meal time. This latter turned out to be a never-ending routine. Even compassionate Dave came to realize that this state of affairs was not good for the robin nor for the hard-working worm diggers.

He attempted to rectify this dependent condition and after many attempts to shoo the bird away had failed, Dave took him to the nearby wooded ravine, only to have Mr. Robin return to his back porch railing within minutes of his release. In desperation, Dave finally took him by car to a distant wooded area. Three days later, the bird made it back to his favorite perch once more. As Mr. Robin figuratively said, "Why be an early bird who has to scratch and dig when it is so much easier this other way."

Realizing some drastic action was required, Dave came up with a solution for the robin's welfare state which turned out to be a stroke of genius and one that could be copied by our politicians in their attempts to solve our country's welfare reform legislation. He simply and very gradually reduced the number of worms furnished each day to his client.

The end result was that finally Mr. Robin's hunger increased to the point where he had to start looking for some of his own rations. The initiative and industry required for his labors had definite side benefits for him. Replacing his feelings of dependency came a sense of independence and self-confidence which had been sadly lacking after his injury. Accompanying this increase he regained his self-esteem and his desire for the freedom of the skies.

Shortly thereafter he flew off to be with his former friends—which is just the way it should be.

An Apple from the Teacher

With a wild triumphant shout, he leaped from behind the bushes and yelled, "I've finally caught you!"

When he grabbed each of us by the back of our shirts, he ripped mine nearly its entire length from the collar to the tail. He was strong and held us firmly in a vise-like grip. Our first thoughts were that we were in the clutches of a maniacal inmate of the nearby hospital for the insane who had somehow eluded his guards. And who, in a deluded or psychotic state, had confused us with some imaginary foe.

As he held us, his eyes seemed to bug out. Big drops of sweat covered his forehead, cheeks, and neck. In his unshaven condition, with his uncombed hair wildly askew, he looked truly savage. His trousers were dirty and wrinkled and were topped by a smudged, grayish-white t-shirt which was torn and covered with brambles from the bush in which he had been hiding. He kept yelling excitedly and in what seemed to us an incoherent manner, "I'm sick and tired of you kids stealing my apples! I've finally caught you, and I'm going to make an example of you both."

As this was our first visit to this area, we were understandably confused, to say nothing of frightened, by all of his ranting and raving.

This little tableau took place on our last few days of vacation before we were to start our high school careers. As a final summer celebration, two of us had been swimming in the nearby lake and were making our way up a trail from the lake to the highway. Just before reaching the road, we came upon a clearing in the woods. In this cleared area, we passed a small fenced orchard. Outside the fenced area was a lone apple tree. Several apples were lying on the ground under the tree. As the day was hot and we were tired, hungry, and thirsty, we each picked up two of the apples from the ground, then continued on our way across the clearing. Just as we entered the woods on the far side of the open space, this wild man leaped upon us.

While he was shaking us and acting completely demented, I could see my friend drop his two apples into the bushes behind his back. I, because of my Scotch ancestry, being by nature and training rather frugal and not wanting to waste such tasty morsels, continued to hold mine, one in each hand, behind my back, trying to conceal them as best I could.

As time passed, the maniac became somewhat exhausted by all of his yelling and wild actions. With this change, I thought perhaps there might be a chance of finding a way to escape from his clutches. However instead of trying to make a run for it, I felt perhaps the best tactic was to try to calm his mania; to persuade him this was our first visit to this area; that we meant no harm; and that the apples we had taken were from the ground under the tree outside the fenced area.

As I explained all this, a look of reason began to appear on his face. After several minutes, he released his hold on our shirts. Still later, after considerable talking and explaining on our part, he told us to be on our way. We lost no time in so doing. On reaching the highway, we shared the two apples I had secreted during our ordeal.

This event occurred on a Saturday. The following Tuesday was to be our first day in high school, an occasion that, by itself, for most individuals tends to cause some anxiety and dryness of the mouth. As I walked into my first class on that fateful morning, I was nervous and tense, but what I saw on entering the room made me freeze in my tracks. The instructor was none other than the previously maniacal wild man of three days before, only now he seemed to be calm, shaven, well dressed, and very normal in look and manner. Probably, because of my different apparel and more civilized appearance, he didn't seem to recognize me. At least, he gave no sign if he did so.

As the years passed, he proved to be a very sane man and an excellent teacher. I took several courses from him and we became good friends. Shortly before my graduation, I mentioned the apple stealing episode to him. He merely smiled, but did not make any comment nor give any sign as to whether on not he remembered me or the incident.

Be that as it was, the above tale is somewhat of a reversal of an old custom. Instead of an apple *for* it was an apple *from* the teacher.

Rock-'N'-Roll Racket

The rock and roll noise (it can't be called music) from the overhead speakers blasted my old sensitive eardrums. In spite of the thousands and thousands of recordings in this store, it soon became apparent that this establishment was not really geared to nor interested in the tastes of those of us in the older generation.

On this trip my main mission was to find a few musical comedy recordings by the composer, Jerome Kern. It immediately became apparent this was to be no easy task as the preponderance of the store's inventory was in the rock and roll category. Not seeing any clerks readily available, I searched and searched for the section that might contain the classical or semi-classical numbers.

All during my explorations, the rock and roll blasts continued to assault my by now rapidly fatiguing hearing apparatus. While this was occurring the thought finally came to me that perhaps a hearing loss was, in reality, a good defense, and the only way any normal person could tolerate the intolerable noises was to finally lose his or her auditory functions completely.

As time passed and my search for the Jerome Kern section met with a complete lack of success, I finally spotted a young lady clerk. She proved to be a gum-chewing, fake platinum blond who I surmised must be the one responsible for the selection of the recordings which were currently emanating from the overhead speakers. Confronting her, and because of the noisy atmosphere plus my present hearing loss, I shouted, "Where might I find the Jerome Kern recordings?"

She, with a blank look on her already blank-looking face, shouted back, "I'll get the manager."

Several minutes later, the manager arrived. She looked like a clone of the clerk, even chewing her gum with the same maximum intensity. She must have been on her coffee break because she was holding a half-empty cup in one hand and a cigarette in the other. Having been interrupted in her free time, she wasn't in the best of moods. Her whole attitude gave me an eerie sense of impending failure for my present mission, but again I shouted, "Where can I find the Jerome Kern records?"

She gave me a quizzical look, but being the manager she had to put up a good front and have an answer to my query. Her response did little to bolster my confidence in her store when she asked, "Which group does he play with?"

As I didn't have the ghost of an answer to her question, and being considerably weakened by the bombardment of sound, I realized my impending complete defeat. Thanking her for her efforts, I beat a hasty retreat.

As I stepped into the real outside world I was amazed to find an atmosphere of complete silence. None of the usual street noises were present. The automobiles seemed to coast by without any apparent motor or tire sounds. People on the sidewalk were completely silent although they seemed to be in conversation with each other. Puzzled at first, the truth of my situation finally struck home—I was stone deaf.

At first I became a bit panicky, but with some effort I was able to compose myself. Fortunately, this state of affairs proved to be only temporary, and as the day wore on sounds began to return, and gradually my hearing became normal once more.

Several days later, in a quiet record section of a department store, I found a wide selection of classical and semi-classical recordings, including several by Jerome Kern.

However, I never did find the answer to the record store manager's question as to "Which group does Jerome Kern play with?"

A Few Good Tips

Have you ever had a waiter or waitress who acted like he or she was doing you a favor and you were lucky to have them at your table?

Most individuals in this line of work are pleasant, efficient, and seem to enjoy their work. As much of their income is derived from tips, they do their best to please their customers and to give good service. Personally having waited table in my early days, I learned quickly how important this aspect of the job was and found that to be successful required a bit of extra effort.

In contrast to the usual type of waiter, occasionally the opposite ones may appear. They, by their demeanor, act like they are superior to their customers and give the impression they are doing them a favor by waiting on them. A case in point follows.

One evening several couples were at dinner when we encountered one of this type. Through no fault of his own, he wasn't much to look at. He had a long, horse-like face with a large nose with flaring nostrils which conveyed the feeling to others that there was some noxious odor emanating from the nearby surroundings. In contrast to the heroes of many western novels, all of whom had narrow waist lines and broad shoulders, this man's were just the reverse. He had a broad waist and narrow shoulders.

In addition, he did not appear to be a happy person. While not known for sure, the causes of his unhappiness may have been multiple, such as a nagging wife, too many debts, or some past experience which had embittered him. Possibly it may have been due to the fact he didn't like the looks of his present customers because we didn't happen to live up to his expectations and didn't look as prosperous as some of his other clients. Whatever the cause of his discontent, he approached our table with a look of distaste as well as a manner which let us know that he was our superior and we were fortunate to have him.

Our group of five couples had just come from a university football game in which our team had been victorious. We were all in a somewhat festive mood. Our euphoria may have contributed to our waiter's glum approach to his forthcoming tasks. On second thought, he may have been a rooter for the other team and may even have lost a wager. In any event, he seemed determined to be miserable.

In spite of his several negative characteristics, he was an excellent waiter and didn't miss an order. After we had finished dinner, it was decided each couple would leave its own tip. In those days, a good meal could be had for two or three dollars, so most of the charges were about four or five dollars per couple. For some unknown reason, I was elected to handle the payment of the various bills. As a result, money was thrust at me from all sides. I had five and ten dollar bills, plus some ones, protruding from between my fingers. It was all very confusing.

Everyone else had left the dining room and the waiter and I were the only ones remaining. He was working on the opposite side of the table from where I was trying to sort out my financial confusion. I had put my tip by my plate and when I looked up, our previously sour-looking friend had a broad smile on his face. This expression was so misplaced it was sort of like an errant crease on a newly pressed pair of pants. In fact, his smile seemed so out of place I wished he would go back to his previous dour expression.

Wondering what had triggered this sudden change of mood, I started looking for its cause. Nothing was apparent until I glanced down at my place setting and saw that, by mistake, I had put one of the ten dollar bills there as a tip instead of the one I had intended. At that time, a 10 percent tip was considered appropriate. Being of Scottish descent, I wasn't about to leave a 200 percent gratuity. Somehow I had to rectify my error. By waiting until he turned to put some of the dishes on the tray, I was able, with a fast shuffle, to grab the ten spot and slip a one into its place. Then I took off with haste and didn't look back.

Later on I wondered how he took this sudden change of fortune, but figured that he did get a 20 percent tip so he didn't suffer any great loss. On second thought, perhaps I should have left him a much bigger tip by telling him the secret of happiness, and even of financial success, was for him to treat his guests with a smile and pleasant manner; to put aside his arrogant airs and to stop acting like he was so superior. However it is very unlikely such advice would have been heeded or such thoughts would ever enter his mind.

"But, I Had the Green Light!"

At the busy Chicago intersection, as he was pulled back from the path of a speeding truck, he kept yelling, "But, I had the green light!"

"Of course you did, and if you had kept on going, you also would have had a ready-made inscription for your final headstone."

Speaking of headstones brings to mind some of the unusual inscriptions to be found in older western cemeteries, often dating back to the days of the rugged individuals in their western migrations. Some examples are:

> I DID THE BEST I COULD WITH WHAT I HAD TO DO WITH.
>
> SHOT BY A JEALOUS HUSBAND.
>
> STABBED IN A DRUNKEN BRAWL.
>
> I EXPECTED THIS, BUT NOT SO SOON.
>
> I STOLE A HORSE, AND THEN HUNG AROUND TOO LONG.
>
> I KNEW I COULD DRAW FASTER THAN HE COULD.
>
> UNDER THIS GRASSY SOD,
> 'PON WHICH YOU HAVE JUST TROD,
> LIE THE BONES OF LES MOORE,
> KILLED BY TWO SLUGS FROM A 44,
> JUST TWO SLUGS—NO LES, NO MOORE.

Anon

In more modern cemeteries, the inscriptions are a bit more dignified and certainly less graphic. However if we are to be completely fair in this day of crowded streets and highways, multiple traffic signals, drive-by shootings drive through fast food stops, as well as our hectic life styles, some of the following grave side inscriptions seem more appropriate. First of all is the familiar one,

AS YOU ARE, I ONCE WAS,

AS I AM, SOON YOU WILL BE.

TOO MANY COCKTAILS AND ONLY ONE LIVER.

I TRIED TO PASS THE TRUCK ON A CURVE.

ALL I HAD WAS A COUPLE OF BEERS.

IN SPITE OF WHAT THE OTHERS SAID, I KNEW THEY WERE GOOD MUSHROOMS.

SHARK REPELLENT? WHAT IS THAT?

THE FREIGHT TRAIN AND I WERE TIED AT THE RR CROSSING.

I DIDN'T KNOW THE GUN WAS LOADED.

BIG MACS AND FRENCH FRIES WERE MY NEMESIS.

A SECOND PARACHUTE REALLY ISN'T NECESSARY.

A LITTLE MARIJUANA NEVER HURT ANYONE.

I DIDN'T SEE THE ARROWS ON THE ONE WAY STREET.

THEY SAID THAT BUNGIE JUMPING WAS PERFECTLY SAFE.

SEE, I TOLD YOU THAT I WAS SICK.

And finally, BUT, I HAD THE GREEN LIGHT!

Soothing Melodies

The hospital had installed a piped-in musical service in an attempt to calm the nervous patients. In the surgical rooms the volume was always kept very soft and low. One morning, while being operated upon under local anesthetic, the patient and his doctor, one of Scottish ancestry, heard coming from the overhead loud speaker the piece "Mack the Knife." As appropriate as this piece happened to be at that time, there was one song which was definitely banned from the hospital sound system at all times, namely, "I'll Be Glad When You Are Dead, You Rascal You."

A Handful of Thorns

How would you like to have to work three times as hard as you do now? There are those who do. I once knew a man who every day did just that. Each day he did three day's work. You might ask, was he a workaholic and did he accomplish a lot by his efforts? Not really. His problem was he lived each day three times. For example, each day he was frustrated by what he had done or not done on the previous day. He then had to cope with the complexities of the present day and, in addition, had to worry about what he thought would happen on the morrow. Needless to say, he became embroiled in the accumulations of all three days. With these triple burdens imposed upon him, he had no time for pleasure nor relaxation. Naturally he became old before his time.

On one occasion during World War II while stationed in California, he was ordered to a distant post for temporary duty. As this occurred during the Christmas season, one of his fellow officers whose home was in the area of his new assignment offered him the use of his house which at the moment was unoccupied. With this offer, just momentarily a smile crossed the worrier's face. It would make possible for him to send for his wife and give her the chance to come from New York for the Yuletide. However within seconds, his expression changed from one of pleasure to one of frustration. With this, he replied, "If I send for her she will have to travel to the airport through the snow. Her car will undoubtedly skid off the road, and she will be killed or injured."

While the above may seem ridiculous to the average person, not so to him. To him his logic was sound and was typical of his life style and a good example of the way he confronted each day. In some ways he resembled an automobile parked at the curbside with its throttle set at the maximum speed. A lot of noise would ensue, but there wouldn't be any progress. By not functioning as its designers intended, the motor would soon become overheated and would eventually destroy itself.

In my medical practice, I frequently heard young mothers complain in the following manner: "I don't think I can stand all the meals I am going to have to prepare, nor all the dishes I am going to have to wash during the next twenty years."

When life is looked at with this attitude, the future does take on a very bleak appearance, and the tasks ahead do seem a bit overwhelming. My answer to the above was one of understanding and sympathy, but it was also realistic. I used to reply in somewhat the following manner: "I know just how you feel. Sometimes when I think about all the house calls, office visits, hospital rounds, late night surgeries, and obstetrical deliveries I will have to handle in the next twenty years, I feel like giving up the ghost. Fortunately, I have only today and tonight to cope with. I know I can handle the next twenty-four hours. This makes the tasks much more reasonable, and very attainable."

For most of us it is very easy to fall into the trap of needless worry about the past and especially about the future. Obviously we cannot entirely exclude from our thoughts what has occurred and what may occur. Some thought is necessary for learning from our mistakes and for planning for the morrow. The true answer is to profit from the past and then get on with living. Nothing is accomplished by constantly dwelling on yesterday and subjecting ourselves to continual self-flagellation.

As far as the future is concerned, each of us must make plans and prepare, as far as possible, for whatever problems may arise. However needless worry about tomorrow is a waste of our energies and detracts from today. As the Holy Bible so succinctly states in Matthew 6:34, "Sufficient unto the day is the evil thereof."

We all have a choice. We can enjoy our many blessings and make the most of each day, or we can sit in the corner and mope while we hang onto our little HANDFUL OF THORNS.

To Quill or Not to Quill?

Following the strident ringing of the telephone, a frantic voice pleaded, "Please come in a hurry. My daughter has had a heart attack and is lying unconscious on the living room floor."

A few minutes later, on arriving at the home I found the front room crowded with a whole host of sad-looking relatives and neighbors. They formed in a silent circle around the body which was spread-eagled on the rug in the middle of the room. The patient, a portly young girl in her late teens, was nearly square in shape. Obviously she had been over-indulgent in her dietary habits. Lying on her back, face upwards with eyes closed, her skin color was a rosy pink, and her respirations were regular and normal.

When I knelt on the floor to examine her, I could see her eyelids flutter slightly as she peeked out through her lashes in an attempt to catch a glimpse of this new arrival. It became immediately apparent to me her "heart attack" had not done her in.

While I was evaluating her present condition and the proper course of action, I recalled an old remedy, now archaic, called "quilling." In the past this treatment had been used on rare occasions with dramatic results. At that time, it was customary for gentlemen to carry a quill toothpick in their vest pocket. It was made from a hollow goose quill, sharpened at one end. Being quite sturdy, it could be used and reused many times. When employed for therapy, it could be filled with ordinary black pepper. One end was then inserted into one of the patient's nostrils. Then a slight puff of breath by the therapist usually achieved rapid and remarkable cures in any pseudo-comatose patient.

In the present situation, not having a quill toothpick as well as not wanting to embarrass my rotund patient, I decided a more subtle approach was called for. Putting my mouth close to the patient's ear, I whispered, "Get up off the floor, and lie on the davenport."

Without a word nor a moment's hesitation, she arose from the floor and did as instructed. The family and many of the other spectators were amazed at her apparent miraculous recovery. I later explained to those present she had not had a real heart attack and her rapid recovery was due to her youthful recuperative powers.

The following day, a complete examination in my office confirmed my original diagnosis, that this was a typical hysterical attack used by the patient to get her way. The girl did appreciate the fact I had not revealed her ruse to those present at her home. She and I subsequently became good friends. I was able to persuade her to lose weight, make herself more attractive, and to cease using such spectacular modes of attention getting in the future.

Several months later, one Christmas morning, I received a call to rush to see an elderly woman who was having a heart attack. When I reached the home, I found the woman lying on the davenport surrounded by anxious sons, daughters-in-law, and grandchildren all looking sad and disturbed. In spite of the gala Christmas trappings and the multiple presents strewn about, the small youngsters were completely subdued by the gloomy atmosphere. Their eyes kept glancing at the exposed toys and dolls as well as at the still unopened presents. It was obvious Grandma's attack had caused an abrupt cessation in the previously joyous proceedings. It also soon became apparent Grandma was enjoying her role as the invalid in her front and center stage location.

An examination revealed that while she had a seventy-five-year-old heart, there was nothing acute about her present condition. She had either consciously or otherwise used this means of getting the attention away from the happy children and their presents, thus focusing the spotlight upon herself.

While "quilling" was not an appropriate treatment here, some other rather prompt therapy was called for if the Yuletide festivities were to be salvaged. After examining Grandma, I assumed a very grave yet sympathetic manner and said, "It's obvious that all this excitement is just too much for you at this time. What is essential for you is complete rest and quietness. I want you to lie down in a back bedroom away from all this noise and confusion."

Then, turning to the sons and daughters, I asked, "Do you have a quiet spot where she can get away from all the excitement? It would be best if she wasn't to be disturbed by anyone for any reason except for an occasional hourly check. As far as her food is concerned, just a little tea and crackers for now. By tomorrow there should be considerable improvement."

We then moved Grandma into the most distant bedroom in the house, put her to bed, closed the blinds, and darkened the room. I carefully appraised the sons and daughters of the true state of her condition and cautioned them to be kind but firm in the outlined treatment regime.

Later that day, when I called to inquire about her condition, I was told she felt much improved and was begging to come out with the rest of the family. Permission to do so was granted with the provision that any recurrence of her symptoms would necessitate her immediate return to the bedroom. On subsequent Christmases there was no repetition of her counterfeit heart attack.

One evening several years later, a call from a distraught mother started with, "Can you come to see my young daughter? She is having a hysterical attack, and it takes four of us to keep her in bed."

I was at their home in minutes. As had been described on the telephone, I found four adults, three men and a woman, struggling to keep a wildly thrashing young lady in a completely disheveled bed. The room was semi-darkened and the scene was quite eerie. The patient's eyes were tightly closed, and no sound came from her lips. The complete silence in the room only magnified the bizarre nature of the entire setting. In contrast to the silence, the patient's legs, arms, and body were in constant violent movement. With her wild gyrations, if she had not been held, she would have thrown herself from the bed. Obviously, no "quilling" of this patient was indicated.

Examining her was somewhat like riding an untamed bucking horse or Brahma bull at a rodeo. A few salient features became apparent during my hasty and turbulent inspection. This was no hysterical attack. Her coma was very real. I found she had a tumor in her lower abdomen, comparable in size to a pregnancy of three or four months' duration. Several possible diagnosis for her present condition flashed through my mind. Could this be some unusual toxicity of pregnancy with convulsive seizures? Was this a weird variation of a diabetic coma? The clinical picture was certainly not a classical example of either condition. I put my nose close to her mouth to try to detect any evidence of "sweet breath" which, if present, would give a clue to diabetes. There was no evidence of this odor. In her present grave and precarious condition, whatever the diagnosis, immediate hospitalization was indicated.

Once in the hospital, further examinations revealed the lower abdominal tumor to be a greatly dilated urinary bladder. Catheterization, with a slow release of the pressure, resulted in an immediate cessation of her violent gyrations. The physical calmness which followed, however, seemed to enhance the apparent depth of her coma. By now it was nearly 1:00 A.M. The quietness and darkness of the night made our problem appear to be even more ominous.

In a relatively short time, with the information from a spinal fluid exam available, I was able to pinpoint the exact diagnosis. The patient had a meningococcic meningitis. Prior to the advent of antibiotics and the sulfa drugs, this illness had had a nearly 100 percent fatality record. Up to this time sulfadiazine had been available only in the tablet form. Because of the patient's coma, the use of tablets, while not impossible, would be difficult, and the onset of its therapeutic action would be slow. I had heard about an intravenous solution of sulfadiazine which had recently been developed. After several telephone calls, some of this drug was found at the local wholesale warehouse. In fact, the solution had arrived there for the first time the previous afternoon. By 2:00 A.M. we were able to start a vial of this via an intravenous drip. Even though the patient was still in a coma, there was nothing more for me to do except to wait and see what would happen.

As I relaxed by the bedside, I suddenly recalled my having placed my nose close to the patient's mouth earlier in the evening in order to smell her breath.

Figuratively speaking, I could visualize the meningococcic bacteria leaping from her mouth to my nasal membranes. These thoughts caused a cold sweat to break out on my brow. Jumping up, I ran to the hospital pharmacy, ordered a large number of sulfadiazine pills, and started gulping these at the maximum safe dosage.

While my response to the fear of meningitis wasn't a true hysteria, it was an anxiety reaction of the first order. Interestingly enough, any thought of "quilling" as a treatment for my own condition never entered my mind.

One lesson I learned from the above three cases, plus my own reaction to the fear of meningitis, was that no one treatment is appropriate for all cases which on the surface may appear to be similar. I also learned that while "quilling" may have had its place in the distant past, it had better be relegated to the back shelf in the therapeutic armamentarium of today.

Incidentally, the next morning when I visited my meningitis patient in the hospital, I found her sitting up in bed, wide awake, looking about, and calling in a loud voice, "Where is my breakfast? I'm starved!"

Have a Good Day

Experts tell us what not to eat,
And if we do, our diet to complete,
All sorts of foods, especially fat,
will seal our fate by this and that.

The worst of all is table salt,
As all our organs it does assault.
It is often said by all its foes,
That it will cause most all our woes.

Next, comes the villain cholesterol.
It's nearly as bad as straight alcohol.
Our arteries it does really clog,
And our bodies, generally, it does flog.

Cyclamates at one time were banned.
Even white sugar was really panned.
The former is now a-okay.
The latter can still cause tooth decay.

Of course spices, onions, and garlic,
Some say do make our dishes slick.
'Tis said the result is food quite tasty,
But when exhaled, they cause an exodus hasty.

It seems that whatever we ingest,
To give our meals some fun and zest,
Is quite bad—without a winner,
And without them—a somber dinner.

While things may seem tough, don't lose hope
By eating oat bran, we can cope.
Add granola, decaf, and niacin.
With all these, we will surely win.

But lest you relax, without strain,
Recall the greenhouse effect, acid rain,
And the dangerous ultraviolet rays.
Will surely limit our remaining days.

All this hearsay can give our brains a schism,
Still there is reason for optimism,
Because as so many are prone to say,
In spite of all, "HAVE A GOOD DAY!"

What's Yours Is Mine, and Mine Is Yours

The following story is told of a farmer in the Soviet Union at the height of the communist regime. When he was asked about sharing his possessions with his neighbors, he replied he would be glad to do so. "If you had two cars would you give one to a neighbor?"

"I'd be glad to."

"If you had two tractors, would you do the same?"

"Certainly."

"If you had two houses, would you let somebody have one?"

"They would be more than welcome."

"If you had two cows, would you give one to a friend?"

"Certainly not."

"Why, after you have been so generous, would you refuse to part with one of your cows?"

"Because I do have two cows."

The above may sound a bit ridiculous, but is it that far from the truth? Many of us, in theory, will share what we don't have, but not what we do possess. This fact is especially true not only for most of us, but also for many of our politicians. Have you ever noticed how these same legislators do not hesitate to share, through excessive taxation, what you own? In so doing, they use any number of different guises to justify their actions. According to them, they are so full of compassion they want to share your property to help the less fortunate. Figuratively, these benefactors wrap their arms around those in need and say, "You can't do it, so we will take care of you" (with taxpayer's money). At the same time they make sure they themselves have many tax-free "perks."

One of the big differences between a liberal and a conservative is based, not so much on their respective financial positions, but on their philosophical approach to someone in trouble. The conservative says, "If you feel you cannot solve your problems, let me try to help you. I'm sure that together we can work our something." His answer is a positive one and helps the unfortunate by encouraging him, with some assistance, to try to solve whatever difficulty exists. This approach fosters a feeling of well being and pride of accomplishment.

On the other hand, the liberal takes a different tactic, which is somewhat negative. He says, "You poor soul. You can't take care of yourself, so I will have to do so." He then gives a governmental handout, and by so doing creates in the recipient a feeling of dependency and a loss of self-esteem.

In addition, there is another more subtle motive behind the liberal's actions. By creating a large dependent segment of the population, many new bureaus have to be formed. The end result is the acquisition of power by those in control. The bureaus, in turn, usually expand and become self-perpetuating. Also, there is a tendency for the employees in the bureaus to encourage their clients to remain dependent. In all fairness, these actions by the workers may be unconscious and not deliberate. We all have a tendency to protect our own self-interests. One other benefit for the liberals is the creation of a large favorable voting block. No one wants to vote out his benefactor. As has been said, "It's hard to beat a Santa Claus."

One economist recently said, "I'd rather be held up by a masked robber than have a politician take my possessions. At least with a robber, you know he will soon be on his way. On the other hand, with the politician, he will spend a great deal of time and hot air explaining to you why you should like his actions."

Jesus said the poor will be with us always, but he didn't necessarily advocate a free ride. He practiced "tough love." Extending a helping hand instead of giving a handout will instill a feeling of accomplishment which will be a benefit to the individual and to the nation. One thing that is essential for us is to reverse the present tendency which exists today, namely, WHAT'S MINE IS YOURS, AND WHAT'S YOURS IS MINE.

Split Seconds and Great Moments

STOP! STOP!

The traffic signal light had just turned green, but without a moment's hesitation I slammed on the brakes just as a speeding car emerged from behind the left windshield post, ran the red light, and zipped by our front bumper, missing it by the thickness of the daily newspaper. We had postponed the hereafter by a split second.

How many of us have had somewhat similar experiences? Experiences which have influenced our longevity, changed our ultimate destiny, and made us realize how important the split seconds and great moments are in our lives. While a few of these events may stand out in our memories, often there is one that is especially significant. For me, the most important one occurred during my third year in college. During several previous winters, I had applied for a summer job on the staff of the Seabeck Conference grounds. Each time I had been told, "No openings. Don't call us, we'll call you."

This year, I decided to try once again and, if unsuccessful, to abandon any further attempts. As before, Mr. Allen, the general manager of the conference grounds, gave his usual answer: "I'll contact you if there is an opening."

As I was about to hang up, one of the university girl roomers who lived in our house came in the front door just as I said, "Thank you for your time and consideration, Mr. Allen."

Betty, the girl roomer, asked, "Which Mr. Allen were you calling?"

When I told her, she said, "He's my uncle. I'll talk to him." With her intervention, I got the job. While working at Seabeck, I met Margaret. By the end of the summer, we were engaged to be married.

In retrospect, if Betty had entered the door a few seconds earlier or a few seconds later who knows what the end result might have been? What happened during those few seconds sixty-two years ago markedly changed both my and Margaret's destinies.

Several years later while in medical school in Chicago, I used to get cheap transportation from there to Seattle by ferrying automobiles from the factory to the dealer. One winter, at Christmas time, I had two cars available. There were four of us students who wanted to head west so we formed a mini-caravan and started off through the snow and ice. Aside from seeing many trucks and cars which had skidded off the icy roads, all went well for most of the journey. By the time we reached Idaho the roads were clear of snow and we felt we had it made. On a beautiful, clear, but freezing night as we sped along, we hit a patch of black ice. Our car went into a 360-degree spin and bounced off the guard rail, hitting all four sides of the car before finally coming to a stop. The icy cold Snake River swirled menacingly one hundred feet below. If we had plunged into its frigid depths with our heavy winter clothing, we wouldn't have had a chance of surviving.

Somewhat shaken by the sudden wild gyrations of the car's spin, I climbed out to survey the damage. When my feet touched the road surface they slid out from under me and I rapidly learned how treacherous black ice could be. On inspecting the guard rail, we found our car had first struck it about ten feet from one end. Our last hit was approximately ten feet from the other end. Either the designers of that rail were very smart or God had further work for us to do. Perhaps it was a combination of the two. The end result of this split second experience initiated a bit of soul searching and inventory taking. Not all the answers were forthcoming, but I know one thing for sure—I didn't shift out of second gear for the next ten miles.

Years later, during World War II, while stationed at Camp Luna, New Mexico, the colonel commanding our station hospital called three of us medical officers into his office. "I have to ship out six medics. I have picked the first five. You three step out into the hall and decide which of you will be number six."

In the hall, we decided we would match pennies, with the odd man the one to go. Captain Angus Clark was the odd one and was transferred from the air force to the infantry. He ultimately ended up in Germany with the troops who liberated the concentration camp at Dachau. He was subjected to many dangers and considerable hardship during his last few years in the army. I, on the other hand, stayed in the air force, went to flight surgeon's school at Randolph Field, Texas, and in general had a relatively soft tour of duty. The contrast in our destinies had been decided, in seconds, by the flip of a coin.

At this same Camp Luna, very early in my army career, one morning as I headed for the hospital, I remembered I had forgotten to bring my daily letter to Margaret. When I ran back to the barracks to pick up the letter, the head of the surgical department, Major Lewis, spotted me and asked, "Could you assist me at an abdominal surgery?"

This question was on a par with asking the average child if he would like a piece of candy. I jumped at the chance. The surgery went well, and the major seemed pleased with my assistance. As a result, he assigned me to the "plum of plums," the surgical service, and also put me in charge of the general surgical ward. A year and a half later and hundreds of surgical cases followed. These furnished an excellent basis for my post-war medical and surgical practice. Thank goodness I had forgotten to take Margaret's letter and had to return for it. Could this have just been a coincidence or was it a prearranged split second event?

Many years before, while an intern at Swedish Hospital and while making my routine evening rounds, I came upon two nurses who were discussing and arguing about the dosage of a medication they were about to give to an elderly patient. The attending doctor had ordered a sixty-fourth of a grain. The argument was whether a sixty-fourth was half of a thirty-second or was two thirty-seconds. The more persuasive of the two nurses thought the dosage was the latter and the student nurse was about to give that amount. If she had done so, the patient would have, figuratively speaking, hit the ceiling. Without putting either of the nurses down, I was able to convince them a sixty-fourth was only one half of a thirty-second.

A year later, while I was a resident at the Pierce County Hospital, this same student nurse, who was now working for an older doctor in Tacoma, called me and asked me if I would be interested in joining him in his practice. As he needed help, she had persuaded him to give me an interview. The end result was that I moved into his office. This move gave me a running start for my future career. The year before, little had I realized how much a sixty-fourth of a grain could influence my destiny and lead to another great moment in my life.

One of the earliest events which proved to be an important turning point in my life's journey occurred in the eight grade. Like many boys of that age, I was the bane of my teacher, Miss Mullane. She was a patient person, but I'm afraid I pushed her past her limit of tolerance. At that time, one of her practices with the eighth graders was to advise each of them on an individual basis about their forthcoming high school class assignments. These interviews took approximately half an hour for each pupil. During these sessions, Miss Mullane would ask questions and make suggestions for changes in the proposed schedule.

When it came my turn, she barely glanced at my program and with a terse comment, said, "That's good." She didn't suggest any changes or ask me if I had anything else to say.

As I had some doubts about some of my choices, I asked "Do you think I should take Latin my first semester?"

Her reply took me aback. "Go ahead; it won't make any difference as you won't pass anyhow."

Her brusque manner indicated either she really felt that way or else she was a master psychologist and knew I needed a bit of shock therapy. Whichever was true, she got the desired results. From that moment on, I resolved I would show her I could, and would, pass not only Latin, but the other courses also.

Thirteen years later, during my medical internship at Swedish Hospital in Seattle, I met Miss Mullane on the street. She recognized me, as I did her. When she asked me what I was doing, I told her I was a medical doctor in my internship. The look of astonishment on her face made all the years of study and long hours of duty at the hospital well worth the effort. However my one regret was I didn't think to apologize to her for all the trauma I had caused her in the seventh and eighth grades or thank her for her timely and necessary "kick in the pants" she had given me during our few minutes' interview those many years before.

Most, if not all of us, have had many great moments and split-second experiences. Some of these may have been positive and some may have been just the opposite. Whichever, they all have had an impact on the future course of our lives. From them we have had a chance to learn and, if we are wise, to profit.

From a personal standpoint, the above-mentioned examples are but a few of the sign posts and direction pointers which have led to the present situation. Without them, there might not have been a chance to meet Margaret and without her, there wouldn't have been Betsy, Barbara, and Molly. Without them, plus Jack, Jack, and Jim, there wouldn't have been Susan, John, Amy, Anne, Marybeth, Greg, Brian, Scott, Laurie, and Marc. All of these last ten plus Karin, Dean, Bob, Michael, and Jennifer have resulted in Drew, Gracie, Lauren, Andrew, and Michael. These, and others not known at this time, have and will continue to have many far-reaching ramifications.

In retrospect, it is somewhat overwhelming to think that all of the above originated from a few seconds in timing during a telephone call away back in 1934. It would be easy to speculate on the "what ifs," but I am convinced there was a *guiding hand* which long ago had planned the total picture.

For this *guiding hand* I am very thankful for all the "split seconds" and "great moments" of the past. In addition, I feel certain He has more of both of these in reserve and they will be forthcoming in the years ahead.

The Three S's of Death

Ranking closely behind the Seven Deadly Sins are what some people consider today's three most deadly scourges, namely: sunlight, sugar, and salt. Why have what we previously considered old friends now become some of our worst enemies?

The answer to this paradox is to be found in a movement in which a rather large segment of our population, both lay and professional, have come to believe the above three are our triple nemeses and will surely "do us in." While many of the members of this movement are not only very sincere in their beliefs, they also are very vocal and do not hesitate to expound forcefully, positively, and at great length, without reservation, on any or all of the above-mentioned plagues. To them, the sun has changed from a life-giving source into a dangerous adversary. Many medical doctors, especially the skin specialists, have joined in the campaign to malign *Old Sol*. As a result, many who used to enjoy the sun's rays and warmth now bundle up with wrist-length arm covers, gloves, ankle-length trousers, dark glasses, and wide-brimmed hats. In general, they avoid any exposure to what they believe are the supposedly deadly radiations.

One elderly man who always looked forward to spending several weeks each winter in Hawaii, was told by his doctor to avoid sunlight because of its harmful effects. For years, he faithfully obeyed this advice and stayed home during all of the dark winter days, wistfully dreaming of past pleasures in the surf of Waikiki. Now at ninety-two years of age, he is still alive and looks at us with longing as we leave for his long dreamed of sandy shores. Perhaps he might live to be one hundred—if so, for what?

In contrast to the above, Dr. Donohue, in his newspaper column in answer to a query regarding sunlight, wrote, "There is a certain amount of sunlight time needed to convert the vitamin D producer (in the skin) into the actual vitamin. In winter months, many (people) will have such little sun that vitamin D conversion is practically nil, especially for older persons whose skin production has waned naturally anyway. The lesson to be learned is that the elderly have to watch their D levels and be sure they are getting the vitamins through longer sun exposure, diet, or with supplements."

Another of the three S's which has been cast in the villain's role by these false prophets is sugar, especially the simple kind. The doomsayers' theme runs something like this: Natural sugars (fruit sources, honey, etc.) are all right, but one should avoid white sugar like the plague. It has not been ascertained where these experts place cane and beet sugars in the natural overall food spectrum. Some of these soothsayers even go so far as to say that diabetes mellitus is caused by sugar. They ignore any reference to an insulin deficiency. These same proponents of the evils caused by white sugar do not offer tangible proof of its lethal qualities. One poor man whose wife became a "sugar expert" used to volunteer as a plate scraper at church dinners so he could sneak in a couple of extra desserts while in the kitchen.

Let us now deal with the real "whipping boy" of the health faddists, namely table salt. This is often referred to as "white death." To illustrate, once at a dinner party I asked, "Would you please pass the salt?"

Like a bolt out of the blue, one of the women at the table blasted me with, "You, a doctor, asking for salt? I'm amazed. Don't you know how bad it is for you?"

This same woman, plus the rest of the group, was eating ham, pickles, and catsup—all of which were rich in sodium. Apparently, this "expert" felt that salt in a shaker was dangerous but not if it came wrapped in some other guise.

To date, except in some cases of renal disease, there has not been any conclusive evidence that NaCl is the cause of hypertension. Recently the head of the hypertension department of a well-known medical school spoke for over forty-five minutes to our medical society on the subject of high blood pressure. During this lecture and the subsequent question period, NaCl was not mentioned once. When a direct question about the role of salt as a cause of hypertension was asked, it was answered with a smile and, "There seems to be some disagreement amongst the medical researchers on this subject."

Here was a real expert, who had spent years studying the problem of high blood pressure, and yet had some doubts about the role, if any, salt might play in this problem. Not so the pseudo-experts who, without reservation, have no question that salt is the guilty culprit.

These same individuals seem to ignore the role salt has played in the history of the world. The Bible mentions salt thirty-two times. Remember Lot's wife? Jesus referred to the disciples as, "Ye are the salt of the earth." Wars have been fought over salt and nations have sprung up over its sources. The word *salary* comes from the Roman soldier's "salarium" or his pay. The expression "worth his salt" was meant literally in ancient times. Many of the Sahara Desert caravans carried salt as their main cargo.

Even dumb animals have a craving for this substance. They probably haven't been reading any of the modern literature on this subject.

Also, it is doubtful any of those individuals who so glibly condemn salt have ever studied at any length the cellular "cloride shift" or the workings of the kidney tubules, all of which takes place in our bodies minute by minute on a daily basis.

And now after ten years of advice by health organizations and government agencies regarding saline abstinence, a recent article has appeared titled, "The Great Salt Debate." This article states that the needless prohibition of salt intake will not only deprive people of a simple pleasure, but also make them "think" that by so doing they are making an important contribution to their health, when they would be better off losing weight, getting more exercise, and avoiding heavy drinking.

The article goes on to say, "Many of the previous studies regarding salt's relationship to hypertension were based in large part on studies of primitive tribes in the rain forests. It seems that these people eat very little salt and apparently have low blood pressures. From this, scientists concluded that salt must be to blame for hypertension in the industrial world, even though many other factors could explain why the tribe's blood pressure is low. For instance, tribal members generally don't drink (alcoholic beverages), get fat, or sit in traffic."

Dr. William Bennett, editor of the *Harvard Health Letter*, states, "I don't want to advocate an official retraction (regarding salt restriction). We might be confused. The data is not clear."

In other words, no one wants to admit there might have been a mistaken conclusion made in the past regarding the use, or lack of use, of salt.

There are several lessons we can learn from the foregoing. First of all, we should not believe all that we read or hear about the influences of various external factors on our internal well being. Second, when we do read or hear about some theory regarding our health, let us ask ourselves three questions: What are the qualifications of this so-called expert? Is he really bonafide or is he an off-season sports writer or gossip columnist who is trying to "keep the pot boiling"? Is he or she interested in the good of his fellow man or is he just trying to make a little money? Also, remember that just because he or she may be qualified in some other field such as law, politics, or sports doesn't make him a nutritional expert.

There are other steps we can take for our physical well being, such as practicing moderation is all of our various activities. We should eat sensibly of a well-rounded diet with more basic foods and less pizza. Of course, it is wise to avoid alcohol, drugs, and tobacco and to get regular and moderate exercise. By all means, we ought to keep our perspective and our sense of humor.

Finally let us pay more attention to and avoid the three S's of spiritual death, namely Sin, Satan, and Sacrilege and less attention to the supposed three S's of physical death: sunlight, sugar, and salt.

The Turbulent Tutor

When compared to an explosive, she was like liquid nitroglycerine in a lurching truck on a bumpy road. When likened to a volcano, she was a Mt. Saint Helens in mid-May 1990. Like the explosive and the volcano, it wasn't a question of would she explode, it was only a question of timing. When would the eruptions occur?

Psychologists would probably blame her tempestuous behavior on her past childhood experiences or on some inherited genetic aberration. Perhaps they would be correct perhaps not. A more practical explanation might be that she was a middle-aged, menopausal spinster who had been teaching music to seventh and eighth grade pupils for too many years. This occupation would test to the maximum the disposition of even the most saintly. Even the most stable individual, in trying to control a room full of this age group, would be frustrated by these perfect catalysts which could trigger the explosions of any smoldering, inner emotional complex.

The teacher was no physical beauty, and yet she was not unattractive either. Her stern angular face was supported by a long neck which was covered by pale, freckled, partially wrinkled skin. Topping these two was her crown of flaming red hair which seemed to be a perfect culmination for her spells of anger. When activated, her explosions always followed a set pattern. At the onset, her mouth would become a thin firm line. Her eyes, behind silver-framed glasses, would take on a steely gleam. The skin at the base of her neck would then acquire a gradually deepening reddish hue. This coloration would slowly migrate upward like the reflection of the rising sun on the morning clouds. At the climax of her anger, her entire neck and face would become a brilliant red, intensified by the color of her hair.

Over several months, there had been many lesser rumblings and eruptions, but the most violent explosion occurred the day someone sneaked two frogs into the classroom nature display. During the morning hours of class, the frogs were well behaved and seemed content to nestle down among the ferns and plants. Later on, when the music lesson started, they became a bit restless and, with the onset of the singing, they began to croak. As might be expected, they were not very melodious and their rendition was more of a base monotone. With the onset of the discordant background, the teacher stopped the singing. "Someone's not in tune. Let's try that part again."

On the second attempt, the same thing happened. Again she stopped us. Fortunately each time our singing stopped, the frogs also ceased their croaking. With a repetition of this same scenario on the third try, we could see the storm clouds begin to gather. First, the steely eyed look appeared. Then her mouth began to tighten, and the skin at the base of her neck began to redden. It was evident that a violent explosion was imminent. When it did come, it was horrendous. Had it been measured on a seismograph, it would have been in the range of six or seven at the very least. Needless to say, the music lesson was over for that day, and the class was dismissed.

Later on that afternoon when school was over for the day, the frogs were spirited away, never to be seen again. The perpetrators of the stunt were never apprehended, which was lucky for both of us.

Interestingly enough, when one of the pupil's parents invited this same teacher to their home for dinner, we all expected to hear the meal had been tumultuous, to say the least. We were amazed when the pupil reported, "I was really surprised. She turned out to be a very nice lady."

All of which goes to prove that volcanoes can be beautiful when quiescent, and even liquid nitroglycerine can be controlled when it is handled properly.

Computer #2345678

March 21, 1990
Computer #2345678
ABCD Company, Inc.
Anywhere, USA

Dear Computer:

I really feel very silly writing to an inanimate object like you, but in as much as I have been unable to arouse any live human being in my last three letters, I have no other choice. I don't like to incur your wrath by calling you inanimate. However it is apparent by your complete indifference to my appeals for mercy, and by your total lack of empathy for the shattered state of my emotions, that you do not have a soul.

To refresh your binary connections, I am the one you billed for a product I did not order and I did not receive. I have tried to explain this to you each month for the last three months. In spite of my efforts, you keep sending me new statements with precision-like regularity. This state of affairs was bad enough when it pertained only to the original false billing, but now, this month, when you added an interest charge on top of the amount I didn't owe you in the first place, that was just too much.

And so, unless you do something to alter the flow of electrons through your mechanical brain, I will have to take some drastic action. I do not like to be difficult or threaten you, but unless you change your ways, my next step will be to punch some extra holes in your computer billing statement. This action will really shake up your binary calculations and electronic controls. I fully appreciate the consequences of such an intemperate action on my part, but somehow I just don't care.

In one last appeal, please do something to remedy this mix-up before I perpetrate an act I would regret very much, namely, to commit computer statement mayhem.

Sincerely,
Glenn G. McBride

There's More Than One Way

In my early childhood, the expression "There's more than one way to skin a cat" bothered me a great deal. Why would anyone want to do such a thing? As time passed and I learned the expression was only a figurative way of speaking, I felt much better. However many years later it took a real live cat to give even a different meaning to this common saying. It happened in the following manner.

At that time, we had two cats, Miss Boo and Muffie. I can't say we owned them. In fact, the reverse would be more accurate. Both were born to the same mother, but came from two different litters. Because of their differences, we assumed the father of each was not the same, making them half-brother and half-sister. Miss Boo was the elder of the two. She was a beautiful calico-colored female and from an early age had a queenly bearing. As she matured this regal aspect of her nature became more and more evident. If, per chance, we happened to displease her in any way, such as taking a short vacation, she would, in effect, on our return banish us for a few days by completely ignoring our existence.

In contrast, Muff was like a little boy and was constantly in some sort of mischief. His fur was a mixture of gray and tan with a light-colored muff at his neck and fore chest. His paws were covered in the same coloration, giving them the appearance of mittens on all four feet. He had an innocent look of wonderment on his face which stood him in good stead as he became tangled in the yarn basket or when he was mixed up in the pens, pencils, and stationery on the desk top. His expression seemed to ask, "What did I do wrong?" He acted like a little boy caught with his hand in the cookie jar.

As Boo was the elder of the two, she arrived at our home first. When Muff arrived a year later, Boo immediately took over as his surrogate mother, caring for and teaching him in the art of self-defense, climbing, and how to play. They became inseparable companions.

As time passed, but when Muff was still in the kitten phase of his development, he became a bit too adventurous and climbed to the top of a telephone pole located next to our tool house. For him, all went well on the way up, but once there he was at a loss as how to come down. His plaintive meows, at first faint, became louder and louder as he crouched atop the pole.

No amount of coaxing from us persuaded him to descend. My only ladder was not long enough for a rescue. Failing to get results by any other means, we put a bowl of milk on the tool house roof. This, too, did not tempt him. Calls to the electric company and the fire departments were rebuffed by such remarks as, "When he's hungry he'll come down," or "We don't have a cat rescue crew available."

Not wanting him to spend the night on top of the pole amidst the wires there, we kept trying to coax him down without success. We were at a loss as to what to do next. Miss Boo finally had had enough. She slowly climbed to the top of the pole. Once there, she spent considerable time and seemed to talk to Muff as if instructing him in pole descending technique. She then backed down the pole, stopping at the bowl of milk level where she lapped up several mouthfuls, looked up at Muff, said something in cat language, then jumped to the ground.

Within minutes, Muff started down the pole in the same manner his elder sister had just used, stopping at the bowl of milk where he drank all that was left, and they hopped to the ground.

Miss Boo had graphically demonstrated the truth of that old adage, "There is more than one way to skin a cat."

The Gladiators

Those who have watched professional wrestlers on TV or at ringside can be classified and divided into two widely separate groups: those who think the matches are a sham, and those who feel every match is a deadly serious battle, even unto death. The actual truth is somewhere in between.

I don't pretend to be an expert in this field, but having spent considerable time as the official attending physician at several of these contests, I have had the chance to observe the standard format of the matches, as well as to examine and treat the fighters themselves. These opportunities have been quite revealing and very interesting. I won't say the fights were ever fixed, but I do feel they were certainly well rehearsed.

From my observations, a few facts have become apparent. First, the participants were all well conditioned and were super athletes. They had to be in excellent shape to withstand the rigors of the fights and the exercise involved. The second fact that was noticeable was in each battle there usually had to be a villain for the crowd to hiss and boo. As a rule this unenviable position was passed around amongst the fighters depending on the locale of the battles. One particular man was always the hero in his own home town, but often had to be the villain in other locations. Third, most of the fighters were ex-college football players, wrestlers, or weight lifters. Their muscle development was somewhat unbelievable. Fourth, most of them were well educated, brainy, and good showmen. In addition, many owned outside businesses in their home territories.

As far as the audiences were concerned, they were something to behold and were often more entertaining than the fighters themselves. I was never able to determine whether there were "plants" in the crowd hired by the promoters and placed strategically in the arena, but I suspected as much. In this group there were those who, in essence, were specialists in their own right: the hecklers, the spitters, and the umbrella wielders. These last were the most dangerous and would often beat or poke the fighters with their bumbershoots.

In the locker room between matches, the fighters would often warn each other about those in the audience with remarks like, "Watch out for the spitter in the right corner," or "Stay away from 'umbrella Annie' on the far side of the ring."

The fighters' backgrounds were markedly varied. One man earned his way through medical school by wrestling under an assumed name. After getting his M.D., he kept himself in good physical condition. In addition, he became world famous in his medical specialty and wrote a widely used textbook about his chosen field. He was in demand as a medical speaker and on one occasion was scheduled to give several lectures in a distant city. One of his close friends was still an active professional wrestler who was, coincidentally, signed to fight in this same city at the same time. The wrestler took the liberty of putting the doctor on the wrestling program for the nights he didn't have to speak at the medical meetings. When the M.D. learned of this he objected, saying, "I'm not in condition to go through a tough fight."

His friend replied, "If you get tired during the match just assume a defensive knee-elbow position. All of the other fighters know about you and will just go through the motions until you have a chance to catch you breath."

With this reassurance, the M.D. consented. As a result, every other evening he would lecture to the medical community about his specialty. The alternate nights he would wrestle at the sports arena under an assumed name. Later on, he said he enjoyed both experiences, but was completely exhausted after the wrestling matches.

Returning to the gladiators themselves, it is interesting to note to what extremes some of them will go just to get noticed and to put on a good show. Many of them will assume ridiculous roles and wear outlandish costumes. Some will even bleach their hair and leave it in long tresses. Others will go to the opposite extreme and shave their heads and wear long beards and moustaches; anything to make themselves stand out from the crowd. "Gorgeous George" and the "Masked Marvel" are good examples of these attention getters.

And so the next time you watch a wrestling match, if you ever do so, just remember, don't judge the fighters by their appearance alone. You may be watching a nuclear scientist, a lawyer, a doctor, a college professor, an engineer, or some other learned man who is supplementing his income or just out for a lark by a bit of "moonlighting." Also, give these men, who ever they are, credit for being able to stand the rigors of the contests.

The Awkward Age?

If asked, "What is the awkward age?" many of us would, without much thought, say, "It's the early teens." Even the dictionary's first definition of *awkward* is "early adolescence." However, is this the only and fair assessment?

We can all recall incidents in our teens which were awkward and, in many instances, downright embarrassing. For instance, there was the time the teenage girl wouldn't sit with her mother in church because the mother had, in her rush to get everyone off to Sunday School, inadvertently put on shoes unmatched in color.

Then there was the admonition given as they left for the football game: "Don't wear your old yellow fishing rain gear, and please, please don't jump up and clap for all the good plays." These remonstrances came, not from the mother to her junior high school-aged son, but the other way around.

In a different setting, another teenager moved from her parents' side at a football game because the father was watching the plays with a monocular glass instead of a binocular one.

As adults, having gone through this stage of life in one degree or another, we can now laugh at these examples of the so-called awkward age. However before we come to any hasty conclusions and tend to confine our definition of awkward to only one age group, let us look further at the definition of the word *awkward*. One of the additional meanings listed in the dictionary is "lacking in skill."

This brings to mind any number of situations we may have encountered in our past. For me, one particular event stands out. It took place at a public golf course where I was playing the game for the first time with three of my friends. The first tee was crowded with many players waiting to tee off. As I had never had a lesson of any kind, I hung back so I could shoot last. With a large audience watching, I was tense and nervous but determined. As I tried to hit a mighty drive, the ball squirted off the end of my club and in a high looping arch at right angles to the direction of the fairway, landed on the club house roof.

There it hesitated for a few seconds and then started to roll slowly down the slope, finally careening off and landing on the back of the gardener who was weeding the flower bed below. This scenario elicited a mixture of laughter as well as numerous complaints from those waiting to tee off. I was completely embarrassed. It was a very *awkward* experience.

A further perusal of the dictionary reveals the word *awkward* also means "to lack in social manners." Again, this brings to mind several awkward situations. There is one such that is very common. This is especially true for men as a group. Try, as most males have, there is one particular phase of the social graces men will never master. This is the ability to balance a plate of food on one knee and, at the same time, manage a cup and saucer of beverage with their one free hand. These same men will watch, with awe, the nearby women who have been able to perfect the technique of this difficult procedure. This ability may be due to genetic factors such as the shape of men's knees, or possibly due to women's long and frequent practice. Whatever the differences, be it the bumpy male knee structure or because of just plain awkwardness, this skill has so far completely evaded men as a group.

When looking for a solution to the above, one answer for the men is to find, without being too obvious, a chair near an unoccupied piano bench or empty windowsill upon which to put one or both pieces of their service. Even so, it is much easier and less awkward for each male to sit at a conventional table. However even at a table awkward situations may surface, such as three forks and an abundance of other utensils when in previous experiences, two forks has been the maximum.

Again, referring to the dictionary, we find the word *awkward* also refers to "lack of coordination." This lack is especially evident on a ballroom dance floor where some of us men seem to be endowed with two left feet.

Often awkwardness surfaces when we have to perform some delicate task or repair an intricate piece of equipment while in the presence of an attentive and possibly a critical audience.

And then there are those awkward situations during the middle years (thirty-five to sixty) when we forget the name of an old friend while trying to introduce him or her to someone else whose name we cannot remember either. Also, when we arrive at an open house before the host and hostess are fully dressed; or when we are late for a dinner engagement; or, even worse, when we forget a dinner date entirely.

Still further, an awkward person can be one who is hard to deal with or to understand. For example, an old, cantankerous, ornery neighbor who avidly guards his property lines and who insists the rose bush you yourself planted belongs to him. If you are trying to preserve a good relationship with him, the situation may become quite awkward.

Sometimes awkwardness can be an occasion for joy. When we watch the first awkward steps of a baby, we can laugh and applaud because we know it won't be long before those same steps will be graceful and steady. So it is with other phases of life. The adolescent will, in most instances, gradually mature and once again join the world; the golfer, with practice, may become more proficient; even the cantankerous old man may, with our prayers and with our patience, become happy and cooperative; and the rest of us may be able to recall the names of our acquaintances. Some men may even become more fluid and smooth on the dance floor.

In the final analysis, we must conclude there is really no one phase of life which is exclusively awkward, and no one phase escapes its awkwardness entirely. There is hope for most of us, but there is one exception. It is doubtful that, even with practice and dedication, very many men will ever master the art of balancing a plate of food on one knee, and at the same time be able to control a cup of tea or coffee during an average stand-up buffet.

"He Sure Spoiled My Dinner!"

He was so tired, so terribly tired, with a tiredness so intense that any mental activity or physical movement seemed to be beyond his ability to execute. His bones and muscles even felt brittle. His skin tingled, hurt, and seemed to be made of parchment stretched over his face, leaving just mere slits for his eyes to peer through. He had been fatigued for weeks, but not as intensely as he felt this late afternoon.

To make matters worse, the day was far from over. He still had the rest of the office practice left, and he had a staff dinner meeting at one of the local hospitals that evening. Then following there would be the usual evening and middle of the night telephone calls which were ever present. In retrospect, he could hardly remember back to the days before medical school, thirty-five years past, when he had not been under constant pressure both day and night. Having had to work nights as a plant first aider during his medical school years, followed by the long twenty-four hour sessions while in his internship, the present pace was just a continuation of his frenetic way of life and had become an integral part of his daily routine. Without it, he surely would have felt somewhat lost.

The immediate question he had to answer was, How could he gracefully skip the meeting at the hospital tonight? He longed to quietly sneak home for some light music on the stereo, a good book, and a fireplace fire. His wife was going to be out for the evening, but he could fry a couple of eggs and have a small snack.

Of course, he really should go to the meeting since it was the important annual dinner with the final yearly reports and the inauguration of the new officers. It seemed that every meeting was important for one reason or another. However on the positive side, this, the Christmas dinner, was the best of the year. The food would be good, the atmosphere festive, and there would be over two hundred of his fellow doctors present for companionship. He wasn't very hungry and not sure he was equal to the task of talking and socializing for another two hours. Should he, or should he not, skip the whole affair? In a way, he wanted to go, but in another, he didn't.

The hospital was located in the same general direction as his home so he could make his decision while on the way. Once in the car, he was still undecided, but when he arrived at the intersection where he would have to make his final choice, at the last second he suddenly made a hard left turn and headed toward the meeting.

Upon arriving at the hospital and upon entering the well-decorated dining room, he mobilized his reserve energy. His fatigue seemed to lessen somewhat, and he was able to greet his colleagues in his usual outgoing and ebullient manner. He found a place at a table with some of his old friends. The whole atmosphere was filled with gaiety and laughter. The table was covered with delicious-looking food, and his appetite was whetted. However as he raised his fork toward his mouth, his arm movement stopped; his eyes took on a glassy, staring look; and he started to slowly lean to his right side. This was the last thing he remembered.

Later on, when those sitting at the same table were asked what had happened, they recalled he had seemed to be happy and had acted normal, but just as he raised his fork toward his mouth, he seemed to lose consciousness and started to fall toward the right. He didn't cry out or utter any other sound. Immediately those nearest to him started CPR, lifted him onto a hastily summoned wheeled stretcher, and rushed him to the intensive care ward.

It is interesting to note many of the doctors present felt the cause of his illness was something related to their own medical specialty. The neurosurgeon thought he had had a brain hemorrhage. One chest surgeon present speculated that a bolus of food had occluded his air passages. An internist was sure he had had a cardiac arrest. When a psychiatrist, who had been sitting directly across the table from the patient, was asked his impression of the cause, he replied, "At the moment, I wasn't sure what the diagnosis was, but I did know one thing: He sure spoiled my dinner."

ADDENDUM

The internist was correct. The diagnosis was a typical cardiac arrest. Within five minutes, the patient's heart rate was restored to normal. The patient eventually made a complete recovery. This incident took place more than thirty years ago, and while the doctor did not return to the rigors of private solo practice, he remained active with other medical employment.

Most of the other doctors present at the banquet felt if he had been any place other than where he happened to be that evening, he probably would not have survived. If he had gone home where he would have been alone, or if he had been in his office or car without immediate help available, he would have become a negative medical statistic.

And now, the doctor is eighty-nine years of age and, while long since retired, is still active mentally, although somewhat slowed physically.

If there is a lesson to be learned from this story, it can probably best be summarized by the following: If you are a doctor, be sure to go to the scheduled medical meetings even though you are tired. If you are not a doctor, a good routine to follow is not only to play golf on Wednesday afternoons, but also to go to weekend football games. At both of these activities, the odds are very great that amongst those nearby will probably be at least one or two medical doctors or paramedics.

The Night Shift

Our car skidded wildly and, with an ear-splitting crash, smashed through the bridge guard rail. After an abrupt, neck-wrenching, shuddering stop, the car's front end projected into space as it, and we, hung precariously balanced over the rushing river one hundred feet below. Only the rear wheels, mercifully caught on a torn piece of the bridge railing, kept us from plunging into the beckoning, turbulent waters which swirled under us. Any movement by either of us in the front seat caused the car to teeter in a frightening manner. All I could do was cling to the steering wheel with a vise-like grip and pray. Try as I might, I could not cry out or utter any other sound. It seemed as if my vocal cords were completely paralyzed. My first thought was, would we survive? Obviously we did survive and are now here to tell this tale today. You see, this hair-raising episode was just another one of my many frequently bizarre dreams.

For centuries, even from the earliest recorded history, dreams have been the subject of much speculation and analysis. Many soothsayers have attempted to read meaningful messages into man's nocturnal sleeping time ventures. Even today, there are those who specialize in dream interpretation and claim that dreams are the most direct route to the person's subconscious. They state these nighttime visions occur when the mind is not on guard as it often is during the waking state. These analysts even go so far as to have universal symbols for their explanations, such as saying insects are illustrative of a person's siblings, that emerging from a lake or sea represents one's birth, that a cave is symbolic of the mother's womb, and many other weird comparisons.

When you consider most of us spend approximately a third of our lives in bed and many of us dream a good deal of that time, we are not being very well compensated for all the energy we expend in these nocturnal forays. This is especially true when we consider this work is all done on the usually more highly paid "graveyard shift." Of course, not all dreams are laborious. Some are pleasant, and some take us to distant, exotic places. Still others are very puzzling, frustrating, and even frightening.

We often wonder not only where these dreams originate, but also whether they serve any useful function. Daniel's interpretation of King Nebechadnezzer's dream and Joseph's answer for the Pharaoh of Egypt about the forthcoming seven years of plenty to be followed by seven years of famine are well-known biblical Old Testament tales and illustrate the usefulness of some dreams. Personally, in one of my dreams many years ago, I was able to solve an especially difficult school homework mathematical problem I had been wrestling with for most of the previous evening. Aside from these examples, until recently I'd have to say dreams did not have any demonstrable or practical value, except occasionally to furnish the stimulation to get up in the morning, if for no other reason than to terminate a frightening nighttime chapter.

However just recently I had an experience which has changed my opinion about the usefulness of dreams. It so happens that in my daily activities, I quite regularly contacted an older man who, while not hostile, had not been easily approachable—this in spite of my attempts to be friendly. After several rebuffs, and for no explainable reason, I happened to dream about him. In the dream, he and I were working on the same job, and he was my boss. The next time I saw him I said, "I dreamed about you the other night." I then recounted the events of the dream. He listened attentively and seemed to be pleased. Following this conversation, his manner changed markedly. He began to greet me enthusiastically each time we met. We even joked about whether or not I could take a little time off from the job or about which duties he would assign to me for the day. He seemed to become a happier person, and I acquired a new friend. One day he said, "Starting the first of next month, I'm giving you a 25 percent raise."

For your own satisfaction, when and if you have the chance, notice what happens to a person's facial expression when you say, "I dreamed about you the other night." Invariably a combination look of surprise, anticipation, and pleasure will appear. Often you will not have to relate what it was that you dreamed. In most instances your relationship with the individual will acquire a new dimension. I'll let you judge for yourself whether or not all the labor, trauma, and anxiety of your dreams are worthwhile. For me, acquiring one new friend has repaid me for all the efforts expended in my night shift adventures.

Have Her Make the Call

In a dire situation and if you really want fast results have your wife, sister, girlfriend, daughter, or your mother take over. The essential ingredient is that she be a female. For some mysterious reason they have the ability to get fast results which so often elude the male gender.

Early in our marriage, I learned this valuable lesson. At that time we lived in our first real home, a small cottage located on a rather busy arterial hard-topped road. All went well until the city decided to install new water mains. This, of course, necessitated digging up the street and destroying the hard surface. In the hot, dry, summer days the resulting dirt road became a source of large clouds of dust which permeated our entire home and covered everything with a fine layer of dirt.

This condition lasted for several weeks. As the road was well traveled, the resulting problems were considerable. The city engineers seemed to be oblivious to the inconveniences confronting us and apparently made no attempt to remedy the situation.

Finally with dust-dried vocal chords, I called the department at city hall and spoke to the engineer in charge. He kindly explained they were so overwhelmed with their various projects they had fallen behind, but would get to our project as soon as possible. To me, this seemed to be a very logical explanation, and I thanked him for his trouble.

As the weeks passed, the condition persisted. The dust became thicker and thicker. Again I called and again I was given a very logical answer. Being a busy professional, I could appreciate the problems the engineers might have.

Again time passed without any remedy so I canvassed the neighbors about our oiling the dusty surface at our own expense. No one seemed interested in contributing any monies for this project, so I resigned myself to the situation.

Shortly thereafter, one afternoon as the clouds of dust kept rolling in, our one-year-old daughter started coughing. Margaret called me at my office about this and asked me to call the city engineers again. As I was swamped at the time,

I asked her to make the call. By this time, it was 4:00 P.M. on a Friday. It seemed to me there would be no possible remedy until Monday at the earliest. Of course I failed to reckon with the persuasive powers of my spouse. I'm not sure what she said to the city engineer, but I am sure it was done in a Christian manner.

Imagine my surprise when, on arriving home, I saw road scrapers busily smoothing the surface, followed by large oil trucks laying down a protective covering over the dusty surface. The work progressed throughout the entire evening and on into the late hours, the last part of the project done under search lights. Like magic, the dust disappeared and the coughing abated.

As the years passed, following this somewhat miraculous demonstration, I was to see repeated evidences of Margaret's powers of persuasion. This was especially true in her handling of me. The remarkable part of the whole process in my transformation was that I usually at the time wasn't aware it was happening.

Finally, the secret of her power became evident when I discovered she was using the Holy Bible's admonition, "A soft answer turneth away wrath."

From a practical standpoint, I had found it pays to HAVE HER MAKE THE CALL.

A Trilogy

He had a rather nasty fracture of one leg. The break had been reduced and casted. All was progressing well, but the patient complained, saying, "I had this same kind of fracture several years ago during World War II while in the Navy, but it didn't hurt nearly as much as this one."

There are several reasons why his present injury was more painful than the one before. First, this one was now. Just as a today's headache is worse than the one last month, so his present pain was greater than the one that occurred several years ago. Second, his entire situation was completely different this time. When he had his first fracture he was taken from his hazardous duty to a relatively safe hospital ship. There he was cared for, fed well, and lived the life of Riley while still receiving his regular Navy pay. Also, he was unmarried and without dependents.

With his most recent fracture, his situation was in marked contrast. He was now married, had two children, and was the owner of a one-man roofing business. With his disability, he would not be able to do his usual type of work for several weeks. He couldn't afford to hire someone to do it for him. The combination of worry about the possible loss of his business and his family's welfare plus his medical expenses all combined to increase his pain.

The compounding of his pain caused by his multiple problems illustrates graphically the interrelationship of the many facets which are present in all of our lives. We, as humans, are in reality a trilogy made up of three basic elements: the spiritual, the mental, and the physical. While each is separate to some extent, the three are all closely intertwined. Each one influences the other two which, in turn, then rebound on the initiating element.

One of the curses of mankind is needless and futile worry. This is not to be confused with thoughtful and careful planning for future contingencies. An example was the woman who constantly worried about all manner of imaginary problems, all to no avail. When she was at last confronted with a serious illness, she was an ideal and cooperative patient with no unusual concern. Later, when asked about this change of attitude, she replied, "Oh, when I really become sick and know what I have to contend with, I know that I can handle it. What usually worries me the most is when I don't have anything to worry about. It's the unknown that gets me."

In contrast, another elderly woman seemed very serene, without an apparent worry in the world. When asked her secret, she said, "I found out long ago that most of the things I used to worry about either never occurred or were much less than expected. What remained I couldn't do anything about, so I turned the problems over to the Lord." The latter woman was a strong Christian.

As we all must someday die, many of mankind's worries are concerned with the fear of death. In some instances this can become so strong it impairs the individual's ability to lead a productive and happy life. In turn, the frustrations which accompany this turmoil can have a direct effect on the body's physical processes. In case there is some doubt in the reader's mind regarding this, let us look at the way our bodies function.

Without going into too much detail here is a brief outline of some of the ways the body's functions can be influenced for the better or for the worse by our mental processes and the strength of our Christian faith. First of all, we as humans are very complex computers—which by comparison make even the most sophisticated modern inanimate computers seem like very crude and elemental toys.

Basically, our nervous systems are composed of two major components: the voluntary and the involuntary, or autonomic. The voluntary is used by us at all times and is subject to our will and conscious thought. The involuntary is much more subtle and is not directly under our willful control. This can be both an advantage and also a liability. For example, it works in the following manner. If a bear were to walk into the room, we would say to ourselves, "There is a bear! Let's get out of here!" A signal would then go from our conscious mind to our autonomic nerve centers. Many switches would automatically turn on without any further conscious direction from us. Our adrenalin production would increase; our heart rate would quicken; our blood vessels would constrict; our muscles would tighten; and we would prepare to flee and move with alacrity.

Let us assume this particular experience had a nervous rating of 10. The response to this 10 would be immediate. Later on, we would say, "That bear nearly scared me to death!" However we wouldn't worry or even think much about the various side symptoms such as our fast pulse, hair standing on end, pallor, or any other reaction which might have accompanied the scare.

In a different situation, let us suppose that on any given day, a person has ten separate irritations or excitements, each with a rating of 1. There are many of these, such as: a letter from the IRS; a friend's illness; newspaper articles about cancer, salt, fats, etc., etc., which appear nearly daily; an irritable husband or wife; a burned hot dish; a traffic delay; and anyone of a hundred minor experiences which occur on a regular basis. On this particular day, let us assume a total of ten units accumulate.

While the total strength of the units is the same as in the bear experience, the response is quite different. Instead of an immediate reaction, there will be a delayed onset—usually of several hours or even days. This response can be manifested in any number of ways, such as: headaches, palpitations of the heart, abdominal pain, nighttime cold sweats, skin rashes, etc., etc. In most situations, any connection with the previous day's events is not readily apparent. As a result, these new symptoms will, in turn, add to the above anxiety and trigger a chain reaction, conjuring up in the person's mind a self-diagnosis of heart trouble, gastric ulcers, or any number of other physical conditions. From the above it becomes apparent that if adverse experiences are encountered repeatedly over a long period of time, the individual so affected will react unfavorably, especially if he or she has no other support upon which to rely.

You might ask, "Why do we have such a nervous system that we cannot directly control ourselves? If we didn't have this automatic or autonomic mechanism, couldn't we avoid all of these functional problems?"

Good question. However without this mechanism it would be necessary for us to consciously turn on our various systems such as our gastric juices and peristalsis with each meal; make sure our heart rate was adequate for each activity; regulate our breathing; control our perspiration; etc. All of these would be necessary twenty-four hours a day, even during our sleeping hours. As long as we have this wonderful self-regulating mechanism, we must learn to live with it and keep it from acting in an adverse or malfunctioning manner.

It should be noted that positive experiences have a beneficial effect and in some instances may even cancel out some of the negative factors. A smile, a hearty handshake, a compliment, a thank you note, and many other little kindnesses may do wonders for an otherwise somber day.

Before going on, it should be noted there are no purely physical nor purely emotional illnesses. Each ailment is made up of combinations of these two components. For instance, as mentioned earlier, a fractured leg has its emotional element. Also, an emotional illness will be accompanied by physical problems such as malnutrition, cardiac palpitations, obesity, digestive disturbances, and any number of other manifestations.

Once there were two men who in many respects were very similar. They both had worked for the same company, had retired at the same time, were of the same age, and in approximately the same condition financially. One man was primarily self-centered and had many functional problems. His general physical condition was good, but he was constantly miserable and worried about the possibility of dying. The second man had an extremely severe heart problem. However he was outgoing, happy, and serene. On leaving the doctor's office one day, he turned to the doctor and asked, "Can you keep me going for a while longer, Doc? I'm working for the Lord and have a lot left to do." Which man would you choose to be if you had a choice?

The following statement is often expressed: "They told me that my problem was all in my head." While the quote may be accurate, the thought behind the statement is far from the truth. A functional leg cramp is just as real and painful as that caused by a blow from a baseball bat. A red skin from sunburn is organic. A red skin from a blush is functional. The signs and symptoms of the above conditions may be similar and equally painful for the patient, but the causes are far different. The blush and the muscle spasm will leave in a few minutes. Not so the organic problems.

Never be ashamed of having functional problems. They simply prove you are human. The only objects which don't have these symptoms are inanimate—like robots and computers.

What can we do to control some of these functional disturbances or at least minimize their intensity? This is where Christianity can play a dominant role. Possessed with true faith, we can smooth off many of the rough edges and help to calm the turbulences of life. Instead of being like a small rowboat tossed hither and thither by each wave, we can be more like a large ocean-going liner—rolling a bit, but for the most part plowing through the storms on a relatively even keel. Christian faith acts like the ship's gyroscopes which help to stabilize the rolling of the vessel.

True faith gives us the strength and vision to properly evaluate each adversity and give each problem the proper amount of attention it deserves. Two quotations from the Bible will help. Proverbs 3:5-6: "Trust in the Lord with all your heart and lean not on your own understanding: in all your ways acknowledge Him, and He will make your paths straight."

James 1:2-3: "Consider it pure joy, my brothers, whenever you face trials of many kinds, because you know that the testing of your faith develops perseverance."

And so, with a smile on your face, a song on your lips, and Christ in your heart, you will have adequate medicine for most of life's vicissitudes and will, in turn, be able to better understand the trilogy of the spiritual, the mental, and the physical.

Life's Totem Poles

We all have our own totem poles. Ours, unlike those large wooden poles of the Indians of the Pacific Ocean slopes of Canada, Alaska, and Washington, are in our minds. Unlike the Indian poles whose images remain in the same relative placements, our images are mobile and often do change places from time to time depending on many different factors. Of course, these changes are a positive factor and offer each of us the stimulation to better our relative standing on our individual family poles.

For instance, in early youth we are willing to accept one of the bottom spots on the pole, feeling that as we mature we will be able to move up one or more spots. We may even aspire to reaching the top of the pole in our later years. The disadvantage of this mobile ranking is that once a person reaches the top rung, there is only one way to go, and that is down. This is especially true for those of us after we retire from our chosen profession.

Once this stage is reached, each of us enters an entirely new world. New challenges appear, and the positions on the totem pole shift somewhat. The time has arrived for someone on the way up to assume the top level. Often the apex is relinquished without any regrets by the previous occupant. With retirement comes a whole new set of activities, many of a manual nature.

There is nothing demeaning in manual activity. In fact, a rugged session of hard work is not only good for the body, but also is soothing to the soul. In addition, the feeling of accomplishment which results makes all the hard work well worthwhile. Even the fatigue and the aching muscles which follow seem beneficial in spite of all the effort expended. However to be completely objective, there are a few drawbacks connected with projects of this kind which should be mentioned.

With manual labor, there are a few tasks which can easily be dispensed with without any regrets. Close to the top of the list is the clean-up work after a session of bush and shrub pruning. This is especially true where rose bushes are concerned. In the actual process of pruning, the snipping and cutting are sort of fun and do help to average out the later pain of picking up the scattered twigs.

Many wives will trust their mates, to a limited extent, with the trimming of most shrubs, hedges, and even some of the small trees. Of course, they do keep a close *eye* on these same spouses during their operations as most men have a tendency to hack and cut back rather severely some of these innocent growths, leaving only a few bare stubs. In one instance, after trimming a cherry tree, the harvest that year was only one cupful whereas the average annual crop was usually many quarts. In some instances, the pruning was nearly fatal to the tree or bush involved, to say nothing of the emotional shock suffered by the hacker's mate when she saw the end result.

Because of this rather cavalier and reckless approach to the pruning process, there are three areas where most men are barred from cutting or doing even minimal trimming, namely: the rhododendrons, the flowering dogwood trees, and especially the rose bushes. In contrast, there are no restrictions to the picking up of the trimmings of the above named.

While harvesting most twigs and snippings is a relatively harmless job, picking up rose bush clippings is just the opposite and can be extremely hazardous and in some situations nearly lethal. Cleaning up and carting them off is one big pain. Any who have had this job will know the risks involved. The thorns present are no minor opponent and the aftereffects of their barbs can last for several days or even weeks.

Recently, the United States Secretary of Education, when giving a commencement address at a university graduation, stated getting an education was the best way of assuring success in one's life. While the meaning of this statement is somewhat obvious and not too illuminating, it does illustrate the advantage of acquiring knowledge and developing skills in all of our activities. For instance in the field of pruning, becoming proficient may convert a person from a picker-upper to the status of a snipper and cutter.

In a way, becoming skillful also illustrates some of the similarities and differences our lives have to totem poles. In our developing years, from early youth to maturity, progressing upward on the totem pole of life the first time presents a challenge and is often fun. Early in our careers, as a rule, we don't mind being low man on the pole for a while as we have the hope of improving our position as time passes. However once we have been up the pole and near the top, it is difficult to find ourselves back on the bottom.

Viewed in another way, perhaps this is all for the best and may act as a stimulant to us to better our position. From a lowly place on the pole we may humbly learn to prune with more discretion and forethought. In this way, advancement up the pole may take place once again, even faster than we might imagine.

At least we, as humans, can all be thankful we have one big advantage over the figures on the wooden Indian totem poles—once they are carved, their relative placements can never be changed.

The Bad News Seismograph

The morning paper headlines figuratively screamed the news the president of our country had an acute pneumonia. On the same front page, in smaller headlines, another article told of the impending invasion of killer bees heading north from South America. Also featured was a story of a man in Australia who had had hiccoughs for two weeks. These tidbits of bad news were also featured on the radio as we breakfasted. They were to be repeated many times during the remainder of the day as well as on television that evening.

In this day of instantaneous world-wide communication, it is now possible to hear about a news event within minutes of its occurrence. Because of this speed of dissemination, plus the repetitions on both the radio and TV and later in newspaper headlines and articles, we may begin to lose our true perspective of each event's importance. By the end of the day, we may begin to feel there must be at least epidemics of pneumonia and hiccoughs forthcoming. We might even peek furtively from behind our curtained windows to catch sight of the swarms of killer bees that must surely be arriving at any moment from just over the southern horizon.

Because of this constant bombardment, our brain cells become fatigued and confused. They lose their power to accurately discriminate and start sending us false information. As a result we begin to think all of these events are occurring in our own neighborhood, and therefore, are of extraordinary importance. At this point it is easy for us to feel our little world is rapidly falling apart.

Our ancestors had one big advantage over us. In their day, because of the slowness of communication, tragic and world-shaking events were not reported for days or even for weeks. (The pony express could only go so fast.) By the time the news of some distant event did arrive, the problem was usually resolved and hardly worth considering.

Today good news is rarely transmitted to us with the same speed as the bad. Newsmen state the sale of their product is much greater for alarming or unfavorable events. For example, it is practically impossible to find a newspaper article or hear a radio broadcast about the safe arrival of someone at his workplace or about how well he did his job on that particular day. The converse, however, would have been reported with alacrity. In all fairness to the reporters, articles about safe trips to work or about jobs well done would be quite boring except to those personally concerned. However the emphasis on the negative does cause us emotional trauma. Here, real optimism is a must.

Because some of us have difficulty being consistently and completely objective, I would like to suggest to you a remedy I have found helps to win the battle against pessimism. I call it my "Bad News Seismograph." The rules for its use are very simple, available to all, and consist of a very few basic procedures. Number one, don't turn on the news broadcasts more than once a day. If the news you hear is bad, start singing or whistling lustily until you hear something more pleasant. Number two, if the newspaper headlines are large and alarming, don't read the accompanying articles during the first three days they appear. This requires a strong and disciplined will. If these headlines persist for longer than three days, skim the articles so you can at least pretend to be somewhat knowledgeable when your friends and neighbors, in great agitation, bring up the subject. Finally, if this same alarming news persists for a week, read about it in depth because by then it is probably of some significance.

During the several years I have used this system, I have found that almost 80 percent of the alarming news of the previous week had completely disappeared from sight. Of the remainder, most of it was either markedly diluted or at least was approaching a solvable stage. Of the small fraction which still persisted, such as inflation, communism, or other everlasting problems, there wasn't much for us to worry about as their solution was probably somewhat beyond our own individual efforts—this plus the fact that worry by itself doesn't solve anything unless backed up by some positive counter action.

Just like earthquakes, bad news comes in different strengths. With the former, a true seismograph records the intensity. With the latter, using the above suggestions as a bad news seismograph helps to record the intensity of the doom and gloom and put them in their proper perspective. For your peace of mind, give it a trial.

Don't Be "Cowed"

As the golfer stood over his ball while trying to make a forty-foot putt, many thoughts must have gone through his mind. He was in the final twosome of a three-day tournament for the President's Cup in a match between the United States and an international team. The score for the two teams was tied at 15-1/2 points. His opponent's ball was closer to the cup and the championship hinged on his pressure-packed performance on this last hole.

The eyes of his teammates, as well as those of the opponents, thousands of greenside spectators, and a vast TV audience were focused on him. With this amount of pressure, it would have been easy for him to be diverted and to miss the shot. Not so for this veteran. With unerring accuracy he ran the ball directly into the cup, won his match, and the team championship. Immediately he was overwhelmed by his teammates as well as some of the local throng. He certainly hadn't been "cowed" by the pressure of the moment. In this and other sporting events, such coolness under fire is the mark of a true champion.

The same tribute may be given to a concert violinist, pianist, vocalist, orator, or other performer on the stage before a large audience. In less publicized settings, an aviator in combat, a fireman in an inferno, a surgeon performing a difficult surgery, a mother tending to the needs of her children—all can display this same coolness and efficiency. While some individuals seem to be born with these characteristics, others have to acquire them with training and discipline. Fortunately, most of us are not "cowed" by these challenges.

In many instances, especially with public figures, a certain amount of adulation may accompany these displays of ability. Often, in fact, the entertainer may not only thrive on but may also seem to require this constant attention and worship. If and when the glamour days begin to fade, he or she will often seek some other avenue to attract a following. For example, a former glamorous actress may become an ardent anti-vivisectionist, an ex-prominent legal judge may set himself up as a nutritional authority, and an ex-athlete may feel he is an authority on finance. While some of their efforts are a bit misguided, in all fairness we have to give them credit for their ambition and "uncowed" efforts.

In contrast to the above, there are large groups who have exactly the opposite attitude. They are the ones who never venture into a new field because of the fear of failure. Once they have been safely installed in their regular routine, they do not tolerate any variations. In other words, they are cowed by any challenge. They, in essence, say, "I'm not gifted as a musician and never could play an instrument." Or, "I never was good in mathematics. I can't even balance my checkbook." And, "I'm no athlete. Sports are entirely beyond me." As many of these individuals are perfectionists, they are afraid to try anything new because they feel they might not excel. With their negative attitude, they are defeated before they start.

One prominent surgeon was forced to give up his work because of a severe heart attack. He became extremely depressed and said he wanted to die. A close friend urged him to adopt some other interest and brought him a beginners drawing and painting set. The doctor said, "That's no good. I can't even draw a straight line." His friend's reply was, "Well, just give it a try." Within a short time, the doctor became so completely engrossed in this new venture his depression disappeared, and he regained his desire to carry on.

Another example of the fear of failure was to be found in a man who enjoyed playing golf but hesitated playing with anyone else because they might laugh at him. He was even nervous while playing if the greenskeeper was anywhere nearby as he was about to make a shot, especially when he was putting. One day while alone on the fairway, he felt he was being stared at and could hardly concentrate on his next stroke. Finally, the feeling became so strong he had to stop and look around. Sure enough, there was a large cow with big brown eyes on the other side of the bordering fence peering intently at him. This "cowed" him so much he could hardly continue his game.

Most of us fit in a category somewhat between the professional golfer mentioned above and the reluctant one who couldn't stand to have a lone cow watch him. We all have our hang-ups and our difficulties coping with one or another aspect of our lives, so don't be easily discouraged.

In reality, many of us may never become a famous actor or actress or fly into outer space as an astronaut. We may never learn to run a computer or even to program our VCR, but there are many new fields of endeavor which we can tackle without expecting to excel therein. However for our own satisfaction and pleasure, starting today, let's give some new venture a try, and DON'T BE COWED by any fear of failure.

Aging Gracefully

A government inspector once asked an employer, "How many of your employees are approaching retirement age?"

"As far as I can tell, all of them are. I don't know of any who are going the other direction."

Speaking of aging, in reality this process starts the day we are born and is largely in the mind and eyes of the beholder. When we are five years old, ten seems old. At sixteen, the twenties are ancient, and anyone over thirty is long gone. This probably explains why some individuals, especially young ladies, feel the best ten years of their lives are between the ages of twenty-nine and thirty.

As the years rapidly pass, those in the decade ahead seem so elderly. Yet when we ourselves reach that same stage it seems quite young. However finally there does arrive that stage of life when we have to admit we have aged. Often the signs of this are quite subtle, such as: when the barber no longer has to use his thinning shears, when boy scouts want to help you cross the street even when you don't want to go, when the supermarket checker asks you if you need help to carry the groceries to your car, or when you find you are short of breath on stairs and hills even when descending same.

While it is difficult for some of us to accept the status of "senior citizen" gracefully, actually the process is quite simple. The secret lies in the proper balancing of our mental, spiritual, and physical capabilities. Each of these should be given its appropriate attention. Overemphasis of anyone segment will disturb the delicate balance. As our physical ability decreases, we may have to change the ratio of the three factors somewhat.

Ideally, with maturity comes increased wisdom, optimism, and faith. Once acquired, these help us to look with different eyes at some of the activities we previously felt were important. A former college professor may be happy with less heavy studies. An ex-athlete who tends to remember the days of his glory may have to be content with less strenuous physical activity and even assume a spectator roll. And a former head pastor of a church may find himself at peace in the roll of visitation minister.

One trap we should all avoid when aging is that of wishing we could live our lives over again by overemphasizing the "good old days." Instead, we should learn to be happy with each phase of our life, especially as we gracefully grow older.

The Other Fellow's Turf

In this modern day of computers, complex business ventures, and a myriad other problems, it's hard to win or even to stay even when we are dealing with someone else in his or her own familiar field of expertise.

To illustrate, a doctor heard about a way to make a good profit without any apparent effort on his part. The proposal was simple and sounded like a sure thing. It consisted of his buying some calves, raising them to be full-grown cows, and then selling them. What could be easier? Buy small and sell big. With confidence he plunged into this, for him, completely foreign field. After two years in the venture, he was asked how it had all turned out. His answer: "Well, I bought the calves from a man who made his living selling calves. I pastured them with a man who made his living pasturing animals, and I sold the cows to another man who made his living buying cows. You can guess who was the one who didn't make anything."

We often are on foreign turf when buying airline tickets. A recent newspaper article pointed out that on a given airplane flight there were nine different fares charged in the first class section and thirteen different fares in the main cabin. On many trips the amount a person has to pay depends on several different factors: from whom he bought the tickets, his age (senior discounts), whether he is in a tour group, on a bereavement trip, the mood of the ticket seller at the airport, the passenger's mileage plus status, and many other intangible factors. The end result is that as he flies along, those next to him may have paid half what he paid, the same amount, or twice as much.

Buying an automobile really puts us in an area of unfamiliar turf. It used to be when we decided to buy a car we paid the price listed on the vehicle. No longer. The other day, a salesman was asked, "Does anyone ever pay the price listed for a car?" The salesman thought for a moment, and then answered, "I seem to remember one customer who did pay it, about six months ago."

It is the custom in some foreign countries to haggle over the price of a rug, lamp, or some other piece of bric-a-brac. In fact, dickering in the market place seems to be a requirement before any purchase. Often, the proprietor of the shop will be disappointed if his price is accepted as quoted without some sort of lively discussion. So it is today in making a car purchase. No one, including the seller, really expects the buyer to pay the posted price. Of course, in the maneuvering the dealer has all the advantages. First of all, he has a considerable dollar mark-up to play with. Second, the different cars have such a variety of options and types of equipment that it is hard for a novice buyer to know exactly what he is buying. It isn't as simple as comparing apples and oranges. It's more like the differences between a Mulligan stew and a complex fruit salad. Again, when the deal is finalized and all is said and done, the dealer is on his own turf.

Speaking of turf, there is one field where the grass is really green. That's in the specialty field of antiques. Here, there are no specific rules and no price limits. It is simply a matter of "What will the market pay?" With a few exceptions, no one knows what an item is really worth. For example, an ex-telephone company employee nearly fainted when he was told green glass pole insulators were being sold for two dollars a piece. Also, an ex-milk delivery man couldn't believe old glass milk bottles were bringing horrendous prices.

Someone once asked why antique furniture costs so much when the chairs and settees were so uncomfortable. The answer—the comfortable pieces were used so much in their day they wore out, and what remained was in short supply with resulting higher prices. In all fairness, it must be conceded some antiques such as jewelry are really beautiful and well worth the asking price. Also some old pictures are priceless, but by and large these are the exceptions. Of course most antique dealers are more knowledgeable about their wares than their customers. In other words, they are operating on their own turf.

One turf that is certainly intimidating for most individuals is in a court of law, especially when experienced for the first time. Here the neophyte is often completely baffled. I recall the first time I had to appear as an expert witness. I was very hesitant and made several errors, such as using the word "possible" instead of "probable." Because of the strange, and what seemed to be hostile, environment I became a bit confused. My mind and tongue didn't always get together. As time passed and these experiences became more frequent, the territory became more familiar and things began to fall into their proper place. During this period it became more and more evident the only requirements for good testimony were four basic factors: always tell the truth, answer only what you are asked and nothing more, keep calm, and don't let the opposing lawyer put words into your mouth.

In my court appearances, when answering questions, I always tried to use language which would be clear to the jury. On one occasion, the adversarial attorney, a "hot shot" from the big city, acted like he was in court to show the small town "hicks" a thing or two. As I answered his questions in laymen's terms, he began to repeat my answers in a somewhat mocking manner. To me this, of course, was more than a bit irritating. When he persisted in this mode,

I decided to switch tactics and began answering him by using as many technical terms as possible. Within minutes he was completely befuddled. In other words he had been pushed off his own familiar turf and onto mine.

Speaking of lawyers, there was one who was antagonistic toward the medical profession and who took delight in handling medical malpractice cases. In fact, he sought them out and encouraged patients to sue their doctors on even frivolous grounds. To most of us doctors, the cause of his antipathy was hidden, but was very real nevertheless. However after several years of this negative attitude there did come a time when his wife suddenly became seriously ill and was hospitalized for a prolonged period. At that time the hospital visitor's waiting room was very close to the front entrance. With due credit to the lawyer, he was very attentive to his wife and spent most of the days and nights either in her room or in the main waiting room. In the latter, he became aware of the goings and comings of the medical staff. As a result, he began to be aware of the dedication of the doctors. He later said, "I had no idea how many hours you men spent on duty nor your constant attention to your patients." This same man, from his position as an antagonist, did a complete about-face and became a booster for our profession. In essence, he switched from his own turf to ours.

All of us have had the experience of being confronted by a dentist on his turf. For many patients, even contemplating such a visit becomes somewhat of a trauma. Actually, the exact opposite view should be taken. We should feel sorry for the dentist. He can't help it if many of his customers look at him with disfavor, fear, and trembling as he practices his profession. To the dentist's credit, he does try to minimize the discomfort associated with the drilling, picking, probing, and scraping that goes on. However in spite of his efforts to ease the physical and mental discomforts, he is not able to completely overcome the reluctances and prejudices which have built up over the years in the public's mind. As a result, he is at a disadvantage even though actually and physically he is on his own turf.

For many, one of the most feared foreign turfs they may have to trod is occupied by the IRS, especially their auditing department. Someone once said that if we all filled out our income tax forms honestly we would never have to worry about being audited. While this may be true most of the time, it is not always so. In spite of our best efforts, there may be situations when we are called upon to visit the IRS to defend our tax compilations. If and when this does occur, we may feel we are really on hostile turf and that our fate is sealed. Take heart. Just remember the agents are human and simply doing their jobs. It's like testifying in a court of law: keep cool, tell the truth, and go armed with facts and figures. If there is anything the IRS really loves it's paperwork and numbers. Usually the reason for the audit is some misunderstanding or other marked variation from your previous year's return. Also, it helps to remember that while you may feel you are on hostile turf, you are really only dealing with your own government (yourself) and that if you do have to make an extra payment, you are supporting a kind and benevolent bureaucracy which needs your money and always spends it wisely.

We all will have many occasions when we will meet with others on their own "turf," namely: the bankers, the butchers, the and even the candlestick makers; the crooks and the con men; the doctors and dentists; the merchants and the musicians; the plumbers and politicians; the salesmen and solicitors; the teachers and tutors; plus many others. In these meetings let us remember each one of them knows his or her own field much better than we do. As the song in the musical comedy *The Music Man* tells us, "You Gotta Know the Territory." However let us also remember to give each of them the utmost consideration when we meet them on our own "turf."

Big Men

He was big, very big. At least six-foot-four with broad shoulders, a rugged face, a booming voice, and what seemed to be a definite "take over" manner. In contrast, his sister was small, thin, pale, and even mousy in manner. She stayed in the background and definitely deferred to him. As we three sat at their mother's bedside during the last few days of her terminal illness, it was comforting to me to know that when the final day did arrive there would be someone strong enough to take charge and to handle all the arrangements necessary at such a time.

They had extracted a promise from me that when the fateful day did arrive I would be present to make the final pronouncement. As promised, I hurried to their home and arrived just minutes before the mother expired. As I turned to the son and daughter to tell them their mother was gone, who took over? It was the small, quiet daughter who became a tower of strength. In short order, she organized all the arrangements required. In contrast, the "big man" became completely incompetent and with much weeping and loud wailing was unable to cope with reality.

What makes a man really big? Some say his stature, others say his brain, and still others gauge his size by his spiritual attributes. To be completely accurate, all three facets must be considered in evaluating the true size of any man. While there is no definite relationship between the physical, the mental, and the spiritual characteristics of any one person, each of the three does intertwine and influences the other two. For example, a person of small physical stature may subconsciously try to compensate by increasing his mental skills and spiritual strengths. Conversely, a physically large man may tend to rely on his size and neglect the other aspects. A truly big man is the one who uses all three elements of his make up to the maximum.

When we consider physical size alone, we must take into account the era of history involved. What was considered large in bygone days would now seem rather small. It is surprising how small many of the suits of armor of the legendary knights of King Arthur's Round Table seem to us when viewed at this time.

More recently, in the 1930s, one of the college football players was known as "The Giant." He was six-feet-four-inches tall. Today he would be considered just average or even small for this sport. The same for basketball. In the thirties a six-four player would be considered a candidate for the center position. Today he'd probably be a guard, having been replaced by someone six-ten or even seven feet tall.

In the mental sphere, the size of a man is largely determined by his ability to utilize his brain to its fullest capacity. Many of the great advances in engineering, chemistry, physics, and in the other sciences have been made by men of small stature or by those physically crippled. Charles Steinmetz is a perfect example of the latter.

One of the crucial turning points of World War II was the Battle of Britain. This was the air war in which the British fighter squadrons were able to turn back the German bombers and was the action which prompted Churchill to say, "Never have so many owed so much to so few." Much of the credit for this victory was the result of one man who developed the strategy used by the British defenders.

This man was a pilot who had lost a large part of both legs in an airplane crash. It was thought he would never fly again, much less fly as a fighter pilot. By sheer determination, he was able to persuade his superiors to allow him to not only return to flying but also to become a squadron commander. In this position, he devised new techniques for fighting which were later adopted by most of the air force and were credited with playing a large part in the final outcome of the crucial battle which saved Britain.

In the spiritual realm, some of the real giants have been those who were small to average-size physically. A Scotchman, William Barclay, who wrote a series of biblical commentaries, is one good example. Of course, other leaders in religion have been large physically. Drs. Mark Matthews and Billy Graham stand out here.

But let us return to examples closer to home. When our daughters were young, we used to tell them not to judge a boyfriend by the length of his legs nor the width of his shoulders, but to pay more attention to how he reacted in moments of stress. For example, his response to a flat tire on a muddy, dirt, hillside road at 10:00 P.M. during a heavy rainstorm.

In the sports field, it is a commonly held belief that one difference between a professional golfer and a duffer is the pro rarely makes two bad shots in a row, while the duffer tends to compound his errors. This may be true in most instances, but there are exceptions. Recently, on TV I saw a top-flight professional golfer take four strokes to get out of a deep greenside bunker. As surprising as this was, what was even more startling was what happened next. After his fourth bunker shot, this usually cool and calculating golfing machine threw his club halfway across the neighboring green. The end result was a score of ten for that hole.

The above incident reminded me of a story one of the doctors told about himself. After finishing his long residency in eye, he went into practice with his father. Shortly thereafter, he was scheduled to perform his first private practice surgery with his father as his assistant. Naturally he was somewhat tense and nervous during this baptism of fire. All went well until near the end of the operation. At this point there occurred a minor "glitch" which was not of any major significance. However the young surgeon's tensions got the better of him, and he threw his surgical instrument all the way across the room. Immediately, a deadly silence descended upon the team. This persisted for the remainder of the procedure. When finally the young man and his father were in the doctor's dressing room changing into their street clothes, the father broke the silence with, "Makes you feel like a big man, doesn't it?"

As this now mature doctor told his story, he said, "I never felt so small in all my life. Incidentally, I have never thrown another instrument of any kind during the remainder of my career."

Fortunately no major casualties resulted from either of the above two outbursts, except for perhaps a slightly ruffled grassy green on the golf course and a few scratches on the surgical instrument. At least there were no human injuries except for the bruised egos of the two throwers.

Aside from throwing things, there are many other less commendable ways of demonstrating how not to be a "big man." For instance, being the kind of a boss who treats his employees in a domineering manner or a person who blames others when things go wrong, but takes credit for all of the successes. Then there are those who belittle the accomplishments of their associates. We are all familiar with the type who is subservient to his superiors, but deals with those under his jurisdiction in the opposite way, or those who are inconsiderate of anyone he feels cannot do him a favor. Then there is the golfer who blames the "grain" of the putting surface when the golf ball doesn't go into the hole, but who claims how wonderful his shot is when it does drop.

Probably the lowest type of the so-called "big men" are those who demonstrate their supposed superiority by beating their spouses both physically and mentally.

In contrast to this last group, there was once a bank teller who was so small in stature he had to stand on a box in his teller's cage in order to be at eye level with his customers. However, what he lacked in height he more than made up in his mental acuity, his interest in his clients, and his fellow workers. Many evenings he would stay long after closing to help a fellow teller balance his books. Because of these positive qualities, he overcame the disadvantages of his small stature and ended his career as the senior vice president of a large bank.

Peter Marshall was only average in size physically, but was a giant in the spiritual realm. With his sermons and his writings he was able to influence many thousands of individuals in their search for salvation. He was, in reality, a very big man.

The make up of a truly big man is influenced by many different factors, namely: his inherited and environmental backgrounds, his present condition physically and emotionally, and his spiritual convictions. The truly big men come in many different sizes and shapes. Some may be small in stature physically, but are large in all other aspects.

In the final analysis, the true test of a man's size is determined by his ability to withstand adversity in the times of stress and trauma.

You Can't Please Them All

To paraphrase a famous man, you can please some of the people all of the time; you can please all of the people some of the time; but you can't please all of the people all of the time.

Several years ago a city councilman said, "There is really no need for any term limit rule for elected officials. I've found that three terms in office is usually the maximum for any one office holder. During each of my three three-year sessions, I happened to antagonized approximately one-third of my constituency by the way I voted. In my first term, I voted for a dog leash law. This upset the dog owners but pleased those who didn't have canines. By the next election, the dog owners seemed to remember my vote which ran counter to their wishes and forgot about the 90 percent of my votes of which they approved. In the second term, I lost another third; and again during my third term, the same thing happened. By that time I found it was practically impossible not only to get a majority but also to please even a minority."

While this type of behavior might seem logical and possible in politics, it certainly shouldn't happen in the field of medicine, especially in cases of long-standing physical ailments which were suddenly cured. Here, most of us would probably assume the individuals involved would always be overjoyed. Such is not the case. Let me illustrate how wrong this assumption might be by recounting two separate cases.

Maria was a very thin—even scrawny—middle-aged black woman who came to our medical school outpatient clinic for an examination. Among her numerous complaints was one she mentioned in a somewhat off-handed way. "I've been deaf in my left ear for the last seventeen years. It started one day when all of a sudden I heard a terrible roaring in that ear. It was really loud, just like an airplane was coming right at me. I was really scared. The noise just about drove me crazy, so I took a regular straight hairpin and poked it into my ear. The pain was really bad, but the roaring stopped. When I pulled the hairpin out there was blood on it. From that time on I couldn't hear in that ear anymore. This didn't bother me too much because at the time I was so glad to get that noise stopped. Later on, I wondered if I'd done the right thing 'cause I've been deaf in that ear ever since."

As a senior medical student, new in the clinic, I expected to find evidence of a ruptured ear drum or some other sign of an old injury. However when I looked into the ear with an otoscope, I saw a petrified house fly wedged tightly against the ear drum. Within minutes, by a simple flushing of the canal with warm water, the fly was removed and, wonder of wonders, her hearing was restored to normal.

Maria was ecstatic and kept thanking me over and over. Her gratitude was nearly overpowering. In addition, she just about convinced me I had really performed a miracle. This being my first complete therapeutic cure, I naturally felt somewhat exhilarated and certainly quite proud of myself. As I left the clinic that day, I walked with my feet at least six inches off the sidewalk and my head well into the clouds.

Years later, when treating an elderly eighty-year-old man for hypertension, I found that both of his external ear canals were completely occluded with cement-like detritus and ear wax. He was very hard of hearing and talked with the characteristic loud, nearly shouting voice of the chronically deaf. "I guess I'm just getting too old and my hearing is getting worse and worse as the years pass by."

After much probing, chiseling, flushing, and considerable effort, I was finally able to remove the material from one of his ears. Just as the last bit came out, he exclaimed, "What's that noise?"

The noise happened to be the street sounds of traffic eight floors below. Following the clearing of the second ear, his hearing was restored to a nearly normal level. He, like Maria years before, was overjoyed, but this happiness was to prove to be short lived.

The following month, he returned for a recheck of his blood pressure. As he was leaving the examining room, he turned to me and said. "You know, Doc, I'm sure that you meant well when you cleaned out my ears last month, but I have been wondering if you could maybe put some of that stuff back where you found it. I guess I didn't know when I was well off. Beforehand I could take my newspaper or book, get into my easy chair in the corner of the living room, read to my heart's content or even doze a little. Now that I can hear, I can't escape the constant noise, the TV, and the kid's rock music. In addition, the incessant chattering going on in the house nearly drives me crazy. I can't concentrate on my reading anymore and dozing is out of the question."

When I thought about his predicament in an impartial way, I could see that perhaps there was a small element of logic in what he had to say. However I couldn't help but contrast his reaction with that of my first deaf patient, Maria. The differences in their responses simply illustrated the fact we can't always predict how any one person will react in a given situation. Maybe this is all for the best, and tends to confirm the paraphrasing of Abraham Lincoln's famous statement mentioned in the opening paragraph.

In the final analysis, if we could foresee all future events and if we could score a bull's-eye with every shot, the game of life would become quite boring and we, in turn, would probably become intolerably egotistical. Let us be content to be wrong in some of our expectations. We can't please everyone all of the time so let us be thankful when we make the least number of errors and have a few humbling experiences.

The Age of Paradoxes

Do you remember when we were known by our given and family names? Paradoxically, our identification procedures have undergone a complete metamorphosis. Our previously long-standing identity labels are rapidly being replaced by sets of numerous and sundry numbers. For example, recently when I called a store regarding my account, I was asked for my account number, not my name. Later on, when I entered a hardware store to buy a cordless device, the clerk asked me for my telephone number; again, not for my name. When I tried to buy government bonds for my grandchildren, I had to give their social security numbers before the bank teller asked for the children's names. Often, when buying something over the telephone, the most important item requested by the seller is our Visa number. At a baby's birth, the primary item required seems to be its social security number, not his or her given name. This list of numbers goes on and on. What has happened to our names?

In a completely different vein, have you noticed how many of our various behavior patterns vary from person to person, age to age, and how often they seem to be at opposite poles? At a time when most of us oldsters are trying to hang onto what little hair we have left, some of the younger men are going in a completely different direction and shaving their heads. Also, when driving our cars, have you been aware of how slowly and carefully we, who have lived the majority of our lives, drive? On the other hand, many of the younger set, who have most of their lives ahead of them, drive like there is no tomorrow. It's a toss up as to which is more of a problem: to be caught behind an oldster who travels ten miles below the posted speed limit or to have a "hot rod" speedster riding your rear bumper even as you are driving a bit over the allowed rate.

Paradoxically, clothing styles often openly reveal the ultimate differences in tastes. In any given situation, women's skirts may vary from ankle length to the mid-thigh mini type. In addition, the present craze for Levi's brings out some odd combinations. A woman may dress in a very feminine fashion from the waist up, but from the belt line down, with her faded and wrinkled denim slacks, look like she just arrived on her horse from the far prairie.

In the health field many paradoxes also surface. In spite of the patient's wishes, the medics won't let them die and even go to extremes to keep them going, even if only at a 10 percent rate. In other situations lives are snuffed out willy-nilly via the abortion route.

In this day of high-speed computers and high tech, we as individuals have relatively little control of our destinies. One of the old-time doctors used to say, "Let them die with dignity." But now with pace makers, defibrillators, organ transplants, chemotherapy, and other technical advances, to a large extent this no longer applies. Many situations come to mind in this regard. One woman, 103 years of age, wanted to die. She was blind and had to be fed by attendants or her relatives. However no one would heed her wishes. When she developed pneumonia, instead of allowing her to join her ancestors, she was given the latest antibiotics and supportive treatment. With some modifications this type of story can be repeated over and over.

At the present time our government is concerned with the rising costs of the Medicare program and rightly so. The inordinate percentage of our medical expenses directed at the older age group is staggering. Many of the so-called senior citizens spend much of their time visiting doctors, podiatrists, chiropractors, physical therapists, oculists, and other medical personnel. In a way, these visits become a big segment of their social life. While some of the treatments are bonafide, many are not. If the patient had to pay for at least a part of each visit, the number would probably be markedly reduced.

A glaring paradox to this attention to the elderly is the fact that the Supreme Court of the United States legalized the practice of abortion. Each year many hundreds of thousands of unborn infants are destroyed at the desire or whim of the mother. While there may occasionally be a really valid reason for this procedure, the vast majority are done as a matter of convenience. I found in my medical practice, prior to the time of legalized abortions, that at least a third of the pregnancies were not planned and, when first diagnosed, were even resented. However at the time of the birth of the child or shortly thereafter, in the large majority of cases, the parents would say, "Our little child is a joy and a blessing. We don't know what we would do without him or her."

In our school system, where information is supposed to be dispensed without prejudice, other paradoxes exist. In contrast to the banning of prayer in the school room, some school districts freely give out information regarding abortions without parental consent. Also, contraceptive devices can be issued, again without parental consent. The paradox—aspirin cannot be given to a pupil without first getting the permission of the parent. Seems a bit out of kilter, wouldn't you agree?

It used to be a simple handshake was all that was necessary to seal an agreement. At the present time, paradoxically in many situations, even a signed and witnessed contract is often broken without penalty.

And then there is the paradox of the federal bilingual school program. This started as a one hundred million dollar well-intentioned plan designed to help foreign children make the transition in their studies from their native language until they could master English. This program has now burgeoned into a five and a half billion, *repeat billion*, dollar compulsory bureaucracy which often *requires* foreign-speaking students to participate, even though they speak and read English well. Not only is it wasteful, but also it is divisive in that it encourages the process of separation of the various ethnic groups from the mainstream of American culture. Instead of the United States being the "melting pot" of the world, it is in danger of becoming a collection of separate groups based on racial backgrounds.

And now comes the biggest paradox of all. In spite of the somewhat negative connotations of some of the above examples, we all have much about which to be happy and thankful. There are many positives. We live in the greatest country in the world. We have freedom of worship, freedom of movement and occupation, freedom to vote, an adequate supply of food, and many other blessings untold.

On second thought, perhaps some of the apparent paradoxes in our society are not such, but are simply examples of a misplaced emphasis on our various activities and routines. For example, one day a woman frantically called her doctor and cried, "I have an emergency. Can I see you?"

"Of course, come right in."

"Oh, I can't come in right now."

"Why not?"

"Because I have an appointment with my hair dresser."

Trying Triads

There are those individuals who swear all problems occur in groups of three. To back up their claim, they then quote Aunt Abigail's asthma, Uncle Arthur's arthritis, and Cousin Charles's chronic colds.

While there may be some truth in their contentions, there is considerable evidence that trying situations can occur singly, in duplicate, in triplicate, or even more often. One example of this variation was noted during World War II in New Mexico. Here, we learned early that on payday, problems seemed to increase in number. If payday happened to be on a Saturday, the problems almost doubled in number, and if payday, Saturday, and the local annual fiesta all coincided, the problems seemed to increase in geometrical progression.

It so happened it was my misfortune to be OD (Officer of the Day) when this triad did occur. The fiesta was an annual affair which was eagerly looked forward to by all the local residents. It was a time of much levity, Spanish dancers, singers, Mexican food, balloons, and much drinking, especially of tequila. Before my first fiesta I had heard rumors of the effects of this liquor; that it tended to cause considerable belligerency in the early stages, followed by feelings of extreme remorse later on. This latter stage was often accompanied by copious crying and self-recriminations. Because of my lack of any precious experience with this drink I anticipated, with some trepidation, a rather hectic evening and night of medical duty. As far as the hectic aspect of the forthcoming night was concerned, I was not to be disappointed.

At the dispensary, shortly after the start of the fiesta, we began to receive a steady stream of patients. Many had multiple injuries and lacerations, mostly the result of disagreements and scuffles. Some of them were brought in by the MPs for repairs en route to the guard house. Others came in on their own power. As some were still in the bellicose phase of the tequila, they were so belligerent we had to send them on to the stockade once they were repaired.

Late in the evening, one soldier arrived with a rather nasty laceration of his upper lip the result of a fist fight. As he was a "regular" sick call patient, we were well acquainted with him. When normal, he was a pleasant, outgoing person, usually very talkative. Under the influence of the tequila he was especially verbose. As I started to repair his wound he kept up a steady stream of conversation, telling us how he had sustained his wound. With the constant movement of his mouth it was difficult to suture this mobile part of his anatomy. In spite of my efforts to get him to keep quiet long enough for me to bring the wound edges together, he rambled on and on. Finally I said, "If you don't stop talking I'm going to call the MPs and send you to the guard house." This threat quieted him long enough for me to repair his wound and then send him on his way. As he left, he was still talking.

About an hour later, the guard house sergeant called to tell us they were full to overflowing and not to send anybody else their way. A few minutes after this call, our talkative patient returned. By now, he had entered the remorseful phase of his tequila and was crying profusely. Through his tears, he pleaded, "I've been acting terribly. Please send me to the guard house where I belong."

"You haven't been terrible. Why don't you just head for your barracks, crawl into bed, and have a good rest?"

"Oh no, Captain, I need to be punished. Please send me to the guard house."

In spite of all my reassurance, his remorse persisted. Not wanting to reveal the fact the guard house was full and that they didn't want any more bodies, plus the fact this soldier didn't need the guard house stigma on his army record, I called one of our ambulance drivers and quietly told him, "Take this fellow down to the far end of the field near the warehouses and let him off to find his way back. The cold night air may help to sober him a bit."

The remainder of the night was so busy I forgot about our weeping friend, but the following morning, bright and early, he appeared at sick call. He was still talkative, but acted a little puzzled. He had a complete amnesia for the previous evening's events and asked, "How did I get these stitches in my lip? The last thing I remember was leaving the post for the fiesta. From then on all is a blank until I found myself wandering around the warehouses. I do know one thing though. I'm never going to go to another fiesta."

I was not stationed at this same post at the time of the next fiesta so I didn't have another trying triad with which to contend. However I feel sure the chaos of pay day, Saturday, and the fiesta would not have been so bad if it hadn't been for the fourth element present, namely the tequila.

Our Blind Side

Mentally and visually we all are two sided—the seeing side and the blind side. Unfortunately, the latter often predominates. Many of us have a tendency to turn away from anything unpleasant or anything which threatens us, be it an emergency, an accident, or any other event which might threaten to disturb our daily routine. Often it takes considerable effort on our part to overcome this somewhat selfish blindsidedness.

This fact was graphically illustrated to me one day as I drove along a busy city street to my next appointment. I noticed two small children approximately four and six years of age standing on the opposite curbside. They appeared to be anxious to cross to the other side but were hesitant to do so. After passing them, I watched them in my rearview mirror and was horrified to see them suddenly make a mad dash into the oncoming traffic. The other drivers tried to avoid them but one car was unable to do so and hit both of the children, throwing the little boy aside like a discarded rag doll. The girl was not as fortunate and was struck full force, throwing her to the pavement.

This gruesome scenario was so shocking to witness my first impulse, in my hurry, was to turn my blind side, knowing someone else would stop and come to their rescue. Fortunately my seeing side came to the fore, and I pulled over to the curb, jumped out, and then ran back to the injured twosome. The little boy was crying lustily, but apparently was not hurt seriously. On the other hand, the girl was obviously in exactly the opposite condition. She lay inert on the pavement, unconscious and very seriously injured. A large bluish welt was already forming over her right temple. On palpation her skull felt somewhat like an old-fashioned childhood beanbag. In addition, she had several bleeding skin abrasions as well as numerous contusions. While her pulse was strong and her breathing was not impaired, she definitely needed immediate hospitalization and intensive care.

At this same moment, from the nearby gas station a man ran out with a blanket with which we covered the little girl. Although she was lying in the middle of the busy street, we did not attempt to move her even to the curbside.

As there was no "Medic One" in existence at the time, I asked the man to call for an ambulance and to notify the nearest hospital emergency room. By now the police had arrived. In a short time, we could hear the wail of the siren as the ambulance sped to the scene. About all I could do was to try to minimize her shock and to keep her airway open.

Once the ambulance arrived, we gently lifted her onto a stretcher and sent her on her way, only after making sure the emergency room doctor would be available to care for her. By now the children's mother had appeared and had taken over the care of the little boy, who was still crying loudly.

Having done all I could do, I then tried to quietly and anonymously be on my way. As I approached my car, a policeman stopped me and asked if I was a medical doctor. He then took all the pertinent statistics he required. Finally I was able to proceed to my somewhat belated appointments. However I was thankful my seeing side had prevailed, and I prayed the little girl would recover. Several weeks later the mother wrote me a very nice note thanking me and confirming the fact of her recovery. While the child had had multiple fractures of her skull and a severe brain concussion, she did return to a completely normal condition.

At a later time, after a hard day at the office and hospitals, I was at a midweek church dinner and Bible study. Following a good meal, it was a nice feeling to be able to sit back and relax. However this feeling was short lived, for just as I settled down there was a loud crashing sound at the front of the hall. Knowing that the commotion signaled trouble, my first impulse was to turn my blind side and, if possible, flee. Of course I knew this was only wishful thinking on my part.

Jumping up, I ran to the site of the disturbance only to find an elderly woman lying unconscious on the floor. A hasty exam revealed a complete lack of pulse as well as of respirations. Fortunately a registered nurse was present. The two of us immediately started CPR. In short order, the woman's two vital functions returned, only to stop once more. Again, with additional cardiac massage and mouth-to-mouth breathing we were able to restart her heart and respirations. All during our labors the woman's husband, who was just behind us, kept repeating, "Keep her alive, Doc. Keep her alive."

In the meantime, someone had called 911. Shortly thereafter the paramedics arrived and with their modern equipment took over, thereby relieving two tired resuscitators. After they transported the patient to the nearest hospital it was discovered one of the patient's pacemaker wires had become disconnected. Apparently in giving her cardiac massage, we had accidentally reestablished a connection of sorts and restarted the pacemaker's function. The following day, a new pacemaker was inserted allowing the patient to have ten more years of active life.

Not all seeing side efforts are life saving. Some can even have a humorous twist. Many years ago while I was still in my premedical training, Margaret and

I were on a tour of the Seattle City Light dams and power plants. As our group walked along a wooded trail, one of the women slipped and fell, turning her ankle. I, having had courses in first aid as well as for athletic injuries, rushed forward to offer my assistance. On arriving at the woman's side I found a man bending over her. When I announced my qualifications, the man immediately stepped aside and let me take over. I then examined the ankle and bound it snugly with a scarf the woman had been wearing. Once back at the bus, I cautioned her to be sure to see her doctor as soon as she returned home.

Later, as we left the bus, the man who had originally been standing over the patient stopped me and said, "You did a good job with the lady's ankle." This, of course, made me feel good. He then continued, "I was interested to see what you were going to do. You see, I'm an orthopedic specialist." I then felt like two cents. I should have originally surveyed the situation more thoroughly.

In some instances doing a good turn can backfire. One of the doctors was vacationing at the ocean shore when a swimmer became distressed and called for help. The doctor, without hesitation, was able to rescue the man, resuscitate him, and treat him for shock. Once the ambulance arrived to take the victim to the neighboring hospital for further examination, the doctor returned to his family and continued his vacation. A few weeks later, he (the doctor) was notified that the family of the rescued one were suing him for abandonment because he hadn't ridden in the ambulance with the patient.

In another instance, a medical student came upon a couple where the man was beating the woman in a brutal manner. The student didn't know any of the circumstances of the altercation, but did realize the need for his intervention into the fray. Accordingly, he reached in, grabbed the man by his arms, and pulled him away from the woman. Once this was done he had little trouble with the male and was beginning to feel like he had performed his good deed for the day, when he suddenly felt multiple blows raining upon his head and back as the woman, the victim of the original assault, began beating him with her umbrella. As the student later said, "It sure doesn't pay to get mixed up in domestic disputes."

In contrast to the foregoing, one evening as two doctors were dining with their wives in a hotel dining room, the man at the next table suddenly fell from his chair. His facial expression was one of panic, but no sound came from his lips. Immediately the doctors recognized the symptoms of a bolus of food caught in the larynx. Both of the doctors sprang into action and with a sharp knife from the kitchen were able to open the man's windpipe, dislodge the piece of meat, and restore his breathing. They then accompanied him to the hospital. When they returned to their wives in the dining room the hotel served them a very fancy meal all "on the house."

While the examples mentioned above have largely been about medical problems, there are many other aspects of life which may require the use of our "seeing side." Included here are loneliness, fatigue, depression, financial problems, and some mental conditions, just to name a few. Often a word of encouragement, a smile, a written note, a simple "I'm sorry," or a helping hand may make a great deal of difference to the one in need.

In order to overcome our all too human tendency to turn our blind side to difficult or distasteful situations, we may have to expend considerable effort, but once done it is doubly beneficial, not only to the recipient but also to the donor. Remember the story of the Good Samaritan in the Holy Bible. His curbside diagnosis and treatments were a great help to the injured man. In addition, while not sought by the Samaritan, his actions assured the giver of the good deed a permanent place in the history of mankind.

Our Fantasies

In one degree or another, we all have fantasies. These may change as we pass through the various phases of our lives, but they are an integral part of our development. While some fantasies may be transient, others are permanent and influence our final destiny. In other words, they are essential in the charting of our life's journey.

For example little girls dream of dolls and lollipops. As they grow dresses, ballet dancing, and becoming an actress fill their thoughts. Later on modeling, falling in love, and boyfriends occupy their thoughts. At the present time, women's sports have become popular. No longer is this a man's exclusive domain. Volleyball, swimming, track, basketball, soccer, and baseball are very important for some girls. Some may want to become musicians, scientists, doctors, lawyers, and business executives. A few may even aspire to become Christian missionaries to foreign fields. Of course, during all of these various phases, the desire to become a mother is usually close to the surface. As time passes some bring to fruition at least a part of these dreams. Even with old age, some fantasies may remain and become reality.

Little boys go through similar phases. Fire wagons, cars, airplanes, toy soldiers, baseballs, footballs, and anything else that is round and bounces occupy their dreams. Later on becoming a policeman, fireman, locomotive engineer, or airplane pilot plays a prominent part in their thoughts. Later for some, becoming a scientist, lawyer, doctor, minister, or singer may come into the picture. Of course, during much of this time the opposite sex occupies a prominent part of their thoughts.

Eventually there does come a time when both boys and girls have to dismiss some of their previous fantasies, either because these dreams are beyond their reach or because they are no longer desired. With their dream fields somewhat narrowed, it then becomes necessary for the individuals to focus on a limited number of choices and concentrate their efforts into one or two of these channels in order to excel. A champion swimmer must spend many hours in the water; a brain surgeon must dedicate himself for many years to acquire the skills required. In other words, no fantasy becomes a reality without a great deal of effort expended.

While many of us are satisfied with becoming proficient in one category, others are capable of mastering more than one specialty. For example, one all-American football player later on became a United States Supreme Court Justice. Another all-American became a dedicated Christian minister. Several medical doctors were also accomplished musicians. In addition there were several United States Army generals who later on were elected to the presidency of our country. There was a licensed dentist, who because of ill health, became a railroad pullman porter. There are many other examples which could be mentioned. While many of these individuals were very gifted, much of their success was due to hard work and dedication. They were willing to expend the effort and had learned to concentrate their energies in a specific direction. Also they were able to use their God-given talents in a more efficient manner than the average person.

Sometimes it is difficult to know how to interpret our fantasies and which of these to take seriously. For example when I was in the second grade, the teacher told my parents I should be given singing lessons. There were two different interpretations that could be used for this advice—did I have a potential or did I really need help? I'm inclined to think the latter was her intent. The exact answer will never be known for sure. As for singing, aside from an occasional wish to be able to sing like Nelson Eddy, Mario Lanza, or even Bing Crosby, this art was never one of my great fantasies. At the present time, any questionable ability I may once have possessed has completely left me. In fact at one time I did sing in our church choir for part of one number because I had been called to attend one of the choir members who become ill during the service. Later a man on the building committee suggested the church organ be checked for a defective reed. When I heard of this, all my thoughts of being a singer completely evaporated.

And so, while daydreams and fantasies may be an essential part of each of us in our development, there does come a time when we have to face reality and acknowledge that we all do have some limitations. In the final analysis, to dream may be a lot of fun and may even lead to real changes in our lives—just don't take all of them too seriously.

Dr. Jonas Salk

A short time ago, I read that Dr. Jonas Salk had died at the age of eighty-nine years. His passing brought to my mind what he had accomplished and how much he had done to overcome one of the most dreaded diseases of our times. As a dedicated scientist he had been responsible for the development of the acute anterior poliomyelitis vaccine. This vaccine had markedly decreased and nearly eliminated this disease.

Poliomyelitis, commonly known as infantile paralysis, was one to the most mysterious and feared diseases in the world at the time. While not exclusively a childhood ailment, the majority of its victims were young people. Its muscle wasting residues and resulting weakness or paralysis were devastating and in most cases permanent. In the early years of the twentieth century, its cause and its mode of spread were unknown. Its capricious appearances tended to cast a dark cloud of fear worldwide, more so in homes where there were small children.

During the summer months when the disease was most rampant, many calls to the doctors would be made practically every evening by parents worried because Johnny or Susie complained of leg aching. While in most cases the aches were due to some unusual physical activity by the child earlier in the day, such was never a sure thing. In many instances it became necessary to check the child to be sure. In some cases a spinal tap was indicated to either confirm or to rule out the disease.

The differences in the onset of polio often presented mysteries which were difficult to solve. One such occurred when one child in the family developed the disease while his siblings, who slept in the same bed, did not. In some cases the acute disease would occur in conjunction with some other problem such as an automobile accident. Because of the protean nature of the onset and course, much time and energy, to say nothing of the apprehension involved, was spent by all concerned. For many the uncertainty of an impending attack was the cause of much anxiety. The parents of small children were, figuratively speaking, living with a sword of Damocles hanging over their heads.

It was during this period of uncertainty that Dr. Salk and other researchers were working frantically to determine the cause and, if possible, the prevention of this dread disease. As is true in most discoveries, the final solution of the problem is the result of the work of many different individuals. In the case of polio, once it was possible to grow the virus *in vitro* a whole new field of research was opened. After much work Dr. Salk developed a vaccine for injection which was made with dead viruses. The importance of this discovery of a non-viable vaccine was that there was no possibility it could transmit the disease.

With the approval of the FDA and the release of the vaccine for the general public, several questions arose. Was it safe? Could a recipient of the vaccine then transmit the disease to another? If a person received the vaccine and then developed polio the next day, did the shot cause the onset? As the vaccine at first was in short supply, who should be given preference? These and many other questions surfaced. I remember sitting in a meeting of our county medical society board and pondering all the above as well as other unknowns. After several hours of discussion, we unanimously voted to endorse and to promote this new product. We felt children should be given preference in its use until the vaccine supply became adequate for all.

As with anything new, at first there was considerable skepticism by the public. Some of our anticipated situations did arise. In more than one case a close friend of a vaccine recipient did develop polio a day or two later. Also, occasionally a vaccinated person developed polio a day or two after receiving the vaccine. Naturally these incidents caused some doubts to surface in the community. However gradually the public realized the importance of this new preventative procedure and accepted it with enthusiasm—except for a few hard-core skeptics.

With an adequate supply of vaccine, we began to give it to the older generations. Of course many adults felt it wasn't necessary for them. After all, it was called "infantile paralysis," wasn't it? In one instance one of the doctors was a bit slow in giving it to his wife. A short time later, before he got around to giving her a shot, she developed the "bulbar" form of the disease and expired. He never forgave himself for his tardiness.

Later on another M.D., Dr. Sabin, developed an oral attenuated vaccine. The big advantage of this was it could be given in areas like some Third World countries more easily than an injectable. While the two vaccines were different, their aim was the same—the eradication of this illness. Both of the doctors received considerable well-deserved acclaim. Regardless of who received the most credit, our country and much of the rest of the world is indebted to both of these great men for their contributions.

Today many of the crippling aspects of this disease have been eradicated. To a large extent, long gone are the braces, the crutches, and the wheel chairs; long gone are the iron lungs with their human occupants; long gone are the many months of physiotherapy, rehabilitation, and confinement. Also, and just as important, long gone are the anxieties and doubts about when and where this disease will strike. Once again, the childhood leg aches and crampings can be handled in an appropriate manner. For these blessings, we all should be eternally grateful to Dr. Salk and to other men of his caliber.

And so because of the dedications of these men, as well as many other scientists, we all can breathe easier and be more at peace. As far as polio is concerned, the Sword of Damocles has been removed from over our heads.

Measles!

What do measles and Dr. Ivan Petrovich Pavlov have to do with building modern jet airplanes? In order to find the answer to this question it will be necessary to backtrack in history to the early twentieth century. At that time, Dr. Pavlov, a Russian physiologist, won the Nobel prize in medicine for his experiments in conditioned reflexes.

In the experiments the doctor was able to demonstrate this reflex in dogs by performing, on several separate occasions, the ringing of a bell and then feeding the dogs a piece of tasty beef steak. During these tests he noted the dogs would begin to salivate prior to getting the meat. Once a pattern of this reaction was well established, he found all he had to do was ring the bell, without the steak, in order to cause the dogs to salivate. This reaction he called a conditioned reflex.

While these experiments may seem of little importance to the average person who has only a passing interest in medical matters, and even less so in whether a dog drools or does not drool on hearing the ringing of a bell, they do have far-reaching effects and play an active role in our everyday lives. For example, many times each day conditioned reflexes govern our responses. We may see a large piece of three-layered chocolate cake with a scoop of vanilla ice cream lying along-side and immediately begin to salivate. We know from past experience how delicious such a dish can be.

Conversely, we may be repulsed when we witness someone injured, even in a minor accident, because we may have previously experienced a similar discomfort ourselves. Even hearing about something of this nature may cause us to cringe with pain. These and many other events each day are simply conditioned reflexes at work based on past training.

Even our social contacts and friendships are influenced by past experiences and conditioned reflexes. We say, "I like his or her looks," or "He looks a bit creepy to me."

In addition our perception of everyday objects is based on these same reflexes. When we look at a large metal dumbbell we think, "That sure looks heavy." If, without our being aware, a similar-looking object happens to be made of sponge rubber, we will still perceive it as being heavy. Artificial, plastic fruits and flowers, if made skillfully, will often fool even an experienced gardener. It has been said the makers of artificial flowers try to make them look like the real thing and that, in contrast, the average gardener wants his product to look as good as the artificial ones. Again the perceptions of each are based on conditioned reflexes and Dr. Pavlov's canine friends.

Often our perceptions vary in what may seem to be similar situations. The flashing lights of a police car will invoke a feeling of relief when we are stalled by the roadside. An entirely different response is forthcoming if those same flashing lights appear behind us as we speed down the highway.

And now, after this brief review of the mechanism of these reflexes, let us see how they might have a connection with the building of jet airplanes. One day while on a conducted tour of a large aircraft plant we were amazed to see the assembly lines, each of which started as only a few pieces of metal, gradually grow and grow at each different station until finally at the end of the line they became a complete large jet aircraft. As each line progressed, new parts were added—first the fuselage, then the wings, the motors, the interior wiring, and in rapid progression the insulation, the instruments, cargo compartments, galleys, seats, lavatories, and all the other component parts necessary to make this large structure a workable flying machine.

On the factory floor the progress of each new plane was a thing of precision and the result of highly skilled engineering. The last step in the process was the exterior painting which varied from plane to plane depending on which airline the final product was destined to join. As we approached the end of the line, and stood by the side of the nearly completed plane, I noticed a large sign which figuratively shouted MEASLES. This sign seemed so out of place I asked our guide, "What about this 'measles' sign?"

His reply was, "We have found that if we post a 'Wet Paint' sign, invariably there is a tendency for someone to reach out and touch the plane. If we put up a 'No Admittance' sign usually more than one tries to peek in. However, we have discovered that the 'Measles' notice elicits an immediate tendency for everyone to back away."

And so, in the final analysis, no matter what each of us may think about Dr. Pavlov and his collection of dogs, if we ever do stop to do so, we will have to admit he did all of us a big favor when he illustrated the underlying principle of the conditioned reflex.

Miles Per Apple

When compared with present-day models, our first car wasn't much to look at, but in our eyes it was a thing of beauty with its angled brass radiator, its flat-black front fenders, and its large running boards. It was a wonder of wonders and at our tender ages, it filled us with awe. More importantly, it took us to many distant places previously inaccessible and unexplored.

For us, no regal carriage or ancient chariot had more to offer. While its actual age was unknown, it was probably built sometime in the mid-teens of the twentieth century. It had only one seat, just large enough for two people to sit comfortably. As there were four of us in our family, things became a bit crowded at times. If the weather permitted, we boys could ride in the truck-like space in the back. This was similar to a modern pick-up truck. When it rained we all crowded into the cab, often with one of us kids sitting on the floor boards. We didn't worry about its gas consumption or miles per gallon since gasoline was fairly reasonable at that time (twenty cents a gallon).

One of the best features of the car was its simplicity. There were no power windows or power door locks since there were no windows or locks of any kind. Celluloid side curtains could be put up if the weather worsened. Otherwise fresh air abounded. We didn't have to worry about the windshield wiper failing to work because it had to be hand operated. Of course windshield water sprayers were unknown and would not appear for many years in the future. There was no chance the foot throttle could get stuck because there was no foot throttle present. Instead the speed of the car was regulated by a small hand lever on the steering post. Of course there was no heater and no heat available except that which penetrated through the floor boards from the hot motor—both summer and winter.

In addition we never had to worry about a dead battery since there was no battery. The motor had to be started by hand cranking. There was a wire loop located near the crank. This served as a choke, but it had to be used sparingly because it was too easy to flood the carburetor if the loop was pulled too often.

The hand-cranking procedure was fraught with a few hazards such as an occasional sprained back and the not-rare crank "kick-back" which often resulted in a fractured arm. We learned early not to hold the crank with too firm a grip so we could let go fast if this occurred. Electrically speaking, the headlights were powered from the magneto. One disadvantage of this power source was the intensity of the headlights varied with the speed of the motor. The slower the speed, the dimmer the lights, and vice versa. Of course this variation could lead to complications if the traffic was very slow or if the competition of the lights from the oncoming traffic was too bright.

One such complication occurred one dark rainy Sunday night as we were driving home from church on old Highway 99. This road, at that time, was the main route from Seattle to Everett and had only one lane for each direction. From the wet pavement, the reflected lights from the southbound cars were nearly blinding. All four of us were squeezed into the cab of our car with Fred sitting on the floorboards. Suddenly, as we rounded a curve, there appeared before us the form of a man running in the middle of the road. Dad tried to swerve to miss him but was unable to completely do so. The left front fender and headlight struck him and tossed him like a rag doll onto the middle of the busy highway.

With the loss of the left light, all of the remaining lights were extinguished, much like some strings of Christmas tree lights; one off, all off. As we were not traveling very fast, Dad was able to pull off the road and stop in a hurry. Fred, from his seat on the floor of the car, jumped to the ground. With quick thinking he ran back to the prostrate form and pulled him from the path of the oncoming traffic. Once on the grassy side of the road, we were able to determine the unconscious man was still alive. There was a strong odor of second-hand alcohol on his breath. In the utter darkness, except for the flickering flashes from the lights of the passing cars, the scene was frightening for all of us, especially for me, an eight-year-old.

Realizing the man was still alive, Dad started to run to the nearest gas station for help and to get a new globe for the defunct headlight. The rest of us stayed with the victim, who within a short time began to revive. In spite of our efforts to keep him quiet, he insisted on arising and kept saying he was all right. In his drunken state, his words were slurred as he kept saying, "Yur husbun ish a purfic jetlmum." This statement he kept repeating over and over. How he knew anything about Dad is somewhat of a mystery since Dad was long gone before the victim regained consciousness. Finally, after his multiple declarations about Dad's many fine qualities, he insisted he was all right and needed to be on his way. With this, he disappeared into the murky, moist darkness.

Shortly thereafter Dad returned with the new headlight. When this was installed, the lights of the car once again came on and we were able to resume our journey home. Just before we arrived at our turn off-road who should we see but our drunken runner in full stride, again hurrying down the center of the main highway. Dad's attempts to try to persuade him to get medical attention or at least for him to run on the side of the road were unsuccessful. At this moment he seemed none the worse for his previous experience, but he was probably going to be plenty sore the next day, providing he was lucky enough to survive the night and live to see the coming sunrise. The following morning, since we didn't see any account of his untimely demise, we had to assume he had been able to make it to his sought-for destination.

Dad usually had the disposition of a saint, but there was an occasional exception to his benign nature. One morning when he left for work, we didn't expect to see him until supper time. However an hour later, as we started for school and approached the garage, we could smell the distinct odor of gasoline. As we rounded the garage corner, we found Dad, who usually was properly and neatly dressed, in a completely disheveled state. His face was streaked with grease as well as covered with perspiration. His hands were besmirched, and his suit clothes rumpled. His mood matched his appearance. It seems the old bus was cantankerous and just wouldn't start. Dad had been hand cranking and choking the motor for over an hour. The flooded carburetor accounted for the gasoline odor. Because we had to hurry on to school, we couldn't stop to help, and while we had to leave him to his labors, we felt that was as he would wish in this somewhat embarrassing and stressful situation.

That evening, when we asked Dad about the car and how long he had to spend getting it started, he looked somewhat flustered. Finally he said, "It wasn't the car's fault. It was mine. I had forgotten to turn on the ignition key." Dad was big enough to admit his error and take the blame.

One Fourth of July as Dad and I were getting gas for our car, we saw a stalled car containing three elderly women. Their car was an electric-powered model, not a rarity at that time, and their only source of power, the battery, was dead. Because it was a holiday they were completely stranded. Dad, ever the gentleman, volunteered to give them a tow. He meant to get their car to a garage, and then take the three ladies to the interurban station. They, however, had other ideas. They wanted to be towed to their home on Capital Hill in Seattle, some twenty miles away.

Not wanting to back out of his offer to help them, Dad hooked the cars together with a stout tow rope and off we went. I was told to ride on the truck bed in back. From this position I was to keep track of the tow rope. I'm not sure just what I was supposed to do in case of any problem, but this duty made me feel important. The lady driving the electric car wasn't too astute in the ways of steering or braking, and on two occasions ran into the back of our old bus. It was quite a thrill from my vantage point to see her come crashing into us. Fortunately she didn't cause much damage. Finally, after half a day we were able to make the grade up all the steep roads to their home on one of the highest hills in Seattle. This, of course, required much chugging and straining on the part of our old car. After we had deposited the three, and as we prepared to leave, the lady owner opened her purse and offered Dad fifty cents as payment for his time, to say nothing of the gasoline used or the nicks in the back of our car. I, being eight years old, was willing to take the fifty cents, which for me was equal to over three weeks allowance, but Dad refused. He held his tongue, but I could tell he was nonplussed and let down since he had not expected any payment except perhaps a "thank you."

But let us return to some of the other favorable characteristics of our first car. It should be mentioned it had one important and distinct advantage over the modern automobiles. As it was a Model-T Ford, in addition to the brake and clutch pedals, it also had a third, or reverse, pedal. This not only served its original purpose of backing the car but also could be used as an auxiliary brake in case of failure of the brakes themselves. In those days it was not an uncommon sight to see a Model-T come to a screeching halt with its rear wheels spinning in a rapid reverse manner.

Years later when I worked in a butcher shop, one of my duties was to act as a delivery boy using the owner's old Ford Model-T touring car. As the brakes of this vehicle were never in good repair, on many occasions I had to revert back to my boyhood days and use this same reverse pedal as a brake, especially when descending a steep hill.

While our car did have a speedometer and an odometer, neither of these were really necessary. First, the old bus couldn't exceed the speed limit even on a downhill grade. I recall one time when we felt like we were flying when the speedometer registered fifty as we sped down a hill. Also as far as the odometer was concerned, we were never sure about its accuracy because this was definitely open to question not only regarding its total mileage listed but also about its mile-to-mile figures in ordinary travel. However its accuracy was not of any concern to us since we had a more dependable method of determining our distances traveled. This was made possible by my brother Fred's reputation as a consumer of anything edible, especially when riding in the car. After our first few trips, we were able to determine that with the car's top speed on a level highway, Fred could consume an average-sized apple every nine miles. As a result of these calculations, we reckoned the length of our journeys in apples, not miles. For example, we would say, "Oh, it isn't very far. It's only five apples from home."

I guess the best way to express how we as a family felt about that first old car was that it had a kind of a "peel" for all of us, and especially for Fred and his apples.

"You Get What You Pay For?"

We often hear the expression, "You get what you pay for," but is this true? Do we really get what we pay for? A commonly held feeling is, "If the price is high, it must be good."

There was a time in the not-too-distant past when a pair of dress shoes cost more than a pair of athletic sneakers. No longer. Today it is not uncommon to see a pair of tennis shoes with a price tag exceeding the century mark. For some, paying this figure seems to assure them of a good product, and paying less means a shoddy piece of merchandise. However do those who pay the higher price really get their money's worth? Perhaps the label is worth it to some. In reality, the only sure way of getting what you pay for is to buy common stock in the sporting equipment manufacturing company.

In another field, a few strips of chrome on some large kitchen appliances will often add many hundreds of dollars to their cost. These strips in no way change the efficiency nor the life expectancy of these same pieces. While they may be pleasing to the eye for some individuals, does the buyer actually get what he paid for?

Adding a small fifteen-cent insignia, such as a polo player, a dolphin, an alligator, a Regal crest, or some other completely unrelated label often increases the price of an article of clothing several dollars. Is the small label really worth the extra cost?

One man, noted for his frugality, decided to splurge and buy a topcoat at one of the prestigious men's shops. Prior to his purchase, he had debated with himself about the price he would have to pay, but felt in the long run he would be well rewarded for the price paid. A few days later, at work, he found a similar topcoat hanging next to his. As far as he could tell, the two were alike in every detail. When he asked the other owner if he had been to the same men's store, he learned the other man had purchased his at a well-known department store for half the price he had paid. This was quite a blow to the frugal man. However it did turn out the coats had one difference—the labels over the inside pockets.

You may be inclined to feel that price variations are due to the differences in the quality of the products. Perhaps in some cases this is true, but not always. A doctor who had earned his way through school by selling shoes in a large department store told the following story. It seems the store had three different shoe shops: the Bargain Basement, the Regular sales section on the second floor, and the exclusive Shoe Salon on the seventh floor. While there were some variations in the shoes in each of the three shops, there were also a number of pairs which were exactly the same in all three. The main difference was the prices charged and the wrappings the customer received. In the basement shop, a brown paper bag sufficed. On the second floor, the customer received the original shoe box, and in the salon a rather ornately wrapped package was presented. Of course the price escalated in direct ratio to the height of the floor where the shoes were purchased.

A dentist with a wealthy clientele said, "I have to charge exorbitant prices, otherwise my patients would go elsewhere." He admitted his work was no better than the average dentist. Maybe his patients thought their bite was better than average.

In contrast, a surgeon said he was fired from a case because he didn't charge enough. He also said he knew of other possible patients who didn't come to him for the same reason. This man was no ordinary doctor. In addition to being a skilled surgeon, he was a pillar in the medical profession. He had been president of practically every medical group in his town, county, and state. However he did have one problem. He often forgot to charge for his surgeries, either on purpose or because of his failure to remember. On more than one occasion, the Mayo Clinic told patients from his city to return home because this doctor could perform the necessary surgery as well as they could. In spite of this, some of his local townsfolk felt he must not be very skillful because in their opinion he didn't charge enough. Often, it's difficult to fathom the human mind.

Another prominent surgeon often not only didn't charge his patients, but also on many occasions paid their hospital bills in order to help them. He, like the previously mentioned doctor, was very skillful as well as being completely dedicated to his profession and to his practice. His paying patients were charged a standard fee. As far as could be determined they were very satisfied and felt they obtained what they paid for. Also, his charity patients seemed to be happy. Price was not a factor for either group.

When we attend a symphony concert, the charge for admission is determined largely by the seat location. The row where the price charged changes has to be made by the theater authorities. While in most concert halls the acoustics are relatively equal between the last row of the premium seats and those one row behind in the less expensive section, there might be a question in the minds of some of the patrons about who really received what they paid for.

Today the cost of a obtaining a college degree is awesome, but some students and their parents seem to feel the greater the cost the better the results.

Without belittling the merits of the more expensive universities, the least expensive schools have much more to offer than even the most brilliant mind can absorb. The success of the individual is largely dependent on the desire and ability of the student. One of the best educated individuals I ever knew was a man who had had to quit school after the fifth grade. However his quest for knowledge persisted for the rest of his life as he became self-taught. For most of us, what is paid in tuition is secondary to the end result.

Sometimes what is paid can be important. At baseball or football games, there is usually no question about how the rooters in the box seats and those in the bleachers or the end zones feel. Probably those in the less expensive areas would prefer the more desirable locations. On the other hand, those in the boxes are, for the most part, quite content with what they have received for what they paid.

In air travel, most of us ride in the tourist section. A few are privileged to get into the first class cabin. These latter are probably riding at their company's or our government's expense. There may be a few exceptions and, if so, they probably are willing to pay for all the extras.

In the final analysis, what we each pay for whatever we buy is our own business and not the province of anyone else. However, don't feel that just because it costs more it must be a lot better

What's Par?

In this day of increased automobile traffic and crowded highways, the strain of driving has reached a point where it is not only nerve-wracking, but also borders on the intolerable. This state of affairs becomes especially true at the end of a trying workday as each of us wends wearily homeward. It is at these times we often are confronted by other motorists who also are in the same fatigued mental state and who have adopted driving habits and highway mannerisms that are, to put it mildly, very irritating. In these situations, it is often easy to become upset and distraught.

Several years ago, in order to keep from getting too uptight each evening, I invented a new game which I called Car Golf. The rules of the game are quite simple. The first step required is for each driver to determine the number of bone-headed maneuvers he, or she, can expect to encounter on an average evening commute between the workplace and home. The number can easily be determined within a few days and once determined can serve as "par" for the course. Let us assume the average number on any given trip is six.

The game is then played in the following manner. The first basic rule is as you drive along, you are not to become annoyed by other motorists during their first six infractions. If the figure exceeds six, the next one or two boo-boos become no more than slight annoyances. As in golf, they can be listed as bogeys or double bogeys, which isn't too bad for the average duffer.

Actually, if the number reaches eight or more (triple or quadruple bogeys) the situation becomes laughable and you will find yourself absorbed in guessing what the final figure might become. On one trip, my total was thirteen. Instead of being frustrated and angry, I found myself thinking, "It must be just one of those days."

I feel confident you will find Car Golf is a real break for your nervous system as well as a way of preserving your usually sunny disposition for your family as you sit down to dinner. However in all fairness, and to keep the score accurate, you will have to count the "bone-headed" maneuvers you yourself have made on the same trip.

Second Opinions

Ornately inscribed on his tombstone were the words:
I DIDN'T GET A SECOND OPINION!

Much has been written and still more advised regarding the value of seeking a second opinion, especially in matters of major importance. While most of this advice is meant to be beneficial, there are occasionally disadvantages that can be incurred when so doing. In such situations, it is possible that too many differing opinions can lead to a state of confusion, indecision, and even legal litigation.

In his early youth, one boy was fascinated, even somewhat mystified, while watching land surveying crews plying their trade. With all their paraphernalia—the tripods, surveying scopes, chains, and other equipment—they seemed to be workers of magic. Certainly their results were never to be questioned nor disputed. These feelings were further substantiated when, in school, he learned the father of our country and the first president, George Washington, started his early career as a member of this profession. Because of this early hero worship, it was somewhat of a blow later on when he learned from this same group that getting a second opinion was not always a wise thing to do.

Of course, there are some areas of major importance where a second opinion is warranted. This is especially true in the medical field in any doubtful case in the surgical field or in major illnesses. To illustrate, in one rather puzzling case of fever of unknown etiology, the wife of the patient asked the original doctor for a consultation. When the consulting doctor also seemed to be indefinite in his opinion she, being a good Norwegian, insisted that one particular prominent Norwegian doctor be called in. He had a good reputation and was highly regarded for his astuteness. It was said at that time no good Norwegian could pass on to his or her eternal rest without having been touched or at least been seen by this eminent doctor. The original doctor was happy to comply with the spouse's wishes.

As a result, all three doctors met in the patient's room in order to jointly examine him. They all agreed the problem was a fever of unknown origin, but could not pin point the exact diagnosis. Afterwards as they left the room, the first two doctors told the wife they were still not sure what the exact diagnosis was. When the Norwegian doctor emerged from the room, the patient's wife, with pleading, asked, "What is wrong with my husband? Please tell me."

Without a moment's hesitation and with a voice of authority, he replied, "He is suffering from inflammation."

"Oh, I just knew that you would know the right answer. Thank you so much."

Following this consultation, and without any change in the treatment regime, the patient gradually made an uneventful recovery. Just as important as his improvement was the change in the condition of the spouse. From the moment of the third doctor's pronouncement, she was able to relax and was completely at ease. As is often the case, the reassurance his pronouncement gave her made the consultation all worthwhile.

In many other areas aside from the medical field, obtaining a second opinion may be well worthwhile. When buying an automobile it is practically a necessity to get two opinions and preferable to get a third or fourth. At the very least, a person should study the merits of the various makes and models. Then he should try to get the best available price. In building a house, remodeling, or interior decorating projects and other important ventures, it is certainly a wise move to have two or more opinions.

In contrast there is one field where asking for a second opinion may cause confusion and considerable turmoil. That is in the previously mentioned field of property surveying. In the country's past, at the time George Washington was engaged in this profession, most of the United States territory was rural and in a somewhat wilderness state. As a result, if a surveyor was off a few feet one way or another in his calculations it was not of too much importance. However now that the majority of the population lives in urban areas, even a few inches of difference may be the source of considerable argument and dispute. Of course these variations often necessitate a second survey, and this is where the trouble begins.

To illustrate, in one case the buyer of a building lot had accepted the original survey at the time he purchased the property, but as he was a bit of a skeptic and a doubting Thomas at heart, a couple of years later he decided he wanted a recheck of the boundary lines. In so doing, the second surveyor's results differed from the original by a few feet. The buyer was still in the process of paying the seller and so decided to suspend any further payments. It was decided that in order to rectify the discrepancies, a third completely different surveyor would be employed. He, in his turn, arrived at a third set of boundaries. This, of course, muddied to a marked degree the already previously murky waters.

The final solution of the dispute had to be reached in a court of law. With the several different lawyers, surveyors, real estate agents, and witnesses involved, there was considerable time and expense incurred. In addition there was a bit of acrimony displayed and some loss of faith in what had previously been assumed to be an exact scientific profession. After nine days in court, it was concluded that the basic cause of the dispute was each of the surveyors had used a different starting point for his survey. In the final analysis, it would have been much better if the original survey had been accepted by the parties involved, because that was the court's final decision.

And so while second opinions have a place in our complex modern society, it is best for the average layman to use them with discrimination and only when absolutely necessary. As far as surveyors are concerned, they have a definite and essential place in our world, but it is better for the rest of us to accept their first findings and to be content with the boundaries which they set.

Whatever else happens, never let it be inscribed on your final tombstone, I DIDN'T GET A SECOND OPINION!

They Don't Make 'Em Like They Used to!

How often do we hear the expression, "They don't make 'em like they used to." It seems we all remember our first car, our clothes washing machine, plus any number of other possessions with exaggerated fondness. We have a tendency to forget some of the limitations of many of these products. We forget the fact the first car was, in many respects, somewhat of a "clunker" which couldn't compare with the modern models. In addition, we overlook some of the drawbacks of many of these nostalgic possessions. It's sort of like remembering "mother's home cooking" during our growing years and comparing it to food eaten today during our sedentary years with our flagging appetites. As good as Mother's meals were, they were not always perfect.

In this modern age of electronic marvels such as TVs, word processors, laptop computers, and computerized automobile engines, to say nothing about the advances in the aviation field and smart bombs, it is not possible to compare them with past similar products as there was nothing comparable in the "good old days."

Having said all this, there is one product that does fit in the category of "They don't make them like they used to." The bread toasters of the recent past were definitely superior to those of the present day. Our first toaster given to us as a wedding present lasted for thirty years and produced golden brown slices with unerring accuracy. Finally, because its exterior became a bit tarnished, we retired it to our beach cabin where it continued to function for many more seasons. Subsequent models failed to perform in a similar manner and would either burn the bread to a crisp or, on the other hand, simply warm the slice in a half-hearted manner giving it an undone and somewhat pallid look. One of our new toasters would actually growl if the starting bar was depressed too soon, as if to say, "I'm on a definite time schedule so don't rush me." Even if the timer was set properly, the toaster would often act in a capricious manner with unpredictable results. These inconveniences forced us to return to one of our old-fashioned, rather beaten-up models which, in spite of its somewhat sad appearance, produced satisfactory end products.

Of course we could have reverted to the pioneer days before the electrification of much of our country when toasting of bread was accomplished in a number of different ways: by holding a slice with a fork over an open flame, placing bread on an iron grill over a camp fire, or putting a piece in the wood stove's oven. One ingenious man made a cone of barbed wire which he placed on the stove top. By hanging the slice on one of the barbs, he was able to get excellent results. With this method, all that was required to toast the second side was one quick flip. Although today these procedures would be considered somewhat antiquated, they worked. One of the benefits was the lack of any complicated or breakable parts. In addition, no warranty was required.

You, the reader, might be inclined to feel the problem is not so much the toaster itself, but instead is more likely to be the one operating it; that we do not really know how to run modern electrical equipment. However let me assure you this lack of dependability is not confined solely to private home use, but also is to be found in commercial eating establishments. While most restaurants are satisfactory, we found some that were not. One consistently and repeatedly burned the slices to a dark black. Another cafe's toaster not only failed to brown the bread, but also hardly warmed it. Each of these eating houses was staffed by so-called professionals.

While all of the above may sound unimportant, quite negative, and may even be a bit depressing to you, don't be too discouraged because there is always hope for a remedy. It's possible that either we can return to the methods of our pioneer ancestors, or perhaps the toaster manufacturers may revise their production procedures. Possibly some out-of-work electrical engineer or even a genius computer scientist will some day turn his or her attentions and efforts toward the bread toaster field. The end result may be the development of a dependable product which will produce golden brown slices consistently.

If, and when, that day arrives, we will then, with certainty, be able to say, "THEY DON'T MAKE 'EM LIKE THEY USED TO—THEY MAKE 'EM BETTER!"

Gustatory Gambits

"I'm on a high-protein, low-fat, high-fiber, cottage cheese, skimmed milk diet." This quote, while said in jest by a famous movie star playing the part of a hypochondriacal patient, may sound a bit extreme, but is it so?

At the present time, we are bombarded from all sides by a glut of articles from dietary extremists telling us how and what to eat. Each of these so-called experts has his or her own particular gambit which may or may not be based on any accurate information. In addition the advice given may vary widely from author to author and from day to day.

In the recent past, the dietary emphasis given by these proponents has centered on the harmful effects of sodium, cholesterol, and even on plain white sugar. At the present time, the current culprit is "fat." Practically every other package of food on the store shelves has the label "low fat" or "no fat" prominently displayed. It may not be long before one of these markers may even appear on the butter cartons.

With all this emphasis on specific food elements, there seems to be a woeful lack of attention on the real villain, namely, obesity. While there are many articles and schemes advocating weight reduction, most are either unrealistic, or so extreme they are not practical. You may have heard about the woman who went on a banana and coconut diet. She didn't lose any weight, but after three weeks she sure could climb trees. Then there was the man who ate nothing but dehydrated foods. He lost a lot of weight, but one day got caught in a rain storm and gained twenty-two pounds.

Let us concentrate on the subject of obesity. The world doesn't need another article on weight reduction, but it does need a simple, sound, regime for achieving and maintaining a normal weight. First of all, each of us must be aware that eating is a necessity, a pleasure, and in some respects an addiction. This addiction is a positive factor and is not to be construed as a vice. It is a vital requirement in order to sustain life. No one need feel guilty about liking to eat. It is a delightful pastime. The problems which arise are simply a matter of degree. If a person becomes overweight, it means the addiction has gotten a bit out of control.

It is often somewhat paradoxical that obese individuals tend to remember the one small meal they ate during the previous week. They often say, "For lunch last Thursday, I had an apple and a little sandwich." In contrast, the thin ones remember their one big meal, and comment, "I eat like a hog. Last week I ate a Big Mac, french fries, and drank a Coke."

In some respects weight control is different from and yet similar to keeping track of your bank balance. In the latter, it is necessary to put into the account at least as much, or more, as is to be withdrawn. In contrast with calories the deposits must equal to, or be less than, what will be used. In either case an imbalance in deposits and expenditures will have untoward results.

One important fact to keep in mind is weight control consists of two phases. The first is losing the weight, and second, keeping it off. The latter is the one fraught with the highest failure rate (some studies indicate a 90 percent failure rate in this phase).

With obesity, as it is in alcohol addiction, the first step in the cure is to admit a bad habit exists. It is essential for the acknowledgement that the caloric intake is excessive. Once this admission has been made, the next step is the setting of a desired weight loss goal (don't set an unrealistic figure, however). Next, carve the desired figure with a wood burner or sharp knife into the back of the medicine cabinet or kitchen cupboard door. Otherwise, it is too easy to alter any figure written with a pen or pencil.

After this is done, convert the number of pounds to be lost into weeks in which to achieve this goal. A realistic and desirable weight loss rate should average about one pound per week. Many dieters feel this is not fast enough, but remember a pound a week equals fifty-two pounds a year. Also at this rate a person doesn't have to wait a year to begin to see results. Another advantage is it does not require a starvation regime. Most dietary failures are the result of trying to lose too fast, becoming discouraged, and finally giving up altogether. Often it is a wise move to lose in a step-like fashion. For example, after losing ten pounds, level off for a week before starting down again. This helps to prevent discouragement.

Once this regime is started, it is wise to weigh regularly, preferably daily. This keeps track of the progress and is comparable to balancing your bank account. A word of caution—don't be discouraged by minor upward fluctuations as they are only of a temporary nature.

In cutting your caloric intake, don't eliminate all of your favorite foods. Just reduce the size of the portions. For instance if you are crazy abut chocolate pie, take just a small piece. Also, cut down on the amount of salad dressing. It tends to nullify the benefits of the other salad ingredients. In addition, be aware that macaroni and bean salads are not comparable to head lettuce and sliced tomatoes. Favor bulk foods, and reduce the amounts of such things as cheese, creams, and animal fats, which all have twice as many calories per gram as carbohydrates and proteins. And finally, take one modest first helping, but never go back for seconds.

Other tricks to consider are: Eat slowly and savor the taste of each bite. Put your utensil down after each helping. Don't be like the mechanical dirt truck loader which gets a shovel full ready while waiting for the next truck to back up. Make a game of having to hunt for your fork or spoon between bites. Also if you do indulge in an occasional alcoholic drink, be aware that each cocktail contains a large number of calories—some four hundred plus. One man who had to cut all alcohol consumption because of an infection lost twelve pounds in three weeks without any other dietary change.

A further precaution is to eat three meals a day. Don't skip breakfast or lunch since in so doing there is a tendency to say to yourself, "I didn't eat this morning or this noon, so now I deserve a good dinner." Occasionally a dieter will say he or she eats only one meal a day, but often that meal lasts from 6:00 P.M. until 11:00. Instead, eat three meals, but eat each in a moderate manner.

Now that you have cut your caloric intake, it's time to get moving physically and to increase your caloric burn-up. Exercise has two beneficial effects. First, it does use up calories, and second, it reduces the desire to eat—at least temporarily. Many times after playing a strenuous game, such as tennis, swimming, or walking briskly, the appetite will be reduced for an hour or more.

There is a common tendency to say, "I don't have time for exercise." There are many ways to exercise doing ordinary things around the house. There are stairs to climb, floors to sweep, lawns to mow, walks to take, plus a myriad of other activities available. However these should be done in a vigorous manner. Walk rapidly, sweep with gusto, and if possible take the stair steps two at a time. One advantage of this last is you only have to take half as many. Also, it is possible to do fifty sit-ups or twenty-five push-ups during the average television commercial.

In sitting and lying, some individuals tend to "marry" the chair or mattress. They really really sit or lie. Their relationship with these pieces of furniture is such that in order to move them, it seems it would be necessary to cut the ties binding them to said furnishings. In contrast, other individuals sit or lie in a manner which suggests they are about "ready to fly" when they are supposedly relaxing. A posture somewhat in between these two is to be desired.

One woman, when asked about exercise, said, "Oh yes, I get plenty. I knit a lot." While knitting is a worthwhile activity, it doesn't do much as an exercise unless you want skinny fingers.

It is now time to deal with some of the negatives of dieting. First of all, DON'T MAKE EXCUSES. Don't blame your in-laws for serving such a delicious dinner. Don't blame somebody else's birthday party for the pieces of cake you ate. There are always going to be celebrations like Easter, Christmas, and Thanksgiving to blame. Learn to accept these. Enjoy them, but eat moderately and don't go overboard.

DON'T COMPARE YOURSELF WITH OTHERS. "My sister eats all

she wants and never gains an ounce." A study of obese and normal weight girls revealed the chubby ones actually ate less than the normal ones. In the study, when the two groups went to the same activities, the heavy ones didn't swim as hard or dance as much. Therefore, they didn't use up as many calories. Regardless of what others do or do not do, avoid comparing yourself with them. You don't really know what their intake and output actually has been.

DON'T BLAME YOUR METABOLISM. While metabolic rates do vary from person to person, you are primarily concerned with your own. Again, it's just like your bank account. You have to balance the deposits and the withdrawals. A millionaire can spend recklessly for a while, but even he has to be aware of his bank balance. In order to keep your weight level or to lose you may have to be a bit more frugal in your eating than does your neighbor, but don't compare yourself with him or her. Adjust your intake to your own metabolic rate.

DON'T BLAME YOUR ENVIRONMENT. One professional cook said, "I absorb calories from the fumes from the stove." She completely ignored the fact she constantly "pieced" during her working hours. Another woman, a pregnancy case, blamed the fumes from the bakery, located two blocks from her home, for her extra weight gain.

DON'T EAT BETWEEN MEALS, AND NEVER, NEVER EAT WHILE STANDING. This one precaution will eliminate all snacking prior to, or after, meal time. Never lick the pudding spoon after dishing up. Don't even lick the cake icing off your fingers. There is something about licking that breaks down a barrier in the mind. This tends to open the flood gates of between meal snacking. It's surprising how much food can be consumed between meals. One woman during a TV crime trial series said, "You know, those trials were so interesting this afternoon, I found I hadn't had a thing to eat between lunch and dinner."

Of course, there may come a time when you feel you are about to starve between meals and you cannot wait for the next one to arrive. If this does occur, get busy doing something physical. Often this will cut the desire to eat. If not, then make your snack a formal affair. Put the cracker, cookie, or whatever on a plate. Set the table with knife, fork, and spoon. Then, as with any meal, sit down to eat. Usually, by the time you have done all this you will find you really didn't want whatever it was you had in mind. However if you do eat it, you will remember the fact. Whichever happens, remember this truism— I will never eat while standing.

DON'T REWARD YOURSELF WITH FOOD. If you feel you have accomplished your weight loss objective and you deserve a reward, go buy yourself a hat, a new dress, a boat, or even a new car, but don't buy yourself a big meal. During World War II, six overweight US Army M.D.s decided to follow a ten-day newspaper diet regime. With this, each of them lost ten pounds or more. As they all felt they needed a reward, they went to the officer's club for a hearty dinner. In a period of six weeks they were all back to their original weights or higher. As M.D.s they should have known better.

DON'T GO IN FOR CRAZY DIETS. These are typified by the "eggs and grapefruit," "bananas and raisins only," or other "kooky" diets. Remember, to be successful a diet has to be one you can live with and one you can maintain over a long period—permanently, if necessary.

There are a few additional words of caution. Once you have reached you goal, do not keep losing. Occasionally, losing weight can become just as addictive as gaining. Once acquired, the individual may keep on losing too long—even to the point of cachexia. Avoid this mistake. When you reach the weight figure you had previously carved into the back of the medicine cabinet door, level off and then stay even. One question you may ask, "Do I have to watch my diet for the rest of my life?" The answer is, "Yes, we all do." This doesn't mean you have to deny yourself. You just have to maintain a balance. Again, it is just like your bank account. While you may balance your bank account this month, you can't then go on a "hog wild" spending spree next month without paying the price for your excesses. It's better to keep the balance even and current at all times.

Just remember one important fact—whenever you are near food; in the kitchen; at a party, reception, or other social event, and when you look at all the "goodies" lined up before you, say to yourself, repetitiously, if necessary, "I WILL NOT EAT WHILE STANDING."

In summary, perhaps the hypochondriacal comedian mentioned earlier was not too far off the right path when he said, "I'm on a high-protein, low-fat, high-fiber, cottage cheese, skimmed milk diet."

Grandmother and the Indians

The Indians were big, brown, and brawny. In contrast she was petite and pale, even puny. Puny perhaps in outward appearance, that is. To any casual observer it would seem obvious that if there was to be a conflict between them, the odds the Indians would prevail were so great that in the gambler's parlance, "There was no line."

However what the gamblers wouldn't know was Grandma's background, determination, and fortitude. What was true for the gamblers was also true for the three Indians. To them, the pickings looked very easy and very good. They didn't realize they were in for a big surprise.

Little is known of Grandma's very early years. Her formal schooling was sparse, but she attained considerable wisdom in other ways. By the time she was eighteen, she had had two children, both of whom died in infancy. Five sons and one daughter, my mother, followed.

Like many pioneer women, her strength and fortitude were the result of a rugged existence on the cold, wind-swept, barren prairies of middle Canada. Early in her married life, with her husband and children, she started migrating westward. On many occasions when she was left on the farm while her husband went to the nearest settlement for supplies, she was the sole guardian of the family and their sod house and barn. Equipped with a rifle, which she would not have hesitated to use if the need arose, she learned to be vigilant and wary of any intruders.

Conditioned by her early experiences and near poverty, she developed a toughness that was hard to imagine in one so small in stature. In raising her five sons and one daughter, she was strict but fair and loving. In navy terminology, she ran a "tight ship." Although as they matured her sons towered over her, there was never any doubt as to who was in command. Yet if any of her children needed help, she was there immediately and for as long as was necessary.

Years later, when mother died, Grandma came to live with us to care for Dad, my brother Fred, and me. Here, too, the "tight ship" existed. We all soon learned the ground rules but found that they were consistent arid fair.

Once as a small child, when I stepped on a nail which ran through my foot, the wound became infected and my foot and leg swelled to twice normal size. This was prior to the advent of antibiotics so, around the clock, Grandma applied bread and milk poultices. As I look back from the present time, these did make a nice warm pack and accomplished their purpose, but did seem to waste a lot of good bread and milk.

Each spring Grandma would make a two-quart supply of sulfur and molasses which was to be our "spring tonic." The first day, a tablespoonful wasn't too bad. The second day, it was a little harder to take. By the third day, Fred and I would hold the dose in our mouths until we could spit it out in the toilet. From the fourth day on, we were required to swallow it in front of the administrator. When the supply was gone, we had had our "tonic" for that year.

We never had any question about our doing our chores. Our kitchen had a wood burning stove and Grandma liked bark for the fuel. "It gives such a steady heat," she would say. One of my duties was getting this bark. As there were many old stumps on the neighboring acres, at first the gathering was easy. As time passed and I had stripped off the easily harvested bark, the chore became a real pain. However I never did complain to the "captain" of the ship.

But I have digressed long enough. It is time to return to the event mentioned in the beginning paragraph regarding the three big Indians and their encounter with Grandma. In her migration westward, she and her family had arrived in Regina, Saskatchewan, where they decided to stay. There she started a small bakery business. This required long hours of work, both selling during the day as well as baking during much of the nighttime.

On the night in question, she was alone while baking bread for the following day. It so happened that the three Indians, who had previously been customers at the local pub, happened to pass by the bakery just as she was taking the freshly baked bread from the oven. Like most of us have experienced, the smell probably tantalized them somewhat. Seeing the tiny lone woman working inside, they must have figured the pickings would be very easy. Obviously the three were not aware of the expression "a tight ship" nor did they realize the baker's tough background. Like an overconfident athletic team facing a supposedly weaker opponent, they swaggered into the store and started scooping up loaves of bread. Now if they had just been polite and had had good manners and the good sense to politely ask for a handout, they would have received the same without any question. However to blatantly start stealing was an entirely different matter.

Grandma, seeing this unmannerly conduct, and without a moment's hesitation, grabbed one of her large wooden bread paddles, used for removing the hot bread from the ovens. She then started belaboring the three large hulks over their heads and backs. They, in turn, were so surprised and startled by the sudden turn of events and the fury of the onslaught they dropped their loot and fled in utter confusion.

While it is true the ancestors of these same native Canadians may have won the Battle of the Little Big Horn, it is also true that this bunch, without doubt, certainly lost the Battle of the Little Butterhorn.

What a Way to Go

"If you're going to shoot yourself, go out to the backyard. I don't want you messing up the bathroom or my front room rug."

These harsh words coming from the mouth of the man's wife may sound a bit heartless, but in reality they were a blessing in disguise and a good form of shock therapy. Her husband had been upset because of an illness which had necessitated his retirement. Instead of his accepting the problem and making the adjustments required, he had been making life miserable for all of the rest of the family by his moping and had, in addition, kept threatening to shoot himself.

As he admitted later, his wife's reprimand was the best thing that could have happened. It made him realize how selfish he had been. Following her remarks, he pulled himself together, stopped feeling sorry for himself, and started volunteering his time and efforts to helping others in one of the local hospitals.

It is hard for the average person who is blessed with good health, both physically and mentally, to imagine what dire circumstances could prompt anyone to destroy himself. However when looked at impartially, there are many situations which might seem so overwhelming to a person that he or she would take such a drastic action. These include such conditions as deep depression or other mental aberrations, physical illnesses, loss of a spouse, jilted love affairs, financial losses, loneliness, decreased desire to go on, or numerous other factors.

While the subject of suicide is not pleasant, it is a reality and should be considered. In the first place, the methods chosen will vary depending on multiple differing factors involved in each situation. Once the decision is made, there are several alternate methods which may be used by the victims. Broadly classified, they consist of four categories: the impulsive or fast, the accidental, the gradual or slow, and the weird.

Included in the first group are those common procedures such as self-inflicted gun shots, leaping from high bridges, self-hangings, ingestion of poisons such as cyanide, and deliberate overdosages with sedatives. Many of these acts are done on impulse during a period of acute depression. If this person can be intercepted in time, he or she may often be guided into the right direction and rehabilitated. In some situations the suicide may be due to compassion for a spouse or friend who has a terminal problem. Here a murder-suicide may be the end result. There have been several examples of this combination of tragedies where the wife had an incurable illness and the husband couldn't tolerate her suffering so rightly or wrongly, he resorted to the above. Still other examples are caused by a failed love affair.

The second category, the accidental type of suicide is, in reality, a subdivision of the fast type. The big difference is in this group the individual doesn't consciously anticipate his demise. Included here are those who regularly drive their cars in a reckless manner or those who drink and then drive. The danger here is that, in addition to themselves, they may take out some innocent victims. Also included are those who indulge in hazardous sports such as dangerous mountain scaling, especially those without adequate training or conditioning. One well-conditioned football lineman joined a mountain climbing group. He ignored the need to become acclimated to the lack of oxygen at the higher altitude. As a result, near the top of the mountain he became so fatigued he lost his footing and fell several hundred feet to his death. His failure to heed good advice was, in essence, a subtle form of suicide. And then there are the scuba divers, sky divers, and river rafters who start out without some instruction. Of course, one of the most careless is the bungie jumper who doesn't make sure the top end of the cord is well tied.

In a different vein are those who accidentally take an overdose of certain medicines, as well as those who improperly mix different medicines or those who mix sedatives and alcohol without either of these being in excess. Of course, Russian Roulette should be mentioned here, even though anyone who indulges in this activity has to be a bit balmy in the first place. While those in this overall category may not consciously wish for self-destruction, the end result is just as deadly.

The third group of suicides is composed of those who adopt the gradual or slow methods. This group is by far the largest of the four categories, and while those included in it for the most part may not be conscious of their ultimate destiny, their final outcome is predictable. Here, we find the heavy smokers, the regular alcohol imbibers, and most commonly the overeaters. The evidence about the effects of smoking has been well documented. As far as the moderate use of alcohol is concerned, there is still some argument. The problem here is the definition of the word "moderate." No one ever deliberately set out to become an alcoholic, but one thing is certain—no alcoholic ever became so without his or her taking that first drink. It is said that each beer consumed knocks out one kidney tubule and one brain cell. While there are many thousands of each of these structures, there are not an unlimited number. Sooner or later, a time of reckoning is reached.

We now arrive at the largest group of slow suiciders—the overeaters. We, as consumers, can all be fitted into one of three types: those who live to eat, those who eat to live, and those who eat to die. The first and last types are the ones most at risk. Anatomists have determined that three miles of blood vessels and capillaries are required for each pound of weight. If so, then for ten pounds of overweight thirty extra miles of vessels are needed. For fifty pounds, one hundred and fifty miles will be required. This increase obviously imposes an additional work load on the "pump" or the heart. By way of comparison, if a city increases in size from 100,000 to 150,000 people, the city water system's pumps must either work harder or additional pumps must be installed. Without extra pumps the originals wear out faster. In the human, extra hearts are not possible, only replacements can be inserted, if these are available. In addition, the extra fat in the heart area tends to impede the action of the heart, resulting in a double hazard. In other words, not only is the work load increased, but also the power of the pump is decreased. The end result is a shortened life expectancy.

In addition to the effect of extra fat upon the heart, it also puts an additional strain on the pancreas. This, in turn, increases the chances of the host developing diabetes mellitus which, if it occurs, affects all the body's arteries including those to the eyes, extremities, kidneys, brain, and again the heart. It's a vicious cycle and, in reality, a slow form of suicide.

The story is told of health oriented organization which invited a noted cardiologist and author to speak at their annual banquet. He had written a book and several articles about the benefits of exercise and proper eating in the prevention of heart attacks. When the doctor arrived at the hotel, astride his bicycle, he headed for the stairs instead of the elevator. By the time the welcoming group finally reached the eighth floor banquet hall, the doctor was breathing easily. The hosts were, practically speaking, nearly "done in." The dinner served consisted of prime rib of beef with heavy intramural fat, mashed potatoes covered with gravy, and a chef's salad smothered with dressing. All this was topped off by a chocolate sundae with whipped cream. You can imagine what the doctor said in his talk that evening.

It should be mentioned that in contrast to overeating as an indirect and slow cause of suicide there is an exactly opposite method used by some. This is the route occasionally taken by those who have a terminal illness and no hope of recovery. It consists of refusing to eat anything during their last few days or weeks. Considered in one vein, it really isn't a form of suicide, but on the other hand it does speed up the end result.

The fourth and last category of suicides is the one that for want of a better title will have to be labeled "weird." The methods used here vary considerably and are not nearly as common as most of the above mentioned. Strangely enough, these are often performed by people with relatively high IQs. One such was a medical doctor who placed a plastic bag over his head and then tied it securely with a surgical knot around his neck. What a way to go.

Another was the method used by a man who flew his single-engine plane from the West Coast of the US out over the Pacific Ocean until the gas ran out. What if he had had a change of heart after he had passed the "point of no return?"

A third case and a really truly weird situation was performed by a man who set up his video camera, started it running, and then lay down on the railroad tracks in front of an oncoming train. Both the train and the camera did their parts, but the only thing that showed on the finished film was the bright glare of the headlight of the locomotive.

While most of us may not want to live forever, we, in turn, are not in any big rush to terminate our stay here. We realize eternity is a long, long time and where we spend it is determined by our beliefs and how we live our lives. In contrast, those who intentionally commit suicide and who have no hope of any improvement in their future here on earth or of any life thereafter have no solid ground upon which to stand. In their minds all is bleak, with no chance of any improvement. They have no Christian faith and have only their own strength upon which to rely. This, they realize, is a very weak foundation.

Most of the above-mentioned individuals need our sympathy and understanding. It behooves those of us who for whatever reason are more fortunate to help those less so, to lift up the lonely and the depressed, to encourage and help those who are obese or alcoholics, and to try to convert the agnostics and the atheists by the way we live. No one is beyond redemption. Think of the ex-slave trader who was converted and then composed the hymn "Amazing Grace" or the reformed alcoholic who when asked, "You don't believe that story about Jesus changing water into wine, do you?" replied, "I don't know for sure about that, but since I stopped drinking I know I have been able to change beer into shoes for my children and furniture for my home."

In turn let the rest of us help those in need by changing the expression, WHAT A WAY TO GO into "This is the true way."

A Soft Answer

If we want to keep our minds and hides in proper running condition there is really only one way to go, and that is to follow the Holy Bible's admonition of "A soft answer turneth away wrath." This is a truism which has existed for centuries but which is especially applicable at the present time. While it is indisputable in principle, its practical application is often very difficult to execute in our daily contacts and activities. However in spite of the problems in following this advice, it is usually the better part of valor to avoid confrontations with our fellow man. This is especially true as we drive our automobiles in today's hectic traffic.

Each of us can recall incidents in our lives when a calm discussion got out of hand and became and angry argument of undue proportion. Often in these situations the end result is a state of animosity between friends, or what is worse, between husband and wife. At these times, frequently words are spoken which are not really meant, but once uttered cannot be retracted. When this happens it is usually difficult for each person involved to admit that he or she might be wrong. Obviously the correct approach is either to remain silent or at least to give a soft answer.

A graphic example of the need for restraint occurred when a doctor was winding down at the end of a especially trying day. As all of his assistants had departed from the office, he was anxious to get home to his family for dinner and, if possible, a quiet evening with them. Just as he was heading for the office door, the telephone rang. Strongly tempted to ignore the instrument's strident notes, but then recalling his Hippocratic Oath, he picked up the receiver only to be greeted by an irate patient who started to berate him in no uncertain terms. He recognized the caller's voice as belonging to one of his malcontents. In his fatigued state his first reaction was to defend himself and to argue in return. On second thought, he held his tongue, sat down, and put his feet up on his desk while the tirade went on and on. In the next few minutes, as he listened to the rapid fire monologue, he was able to compose himself and to recall the circumstances of the case being discussed. Finally the caller's source of anger and energy ran out of steam. When finally she paused for breath, the doctor made his first comment, saying, "I'm certainly glad that you called me."

There was a gasp of astonishment at the other end of the line. Then the doctor continued, "If you hadn't called, I would have been unaware that all was not going well with you. As I recall, when you were here last, it was agreed that if you continued to have a problem for longer than three days, you would let me know. As it has been at least a couple of weeks since you were here, I assumed that all was going well. Now, could you tell me exactly what residue of your problem still exists?"

This quiet response to the patient's previous tirade seemed to have a calming influence on the irate caller. As she began to talk in a more rational manner, she listed her symptoms in such a way the doctor could answer with reassurance. Soon, as their conversation continued, she began to respond positively and finally began to laugh. Then, with the immediate crisis under control, it was agreed she should report for further tests. The end result was they parted friends and kept their doctor-patient relationship in good repair.

From a practical standpoint, one of the most common and important areas of testing our ability to keep our emotions under control is our reactions when we are behind the steering wheel of our car. It is a well-known fact that many individuals seem to have a complete change of personality once they get into the driver's seat. It is possible this change is simply a revelation of their basic nature rather than a retrogression to a baser personality trait. On the other hand, this change may be due to the somewhat impersonal relationship of the driver in his various contacts with other motorists. This partial isolation may in turn make the need for good manners seem less important.

Have you ever noticed the common tendency of many motorists to label all of the slower drivers as "fuddy duds" and the faster drivers as "hot rods?" Of course, in spite of the foibles of the other fellow, we often forget to recognize our own idiosyncrasies. Regardless of who is to blame, it always pays to bend over backwards to be considerate of the other fellow. We all make mistakes, many unintentional. Remember this fact when some other driver commits an error similar to our own.

Of course there are many other areas of life where it pays to not only speak softly, but also in some situations to assume a secondary role and to beat a hasty retreat. One such event occurred when a mild-mannered man was asked by his wife to pick up some nylon stockings at a nearby department store where there was a big sale taking place. While this task seemed like a simple mission, the poor guy didn't realize what a hazardous undertaking he had been asked to complete. Once in the store, he was immediately dismayed and found himself being buffeted from side to side by charging female customers. Having been trained since his early childhood to believe in "ladies first" and trying to be a gentleman, he never seemed to get any nearer the sales counter. Finally, in desperation, after many rebuffs, he headed for the nearby luggage department which, at the time, was devoid of customers. Here he quietly asked the clerk, "Would you mind getting me two pairs of nylons from the stocking counter?" Sensing his frustration and feeling sorry for this distraught individual, the clerk did as he had asked. Once these items were in his grasp, with a sigh of relief he beat a hasty retreat to the nearest exit—never, ever to return.

On another occasion, this same man was at a breakfast buffet. As he approached the fruit counter, he found himself swept aside by two Oriental women who zoomed in, one from each side. With haste and to avoid physical damage, he immediately jumped back, again trying to play the part of a gentleman. Minutes later, as he neared the pastry table, he was again threatened by these same two ladies. This time instead of retreating, he decided to try a different tactic. He held his ground and then bowed in a typical Oriental gesture of friendship. This maneuver markedly changed the entire scenario. The ladies, looking somewhat baffled, stopped in their tracks, and then, smiling broadly, bowed several times in return. Once the bowing ceremony had been completed all three moved to the table in harmony. He had inadvertently discovered there is more than one way to be humble and polite and yet complete a successful mission.

And so, no matter what the situation, be it in the home, on the highway, in the grocery store checkout line, in a friendly discussion, even in a argument, or at a breakfast buffet, it pays to heed the Biblical admonition and remember A SOFT ANSWER TURNETH AWAY WRATH.

Medical Practice Hazards

Grandmother once said, "If he becomes a medical doctor he'll take up dope, alcohol, wild women, or some bad habit."

In a way, she was correct, but not completely so. She didn't even mention the many other hazards such as: malpractice suits, the house call dangers encountered in certain neighborhoods, the risks to health from long hours of overwork, the exposure to innumerable virulent germs, or the partial neglect of family because of "dedication to duty."

As hazardous as many of the above happen to be, there is one hazard which overshadows all the others. It is the exposure and ready access to an unlimited supply of hard narcotics. In our present drug-oriented society, there is a tendency by many to treat the threat of drugs in a somewhat nonchalant manner. This was not always the case in bygone years.

I vividly recall my feelings of apprehension when I first received my medical license and my narcotics permit. The fact that I had ready access to any drug without an intermediary was very sobering and even frightening. So much so I resolved to forgo any habit-forming drugs entirely. To this day, except for medications given to me at the times of my two surgeries, I have adhered to this resolve.

The same cannot be said for many others—namely, the drug addicts. In spite of their foolishness, they are to be pitied. The majority of this group are completely mixed up in their thinking. They, as a group, are often quite smart, but not very wise. Many, financially speaking, are successful and at first felt they were being sophisticated and blasé—until it was too late and they were "hooked."

In my practice, the more I saw of the devastation brought on by narcotics, the more I became aware of the similarities to be found in these individuals. There are several of these characteristics which stand out. The average, if there is such a thing as an average, addict is an insecure, confused person. Conversely, he or she is often a desperate individual and dangerous, not only to himself, but also to the rest of society. The danger to others is especially true for the young doctor who is just starting his medical practice.

I'm sure there is a grapevine which alerts the "dopers" to the fact a new doctor has set up shop. Within days of his first "hanging out his shingle," the addicts flock in to see how vulnerable this neophyte might be. If he naively complies with their wishes or falls for their fabrications, the flood gates open, and he is inundated from then on. Most new medics are trusting of others and anxious to help their fellow man. These characteristics make them "sitting ducks" for any slick addict.

Many addicts are very intelligent (not wise), glib talkers, and possess a fairly good knowledge of whatever illness they profess to have. They often are "just passing through town" and have "accidentally" lost their medicine by spilling it into the toilet, down the sink, etc. They always know exactly which pain pill they want (the average patient is willing to accept whatever the doctor prescribes). Most of the addicts want hard narcotics like dilaudid. They are very persistent and become hostile if their demands are refused.

Addicts do vary in some aspects. Some, a few, are content to take their dope orally. Most want it by injection. A few, the real hard users, take theirs intravenously. These last are known as "main line shooters." I recall one of these at the County Hospital. The police had brought him in from the county jail where he had been confined for several days without his usual "fix." He was in desperate shape. He told me what his usual dosage was. As I prepared to give it to him, he said, "I'll do it, Doc." With this, he took the syringe from me, rolled up his sleeve, twisted it to make a tourniquet, grasped this with his teeth, and with a deft movement skillfully plunged the needle into a vein. This was my first experience with a "main liner." While he hadn't used any antiseptic prior to his injection, his one-handed technique was faultless and something to behold.

Occasionally an addict could be a source of amusement as well as an irritation. One such was a woman who developed the habit of calling me about nine o'clock on Sunday evening three weeks in a row. She had the usual story. She was passing through town and had accidentally lost her medicines in the toilet. When I asked her what medication she had lost, she responded, "Oh, I couldn't pronounce those medical names, but I could spell it for you." With this, she started spelling the drug's name with long pauses between letters. "D—I—L—A—U—" I stopped her and said I couldn't prescribe that without seeing her to make a diagnosis. I volunteered to meet her at the hospital, but she declined this offer.

At the end of her third call and after she had refused to meet me for an examination once again, I asked, "Would you do me a favor? If you are rotating through the doctor's telephone directory, would you take me off the Sunday night schedule, and call me on a weekday, preferably during office hours?" I didn't hear from her again.

In my first month of practice, a female addict called from her hotel room with a story that her mother had just died and she had to go to Seattle to make funeral arrangements but was so distraught she had to have a sedative before leaving. She said she had a friend with her at the hotel who would stay with her and then take her to Seattle once she had calmed down. When I arrived at the somewhat run-down hotel and had located her room, I found her alone. As I entered the room, she slipped around behind me, locked the door, and dropped the key down her bosom. To me this was a hazard of the first order, but I put on my bravest front and said, "I don't know what you have in mind, but if I want that key I will not hesitate to go after it. Now tell me, where is your friend you said would be here?"

Her answer was very evasive, but it was obvious she was disturbed, so I gave her a mild sedative which, I'm sure was not what she wanted. After she started to relax, I grabbed my medical bag in one hand and my hat in the other and headed for the door. She did unlock the door, but before I could exit she grabbed me around the neck with both arms. My bag contained breakable vials so I didn't want to drop it, and the floor was so dirty I didn't want to drop my hat. With some effort, I was able to persuade her to let me go, then I made a hasty exit.

The next day, I learned she was not only an addict, but also a prostitute who had just been released from the state penitentiary the previous day. Incidentally, the story of her mother's death was a complete fabrication.

One night, at 2:00 A.M. as I was driving home from the hospital I noticed a car following close behind. No matter what my speed, either fast or slow, it held its position. Even when I changed lanes, it did likewise. On this way home there was one stretch of the road about a mile long which was completely devoid of housing and street lighting. I felt the occupants of the car were planning to waylay me on this deserted stretch of wasteland. At the time, my car had what was then called "jet away." This gave me the power to accelerate from a slow speed to an instant high. I figured my best chance to evade my followers was the element of surprise, so just before arriving at the deserted stretch, I slowed down to a crawl, and then slammed on the "jet away" and was halfway across the wasteland before my pursuers were aware of what had happened.

On the far side was a drug store and theater with lights on, but no humans present. The lights, by their bright glow, seemed to offer me a small feeling of comfort when I parked there and left the car motor running. My would-be assailants stopped on the opposite side of the road and stared at me for what, at the time, was interminable. My plan if they came at me was to speed away or to even ram their car if necessary. Finally, after several minutes, they must have decided I was not worth their time and effort so they pulled away. Somewhat shaken emotionally, but still intact physically, I continued my homeward journey. At least one more hazard of medical practice had been avoided.

Although the narcotic agents would never admit it openly, to keep life interesting for us medics, they would on occasion send a known addict or even another agent in disguise to check on us. If we didn't take proper precautions and if we fell for their ruse, we could be in big, big trouble. The drug agency also had a few other little tests for us doctors. One day a true addict appeared at my office and said the narcotics agent had told him it was all right for me to give him a hard narcotic prescription. When I called the agent, he confirmed the addict's story. However when I asked the agent for a written confirmation of his oral statement, he refused my request. Naturally I didn't give the addict a prescription. In some respects the whole process was a cat and mouse game. The doctor was the mouse.

Aside from the potential hazards we encountered with the addicts, there were several other aspects of medical practice which were a bit risky. One such occurred when making house calls. On these trips there were the frequent encounters with man's best friend, the patient's dog or dogs. I don't blame the dogs for wanting to protect their master's territory, but it was hard to understand why the owners, who knew we were coming, didn't corral their beasts prior to our arrival. I like dogs, but have a problem when two or three of them come charging at me with teeth bared and angry, loud barking in what appears to be an unfriendly manner. Or even worse, when they silently come stalking me in a menacing way.

Fog was also a hazard. Not just a little fog, but the kind that is so thick it becomes a problem to see the front of the car's hood. The kind that when making a 90-degree turn you end up doing a 120 or even a 180. In a real "pea souper," crossing a busy thoroughfare can be a real "hair raiser," especially if there are large trailer trucks roaring by.

In an entirely different field, testifying in a court of law can present problems. While not hazardous in a physical sense, these experiences can be quite trying mentally, especially during the first few sessions. Later on they become easier, but are never really comfortable.

The hazards of a medical practice are not comparable to those which confront many other types of activity such as high rock climbers, astronauts, stunt men, military personnel in combat, firemen, downhill skiing racers, policemen, and many others engaged in truly dangerous work. For that I am thankful I took up the practice of medicine as my life's work, since I probably wouldn't have done a very good job in one of the above-mentioned occupations.

Mr. Gray

I don't know his real name, but to me he was Mr. Gray. Of course, what he called himself really doesn't matter because his name could change at anytime to suit his purpose. In any event, in my eyes he was Mr. Gray because everything about him was gray. His topcoat, with turned up collar, was gray. His hat, suit, and tie were gray. His skin had a grayish tinge. Even his eyes were a washed-out grayish color.

When I first saw him he appeared to be in agony and terribly ill as he entered my treatment room with a slow, shuffling gait. Later I was to learn he was the complete actor. It is doubtful even the original cast of Agatha Christie's record-setting production *The Mouse Trap* could claim the distinction of having acted in one role, continuously, for a longer period of time than this enigmatic man.

At the time of our first meeting, I was a neophyte in the practice of medicine, unaware of mankind's often devious nature and anxious to alleviate the sufferings of others. My sympathies poured out to this miserable man as he described his symptoms, which were classical and a textbook picture of a kidney stone trying to pass.

For anyone who has had this malady, no further explanation is necessary. For the rest of us, it has been said the pain is so severe it is nearly indescribable. I can't vouch for its severity, personally, but women who have given birth to babies and also have had renal stones, say that as far as the pain is concerned, they would opt for the babies any day.

Let us return to Mr. Gray. My examination of him tended to confirm the diagnosis. There were red blood cells in his urine, a specimen which was voided while I was in the room. My sympathy for this suffering man was profound and I said, "I'll arrange for a bed for you in the hospital immediately."

"Thank you. Thank you, Doctor." Then with hesitation and a confused look, he continued, "But how will I take care of Mother? She's eighty-six years old and practically helpless. Could you give me something to help me tonight?

I'll arrange for someone to come in to be with her in the morning."

"I can give you some oral medications, but they may not do the job completely, so if you have trouble during the night, be sure to call me at any hour. Otherwise, report here in the morning for a recheck of your condition."

With this, I gave him two prescriptions. One was a smooth muscle relaxer to help the stone to pass. The other was for morphine tablets for pain—just enough to last him through the night.

The following morning, he appeared as scheduled, looking considerably less gray and much improved. Even his urine specimen showed fewer red blood cells. He thanked me for my help. However as there was no evidence he had actually passed the stone, I cautioned him that he might have a recurrence of the renal colic at any time and, if so, to be sure to call me. I told him we should get some x-rays within the next few days. When I asked him about his medications, he said he could use a few more of the pills that helped the stone to pass (these were not narcotics). He never mentioned the morphine tablets. As I wrote the prescription for the muscle relaxer tablets, I asked, "How about the pain pills?"

At this point his acting talents reached their zenith. In an off-hand, even nonchalant manner, he replied, "Well, I did use all of them. If you think I might need more, perhaps you could give me another prescription. I won't have it filled unless the pain recurs."

With this, big-hearted me, I wrote another morphine prescription, enough for the next twenty-four hours.

The following morning, bright and early, Mr. Gray called to say that, as I had predicted, his pain had recurred. It was terribly severe and not relieved by the second morphine prescription.

"Get to the hospital immediately. I'll arrange a bed for you."

"Okay, but first I'll have to make additional arrangements for mother's care. When I was improved yesterday, I cancelled my previous plans. Could you help me out this morning? I'll be in the hospital by 2:00 P.M."

This delay necessitated giving a few more morphine tablets—the total number of which by now had reached eighteen. As you have probably anticipated, Mr. Gray did not appear at the hospital by 2:00 P.M. that day or any day during the next ten years. I had been taken, literally and figuratively, by a sharp operator. In addition, the theatrical world had been deprived of the thespian skills of a great actor. My naivete had been somewhat buffeted and tarnished, and for the future my skeptical nature had been alerted.

ADDENDUM:

Many years later, in exactly the same setting, my friend, Mr. Gray, appeared once more. Again, I don't recall what name he used this time, but as before, it really doesn't matter. He had the same grayish appearance and wore what looked like that same gray topcoat, hat, and tie. Even his skin and eyes were the same. He walked with the same slow, stooped, shuffling gait of his first visit. He told the same story and hadn't changed his act one iota. Again his urine showed the same findings as before. (I never did see exactly how he was able to get the red cells into the specimen, but I have heard that a secreted pin or other sharp object will produce enough blood to fool even an expert).

I was very solicitous and, with all due gravity, said, "It looks like you have an acute renal colic. This calls for immediate hospitalization. I'll arrange a bed for you."

"Thank you. Thank you, Doctor." Then with the same hesitancy of several years previously, he asked, "But how will I take care of my mother?" (By now, Mother would be in her late nineties and, it seemed to me, was somewhat indestructible).

In answer to this, I figuratively leaped from behind the false facade I had been wearing, and asked, "Don't you remember me? It usually is the doctor who forgets having seen the patient, not the other way around. However in our situation, I have never forgotten you and never will. You were very clever in the way you hoodwinked me many years ago. I suppose you have seen so many M.D.'s since you were here it isn't possible for you to keep track of all those you have fooled. However in all fairness, and assuming you are really suffering, I will arrange a hospital bed for you. Otherwise, you will not get one morphine pill from me now or in the future. In addition, I'm sure that your mother, if she exists, is tough enough to take care of herself."

With a look of antagonism, but without a word, he picked up his hat and coat. Long gone was his stooped, shuffling gait as he walked briskly from my office—never to be seen by me again.

I have often wondered how many other M.D.'s he fooled in his long career. It's too bad he wasted his talents as an actor. Be that as it was, farewell, Mr. Gray, wherever you are.

Inflation Is Now under Control?

These words, uttered by the head of one of the government's fiscal departments, must have gladdened the hearts of many oldsters and others who are on fixed incomes, but is it really true? For the average person it is difficult to dispute the words of an authority who has all the figures at his beck and call. However then again, perhaps he may have been looking only at the short-term picture. Viewed from the long term, the truth is completely different.

For example, the other day an invitation to a banquet arrived with a menu cost of forty dollars, not for a couple, but for a person. While this promised to be somewhat of a gala affair, I couldn't help recall a time when our entire family of four had a complete dinner with soup, salad, main course, dessert, and beverage for two dollars for the entire family.

Speaking of meals, there was a time when political fund raising dinners were priced at one hundred dollars a plate. No longer. A recent one of these was five thousand dollars per person.

In the not too distant past, a ten thousand dollar a year man was considered a big success. Now he would be eligible for welfare food stamps. At that same time, a closet full of hundred dollar suits was another sign of a man's prosperity. Today these same priced suits would be found on the bargain basement racks. It once was possible to buy the best brand of men's shirts for two dollars. Now it costs that much to have them laundered. The increase in the price of neckties is so great it shouldn't even be mentioned.

It used to be a motorist could get free air for his car's tires at the service station. Then special pumps were installed which required twenty-five cents for enough air for four tires. The last time I stopped for air, the price had increased to fifty cents and there was only enough air available to fill two tires.

While in a family bakery a few years ago I overheard the bakers laughingly say, "One of these days the price of bread may even get to a dollar a loaf." From the way they said this, they apparently thought that this was a ridiculous figure. Today, it's hard to find a good loaf as low as a dollar.

Having worked in the distant past for thirty-five cents an hour, it is now a bit disconcerting to hear a young person complain because his job is paying only $9.50 an hour. Of course, he is comparing this figure with some one else's twenty dollars an hour.

It wasn't too long ago that a hospital administrator warned some day hospital beds would be one hundred dollars a day. At that time, this seemed to be an outlandish figure. Now this same amount is fairly standard for ordinary nursing home custodial care.

Forty years ago a good, new, medium-grade automobile could be purchased for one thousand dollars. Today, this is often the rebate figure, as advertised. Now, the price range of twenty to thirty thousand dollars is considered average. Of course, the sales tax and license are added on.

Not too long ago, during a debate about price controls, one of the speakers made the following statement: "Without controls, beef steak may get as high as one dollar per pound." About all we can get for this price now is fatty hamburger.

When I went to medical school in the 1930s, my most expensive year was thirteen hundred dollars. This sum included tuition, books, room, board, and transportation. At the same school today, the yearly total for tuition alone is above thirty thousand dollars.

One of the biggest hikes in value is to be found in property values and real estate. One seventy-year-old house which originally cost thirty-five thousand dollars is now priced for sale at one hundred thirty-five thousand dollars. This type of story can be duplicated over and over.

Long gone is the good hot cup of coffee at five cents. We are lucky to find one for seventy-five cents now. Of course, at the fancy coffee stands like Starbucks the sky is the limit.

Topping all other categories of price increases is to be found in the field of athletics. Of course, no one is forced to attend these events so we cannot feel sorry for the fans if they are willing to pay exorbitant prices for tickets. The athletes are the ones who reap the rewards. In bygone days one of the top-flight golfer's total compensation for his entire career just equaled the first place purse for one of today's events. In 1997, a prominent basketball player made seventy-eight million dollars for playing and for product endorsements. Probably the most flagrant example of excess is in the field of boxing. Here twenty-five million for one fight often is standard.

The list of examples of price increases could go on and on, so I won't belabor the point. What is the solution for the average person who becomes somewhat confused by conflicting reports from our government agencies? Perhaps one solution would be for the different official departments to coordinate their actions before they further confuse the public.

Instead of the Federal Reserve Board telling us inflation is now under control, while at the same time their brother agency, the US Postal Service, is raising the price of a one cent postcard to twenty cents, and the two cent postal stamp to thirty-two cents, they should both remain silent or, better yet, not raise their prices.

Of course, there is one federal agency which remains mum and happy during these confusing times, namely the IRS. They cannot lose, whatever happens, for as prices escalate and salaries have to keep pace, more and more of the public will have to pay more and more of their income in taxes.

Anatomies of Notes

Have you ever noticed how closely the musical and the medical professions are allied? The former seem to have an inordinate interest in the human anatomy, physiology, as well as the psychiatric. There is, in turn, a reciprocal interest in things musical by the medical profession. This mutual relationship between what may seem to be two somewhat divergent professions might lead the casual observer to believe there are factors at play which are not apparent on the surface.

On closer scrutiny, however, there are some similarities to be found. For instance, both professions are divided into two distinct groups: the generalists and the specialists. In this regard there is one minor variation. In the medical field the generalists outnumber the specialists, while in musical circles the opposite is true.

From a musical standpoint, the prime specialty is the one concerned with the heart. This becomes evident when we consider such compositions as: "Peg of My Heart," "With a Song in My Heart," "Heart," "Stout-Hearted Men," "Don't Break the Heart That Belongs to You," "My Foolish Heart," "Heartaches," "Take Back the Heart That You Gavest," "Curse of the Aching Heart," and "Had I a Heart" just to mention a few. Even Bach, nearly three hundred years ago, composed "Heart and Spirit."

Although the heart may be the favorite organ, other parts of the body are not neglected. The eyes come in for considerable attention with: "Jeepers Creepers, Where'd You get Those Peepers," "I Only Have Eyes for You," "When Irish Eyes Are Smiling," "Green Eyes," "Don't Let the Stars Get in Your Eyes," "There's Yes Yes in Your Eyes," and "The Maiden with the Dreamy Eyes." Of course, today the clean air advocates would want to ban such songs as "Smoke Gets in Your Eyes."

Comparable to the orthopedists in medicine, musicians have definite interests in the skeletal structures of the body, Here we find: "Dem Bones," "Hand in Hand," "Tip-Toe through the Tulips," "I Get a Kick Out of You," "Time on

My Hands," Here in My Arms," and "Legs Hang Down." Even DeBuss composed "Fetes." If one stretches the imagination and also likes puns, "Need You" could also be included in this category. The general practitioners in the musical field cover a much broader field and are all inclusive in their compositions, such as: "You Must Have Been a Beautiful Baby," "Five Foot Two Eyes of Blue," "All the Things You Are," "Pretty Baby," "Body and Soul," and "Exactly Like You."

Those with dermatological interests concentrate on the skin and it appendages: "I've Got You under My Skin," "Cheek to Cheek," "Tattooed Lady," "Jeannie with the Light Brown Hair," and "Her Golden Hair Was Hanging down Her Back."

Those composers with surgical tendencies dream up: "Mack the Knife," and the pathologist type compose "I'll Be Glad When You Are Dead, You Rascal You."

Those with a psychiatric bent will be likely to compose: "You're Driving Me Crazy," "You Go to My Head," "Remember," "Didn't I Blow Your Mind Last Night?," "Thanks for the Memory," "Ah, Sweet Mystery of Life," "That Old Feeling," "Memories," "I'll See You in My Dreams," "Melancholy Baby," and "Girl of My Dreams."

In this day of cardiac transplants and other advances in heart therapy, the following compositions take on new meanings: "My Heart Stood Still," "My Heart Belongs to Daddy," and "If I Gave My Heart to You."

The more generous songwriters seem to have no limitations to their benevolence: "Everything I Have Is Yours," "Why Not Take All of Me," and "Love Here Is My Heart." In contrast, the selfish and acquisitive composers often dream up such pieces as: "You Belong to Me," "My Man," and "Yours Is My Heart Alone."

The inquisitive composers might scratch their heads and come up with: "I Wonder What Has Become of Sally?" "Where'd You Get Those Eyes?" and "I Wonder Who's Kissing Her Now?" Incidentally, as far as is known, the "Now" has never been accurately located in the human body by any anatomist.

Probably the most extreme example of lack of memory or at least the utmost example of carelessness in a composer is exemplified in the composition, "I Left My Heart in San Francisco."

Of course, there are always the exceptions which prove the rule. In contrast to the above examples is the musical nihilist who brings forth "I Ain't Got Nobody."

While practically all of the previous comments have been in reference to the musical composers, the ties of the medical profession to things musical should be mentioned at least briefly. It is well known that many medical men and women display not only an avid interest in the musical classics, light and heavy operas, musical comedies, and modern compositions, but also are skillful in playing one or more musical instruments. When a local doctor who was also an accomplished pianist was asked about this, he replied, "In the musical conservatories the 'A' students go on to become the performers. The 'B' students become instructors, and the 'C' students go to medical school."

Today in many hospitals and medical offices, piped-in music is common and is designed to soothe the patients and visitors. It also has the same effect on the medical personnel. It has been speculated that the calming effect of these melodies may even penetrate into the minds of those patients who are under anesthesia. Some skeptics may question this fact however.

In the overall picture, it is gratifying and enlightening to discover the close relationship between the medical and the musical professions and to appreciate the inspirational music produced by the latter group. In addition, on the "flip side" of the record, to be aware of the medical accomplishments of many "noted" doctors.

Speakeritis

In case you haven't noticed, our country is being confronted by an epidemic which threatens all of us. This scourge, while present at all times, is especially rampant during the late summer and the entire fall seasons of even-numbered years. It is not by chance this timing happens to coincide with the major political campaigns. During these periods, there is an overabundance of speakers who bombard us from all angles: radio, TV, telephone, and the public speaking platforms. It is called "speakeritis."

To date, there is no vaccine available to protect us from this ailment. Our only recourse is to be forewarned and to take steps to ward off its effects. A knowledge of its etiology and its varying courses of action will be of some help in modifying the progress of this common affliction.

In the following discussion, the use of the radio, TV, and tape cassettes will not be considered as complete protection from these sources can be achieved very easily by not turning them on. The remainder of our time will be devoted to classifying the various subgroups of the disease and to methods of alleviating the listener's symptoms associated with their contact with public speakers. Try as one might, it is impossible to completely avoid exposure to them. However there are a few ways which can be used to cushion their impact. Here are a few suggestions.

The first step in prevention is to be very careful in the selection of the programs you plan to attend. Be sure to gather as much information as possible about the speaker. Read any brochures, newspaper articles, or other publications available prior to committing yourself. Even so, these may be misleading, so believe only half of what is published.

Second, if you do go, try to sit near the back of the room and always sit next to the aisle.

Third, before leaving for the program, ask your next-door neighbor, the babysitter, or a good friend to telephone you at the box office approximately fifteen minutes after the start of the speech. This will give you time to evaluate the speaker. If he or she is good you can stay. If not, you can gracefully exit in a manner which suggests to others that some important event which requires your immediate attention has arisen. Of course, it helps if you are engaged in some type of work where emergencies do occur. Also, it doesn't do any harm if you casually mention to those next to you beforehand that you might have to leave early.

The fourth and most important step to take is to understand some of the problems which might arise during any speech. These are primarily related to the characteristic and mannerisms of the speakers. It is of interest to note the number of scholastic degrees attained by a speaker has nothing to do with his ability to transmit information in an attractive way. Some of the best speakers are the young who are "on the way up" and some of the worst are those who are at the pinnacle of their scholastic achievement. In the same way, being an author of several books is no guarantee of speaking ability. The only way to really know about a speaker is to hear him in action and, in addition, to know what characteristics to look for in order to evaluate his abilities.

These various traits, or in some cases idiosyncrasies, may overlap. Any one speaker may possess several of them and may use them concurrently. In this present discussion and for simplification, without meaning to offend or to ignore females, only the male gender will be used in referring to each characteristic. The following is a partial list of the most common types the listener will encounter.

THE EARLY BIRD. This speaker's most dominant peculiarity is that he begins speaking from the moment he arises from his seat and starts walking to the rostrum. If his speech is very short, he may deliver most of it with his back to the audience and long before he arrives at the microphone.

THE WHISPERER. This one talks so softly no one can hear him. For the audience, this may be a blessing in disguise.

THE SHOUTER. He is the antithesis of the whisperer. Here we find two subgroups: the MICROPHONE EATER and the BOOMING VOICE with or without the microphone.

THE BROWBEATER. He is often related to the shouter and seems determined to convince you his ideas are the only correct ones, regardless of his listener's opinions. Here, the age of the speaker often influences him. As a rule, the younger he is, the more positive he tends to be, and the older, the less sure he is that he is always correct.

THE "AH-ER." With this type, every other word is interspersed with an "ah," an "er," or an "and ah." In some respects he is just the opposite of the browbeater since he is often hesitant and seems to lack confidence. He may be very learned and factual, but fails to get his message across because the audience is often dozing during his presentations.

THE MACHINE GUN. His delivery is rapid fire and often resembles an automatic weapon. Try as you might, you cannot avoid being hit several times by his words, even if only by a few glancing blows.

THE COIN AND KEY RATTLER. With his hands in his pockets and his constant fingering of either his keys or loose coins he may be unconsciously trying to impress his listeners with his possessions. On the other hand, this mannerism is such a distraction that much of the speech content is nullified by the constant clatter.

THE CONFIDENCE MAN. He is somewhat similar to the whisperer, except he is more calculating. His confidential low tones tend to stimulate your interest and make you want to believe or buy whatever he is peddling. You need to be on guard with this fellow.

THE EXPERT. He is a modification of the confidence man. He often is not selling anything but may simply be trying to convince you of his knowledge.

THE PROPHET. Again, this one may be related to the previous two. His ploy is to predict so many different things he can hardly miss being correct in a few of them. He is often a politician.

THE ALARMER. Instead of pointing with pride, he views with alarm and uses fear tactics. He focuses on the listener's anxieties, especially about health matters, diets, pollution, radioactivity, ultraviolet rays, and electrical magnetic field radiations. He has one advantage—the anxiety he produces does keep the audience awake.

THE BACKER-UPPER. Details are his stock in trade. If perchance he forgets some minutia, he will back up through as many as five or six sidetracks to bring it out. He then will, with unerring accuracy, retrace his steps back to the original line of thought without missing a turn. With this type the audience will have no problem with insomnia.

THE EYE FIXER. Woe if this one's eyes capture yours. In case this does occur, you won't dare yawn or look at your watch. If you happen to become sleepy, you will be dead in the water with this fellow.

THE EYE WANDERER. There are several variations of this species: The FLOOR WATCHER—because of his downcast gaze he is sometimes called the BASHFUL ONE. In contrast, the CEILING GAZER, or at outdoors events, the SKY WATCHER. He's handy to have around if rain is impending or in war zones if enemy planes are in the neighborhood. Another sub subspecies is the OUT OF THE WINDOW GAZER. He gets the audience so interested in what is going on next door, they forget to listen to his words.

THE NAME DROPPER. A common and familiar type and one who tries to impress the listeners with his intimate friendships with famous people. He often makes casual references to Ike, FDR, Charlie Mayo, Bing Crosby, or other prominent people. It is wise to doubt most of the rest of what he says.

THE IN-CONCLUSION TYPE. These are the most insidious and dangerous of all. They promise they will quit and then do just the opposite. They repeatedly raise the hopes of the audience, only to dash these same hopes to bits. These fellows are usually good for at least three "in conclusions" so don't get too excited with the first one or two.

There are numerous modifications of the above types, such as: **THE TROUSER HITCHER, THE TIE STRAIGHTENER, THE SHOULDER HITCHER,** and **THE WATER DRINKER,** just to name a few. These characteristics are merely subspecies and are not really pathological per se. And now, so armed—or vaccinated, so to speak—with the above information, feel free to go to an occasional lecture. However keep your defenses at maximum strength and don't take any unnecessary risks.

Oh, Go Hang Yourself!

With the accuracy of a skilled surgeon, the bullet dissected its way through his neck from front to back skirting by the jugular vein, the carotid artery, all the important nerves, the numerous strap muscles, and the spinal cord. It emerged from below his left ear and entered the wall on the far side of the room. Fortunately the entry and exit wounds were small and of little consequence.

Lying in the hospital bed, the patient, a skinny little man, was in a stable condition. He was conscious and did not display any evidence of severe shock nor ill will toward his attacker, his wife, who sat by the bedside, weeping copiously. His present attitude was not an unusual one for him as in the past he had always manifested complete submissiveness to her and heeded her every command.

In contrast to his small, scrawny stature, his wife was grossly obese and equipped with a domineering, hot-headed, selfish, shrewish-like disposition. She ran their home with a firm though unstable hand. Her fiery temper and undisciplined nature had led her to commit many sudden impulsive acts. These acts were occasionally followed by deep remorse. Because of their diverse natures their marriage had been tumultuous, stormy, and anything but calm and loving. Because of his submissive nature, their partnership had not only survived, but also had produced thirteen children.

Very contrite following the shooting incident, the wife kept asking for reassurance that he would recover. To quote her, "I just couldn't exist without my dear husband."

He, in turn, although the victim, spent what little strength he had left trying to reassure her and to absolve her from all blame. Gradually as the days passed, he did regain some vigor and finally did recover completely.

All remained relatively calm for the next few months, at which time, at 2:00 A.M., I received a telephone call from one of the hospital emergency rooms stating this same forgiving husband had been admitted to the locked ward because of his attempted suicide.

Immediately dressing, I hurried to the hospital where I found my doleful patient locked up in a bare windowless room devoid of all furnishings except for a lone mattress lying on the cold floor. There was nothing in the room, sharp or hard, with which he could attempt to harm himself. Dressed in a thin cotton hospital gown much larger than his skinny frame required, he was, as usual, completely subdued as he crouched passively in one corner. The only external evidence of injury was the circular abrasion on his neck, the result of his attempted suicide by hanging.

When I asked him what had happened, he said he had tried to hang himself by tying a wire rope around his neck and from there to an overhead pipe. He then had jumped from the chair on which he had been standing.

I then asked him if he had been depressed or ill prior to this act. "Oh no," he replied. "We were watching a late show on TV when, for no apparent reason that I know, she started ranting and raving about one aspect of the movie. When I tried to calm her down, she yelled, 'Oh, why don't you go hang yourself?' so I went out to the garage and did so."

Fortunately a few minutes later, during a TV commercial, she went looking for him, found him hanging, and cut him down. Again, as with the gunshot episode, she was remorseful. This new event was just one more stormy chapter in their turbulent marital journey. However like the old movie sequels, there were many other chapters to follow, but they were so numerous they would fill an entire book by themselves.

However there is one which should be mentioned. Several months later, the tables were turned when late one evening she accidentally overdosed herself with sleeping pills and some hard liquor with fatal results.

Following her untimely and accidental demise, I was concerned about the welfare of the thirteen children. My worries proved to be completely unnecessary as this formerly meek, mild, milquetoast of a man emerged, both figuratively and literally, from the shadow of his overbearing mate. He had a complete personality change. Once free from her dominance, his hidden potential manifested itself. He became a real man, bought himself some clothes that fit and replaced his previous yardbird type apparel, took charge of his large brood, and even began to smile a bit.

If You're in Doubt, Don't!

It seems like we have arrived at the time and place in history when and where we can't even faint without running the risk of waking up to find we have just had a coronary bypass operation or some other major medical procedure. It used to be a woman could swoon gracefully or a man could pass out with relative impunity. This is no longer the case. What has happened to bring about this radical change?

In searching for the answer, it has become apparent there are several factors which have recently come into play. First of all, with all the advances in science and medicine, it appears we just know too much. What formerly used to be mysterious is now common knowledge. Accompanying this increased knowledge, there is a tendency to start seeing "ghosts" and to become "spooked out." In addition, doctors can now perform and to make commonplace medical and surgical procedures which just a few years ago would have been impossible. Also the lay public has acquired more "know-how" in medical matters, such as cardiopulmonary resuscitation, medications, first aid, dietary management, and rightly or wrongly the ability to diagnose and treat emotional problems.

While all of this may sound like progress, is it really? Along with the positives there are some negatives. Because of the marked increase in the number of malpractice suits, the doctors have become a bit gun-shy and have a tendency to overtest and even overtreat. In many instances the lay trainees in first aid and CPR have been so impressed by their instructors about all the possible complications which might occur in any emergency they tend to assume each case becomes the most serious and unusual. The end result is an overreaction by all concerned. This overresponse is not the fault of any one facet and is simply due to a lack of experience by a group of well-intentioned individuals.

An example of this overreaction was a situation where a woman tripped over her dog's leash and fell to the street. Sprawled half in the gutter and half on the sidewalk, she was trying to get up when a man jumped out of a nearby parked car, and cried, "Don't move."

"I'm all right. All I need is a Band-Aid for my finger."

"I'll call the paramedics. You'll need an ambulance."

"Please, let me get up," she pleaded.

In spite of her pleas, the paramedics were called and arrived shortly thereafter. Fortunately it wasn't raining so the street and gutter were dry. On arriving, the paramedics took over. These crews do a great work and save many lives. It is not their fault they are called for many minor problems. However once on the scene, they have to do whatever is indicated. In this woman's case, they listened to her when she kept insisting she was all right. Finally after a few minutes they allowed her to get out of the gutter and proceed to her car.

While overtreatment is often common when we are awake, it is sometimes even more pronounced when we are unconscious. Some of us are "vagotonics," the type who have a tendency to faint easily. Unfortunately this malady can be initiated by a wide variety of minor problems. For example, on day while eating lunch with several doctors, a doctor developed a pain in his leg. When it persisted and intensified, he decided to try to walk it off. In so doing he suddenly felt giddy and promptly fainted. Before he hit the floor he had four doctors in attendance. They immediately started rather intensive therapy.

Within seconds he had regained his consciousness and while he did appreciate their efforts in his behalf, he had one complaint. During their enthusiasm to be of assistance they had given him external cardiac massage. As a result, his chest was sore for the next several days. On the other hand, he was thankful that mouth-to-mouth resuscitation had not been used as two of his benefactors had been eating garlic for lunch.

Fortunately there are some partial solutions to the apparent paradox of good training and overtreatment. For example, if you are the rescuer be sure your patient really needs you. Check his pulse. If it is active and regular, no cardiac massage is indicated. Make sure his airway is open. If this is adequate, simply calling loudly in the patient's ear will often elicit a response. Occasionally a firm pinch of the skin ("horse bite") will revive a so-called comatose individual.

Conversely, if you happen to be the patient, it is not always possible to entirely escape overtreatment by a too-avid rescuer. This is especially true if you are in an unconscious state and unable to defend yourself.

One man partially solved this problem—at least he claims he did so. He states he had tattooed on his anterior chest wall in large black letters, IF YOU ARE IN DOUBT, DON'T!

Collectibles

It's very easy to learn a great deal about a person by the way he or she plays poker. The same can be said about their hobbies and their collectibles. There are those who collect vintage cars, and there are those who collect marital mates. Perhaps this parallelism is understandable when we consider that marriages and automobiles are alike in many respects.

First of all, while both are complicated in the make up of their many different components, their basic structures are quite simple. Though some are outwardly fancy and ostentatious and some are quite plain, there is no correlation between their external appearance and their successful performance. In both new marriages and vintage cars, we find there are those which run well without trouble, and those which are misfits and "lemons" from the very beginning. In addition some perform well at first for a short time, but fall apart early and don't last out their "warranty" period.

Both marriages and cars need frequent oiling and lubrication and even more frequent refueling. Also they are equally easily damaged unless proper precautions are taken. Once wrecked they are certainly expensive to repair and may never be restored to their original "mint" condition. Often, minor dents and differences need to be ironed out and, on occasion, a new paint job is needed. In some instances the time may arrive for a major overhaul. With both cars and mates, new models may be obtained by turning in the old one. In fact, there are those individuals who seem to prefer the secondhand, or the used types.

However like most comparative studies, in spite of the many similarities of the two, there are often major differences to be found. For instance in a car, being shiftless seems to be advantageous and denotes progress for some. Not so if this same characteristic exists in a spouse. Also, there are other major differences. Only one license is required for a marriage and this lasts for a lifetime. In contrast yearly renewals are necessary for a car. Even the car driver has to be licensed periodically. No one ever checks on the fitness of the marital partner.

Prior to the sale of a new model car, testing and retesting in every conceivable way is performed. This is not true in most prospective marriages. In fact, quite the opposite is frequently the case. Not only does "love is blind" apply, but also each partner tries to look away from and discount the defects in the other person. We hear, "Once we are married I'll get him or her to change." It is only after the formal ceremony that many marriages receive their principal testing. Some pass; others fail.

Still further differences between cars and humans can be noted. Automobiles are manufactured in factories by professional engineers and skilled workers, while humans are produced by rank amateurs who may or may not be entirely competent. Also for cars, new parts can be purchased to replace those worn or broken. For a marital mate, with the exception of cardiac transplants, some bony joint prostheses, liver replacements, corneal eye inserts, and blood vessel bypasses, this same is not true.

In spite of these many similarities, and differences, the true test of any marriage or any car is the performance on a daily basis. Does each do well in spite of the bumps and chuck holes in life's roads and journeys? How do they react to minor or major breakdowns? There never really comes a time when a car owner or a mate can relax completely and say, "We've gotten over this or that phase. Now we can sit back and rest as everything will continue to go smoothly from now on."

Someone once asked a senior citizen if he believed in "love at first sight."

His reply, "Certainly I do, but what is more important is believing in 'love at second sight' after many years together. That 'second sight love' is the one that has survived the test of toil, turmoil, and time."

We have learned from history that the fall of the Roman Empire was due to inward decay and corruption. In addition, we have read that the old one-horse shay finally just fell apart from lack of good care and proper replacement of its various parts. From personal observation, we all know that most old cars eventually just rust away.

From the above examples, I say, "Let the car buffs collect their vintage automobiles like the 1913 Model-T's or the 1955 Thunderbirds. For me, I'm content with my first and only marital mate who gets better each year after year. I can say, with emphasis, that I don't have any desire to turn her in for a new 'shiftless' prototype."

Sounds a Bit Fishy

Recently, when I was asked to tell some fish stories at a banquet, I was flattered but also puzzled. As I told the asker, "There are probably a dozen others who will be there who know much more than I about this subject. All I know is that I like seafood, have a son-in-law who is an avid fisherman, and a grandson who is studying for his doctorate in fisheries. Otherwise, I'm quite ignorant about the subject."

His reply, "You are exactly what we want. Someone who doesn't know anything and who will be unbiased. Your main function at the banquet will be to keep the audience quiet and under control while the tables are being cleared. You're sort of an ice breaker before the main speaker. Calm them down, but don't put them to sleep." At the time, I wasn't sure which was better—biased knowledge or unbiased ignorance.

Afterwards I realized the asker was right—many true fishermen, not all, have a tendency to exaggerate about the size of their catch and especially the size of the ones that got away. Some of these anglers even have special rulers for their measurements. These rulers are accurate on one side, but have smaller inches on the other side. Because of this tendency to magnify the size of their catches, the old saying, "It sounds a bit fishy" originated. The majority of fishermen tell it like it really is. Here are a few examples of true fish tales.

A retired Internal Revenue Service agent was swimming in the ocean off the coast of one of the Hawaiian Islands when he felt a large object brush against one thigh. When he kicked at the intruder, he felt a sharp pain in his leg. At this same moment, he couldn't help but wonder what his place was in the ocean's food chain. Finally, after making his way to land and after getting his lacerated leg repaired, he revealed that some IRS men do have a sense of humor when he said, "It's probably the only time a shark has tried to get blood out of an income tax agent."

In another instance, an only son who had spent many years getting his doctorate degree in fisheries and whose mother had worked hard to help him during this period, decided he wanted to show his appreciation to her. Consequently, he sent her a bottle of champagne and a jar of caviar. After a few weeks when he hadn't heard from her, he called to make sure the presents had been delivered. "Mother, did my presents to you arrive?"

"Oh, yes they did, son. I haven't called to thank you because I found the cider had turned, and someone left the blueberries too close to some fish."

Several years ago two of our church members went fishing for marlin off the Kona Coast of the island of Hawaii. One of them was successful and after returning to the dock had his picture taken alongside his catch. As marlin are not considered a tasty morsel he was not sure what to do with his prize. Two native boys asked him if he wanted them to get rid of it and, if so, they would haul it away for a reasonable fee. This was agreed to.

The other man had not been as fortunate in his catch, but had caught two sizable fish with which he was not familiar. They were too big to easily transport so he asked the boys if they would take them away. Again, for a fee, they said they would. Later on he discovered he had caught two large-sized mahi mahi. The native boys had had a very profitable day, collecting two fees and selling the mahi mahi to the nearby restaurant and the marlin to the cat food factory.

Fishing in warm water is one thing, but ice fishing is something else again. My son-in-law and his student son both enjoy this latter sport. The term "sport" is used very loosely here. One of the problems in ice fishing is the labor of boring a hole through the ice. This is an arduous task if the ice is very thick, so it was a big event when they bought a power auger. This accomplished the task in short order.

In ice fishing only a rather short pole is used, instead of the longer ones ordinarily used for conventional fishing. One day as they were huddled by their hole trying to keep warm, suddenly their entire gear disappeared into the hole. This loss presented a unique problem. Undaunted, they took their new auger and bored several new holes around the circumference of their fishing site. By lowering a hook and line into each of the new holes they were able to hook onto their original gear and recover it along with a large fish, much larger than the ordinary ones found in ice fishing.

Years ago, an experienced fisherman told me, "From an economic standpoint, never try to calculate how much the fish you catch yourself costs per pound. If you do so, you will find you would have been better off to have stopped by the local fish market."

When I was a high school student I worked part-time in a hardware store. Here there were countless items with which I was not familiar. Many times I would be completely stumped by the customer's requests. In most instances one of the more experienced clerks would rescue me. However one day a man wanted a fishing fly. These were foreign to me, but as no other clerks were available, I steered the fisherman to the glass-covered counter. He was in doubt about what he wanted, as was I. When I peered through the glass top I spied one fly named "Royal Coachman." This name had a nice, somewhat regal ring to it, so I brought it out. He seemed to be pleased with it, bought it, and departed.

Several days later when another man wanted fishing flies, with considerably more confidence, I led him to the proper counter, brought forth a "Royal Coachman" and said, "This is a popular fly." He bought it and departed.

Again, as it was at the peak of a busy fishing season, another man asked for fishing flies. By now, I was practically an expert in this field so when I showed him the "Royal Coachman" I was able to say with authority, "We are selling many of these lately."

I will have to confess that my conscience did bother me for several years about this subterfuge. However at a later time I learned the "Royal Coachman" was considered to be an excellent fly by many experienced fishermen.

I have barely scratched the surface of fish stories. To really learn more it would pay to go where fishermen gather together to swap fish tales. At these meetings there is no limit to the extent of their fabrications. It is there that an outsider can say, with conviction, "It sure sounds a bit fishy to me."

The Causes and Cures of Some Weighty Problems

One of the most rationalized problems of mankind is that of obesity. For those so afflicted, excuses abound. Overlooked in the majority of cases is the basic root cause. Let us explore a few of the excuses used to explain this malady.

One commonly heard: "Doctor, your scales always weigh too much." Never is it said, "Your scales weigh too little."

The doctor having heard this statement many times is immune to the criticism. He knows his scales have been checked and rechecked and are accurate. In addition, he has heard the many other excuses used by those complaining and is somewhat immune to their protestations. While occasionally some are bonafide, many are a bit ludicrous. Amongst the latter are such reasons as:

"My weight is inherited, it's in my genes. All of our family are obese." Ignored are the family's eating habits, exercise patterns, and general life style.

"I gained this month because of my cousin's birthday party." (The reader can substitute Easter, Christmas, anniversaries, etc., for the word "birthday.")

"You know how it is at Thanksgiving time. Everyone eats too much. I'll admit that I stuffed myself. I thought I would die."

"I know I should lose weight. I've promised myself as soon as Easter is over, I'm going on a diet." Incidentally, at the time Easter was six weeks away.

One woman gave herself away when she said, "I got so interested in a crime series on TV last week that on some days I didn't eat a thing between lunch and dinner."

Those who overeat have a tendency to flock together, sort of like alcoholics—they like company in their indulgences. Conversely they tend to conspire against each other. Whenever there is a meeting, no matter what time of day or evening, food is always present—the richer the better. At 10:00 A.M., even though most have just finished breakfast a short time prior, out comes coffee, tea, cookies, and nuts. For luncheons, the sky is the limit. Whipped cream abounds. Each hostess seems to try to outdo the others in piling on the calories.

One group which should be excused from the general classification of the overweight is the young mothers, especially those who are in the stay-at-home category. To a large extent, their days are occupied in food shopping, preparation, feeding of small children, and cleaning up after meal time. Many of them have been trained from early childhood to "clean up your plate." As a result when their young ones leave uneaten food, mother tends to finish off what is left.

Lest the reader feel this missive is somewhat slanted as far as gender is concerned, it should be mentioned that men have just as much trouble as women with weighty problems. With the exception of backwoods loggers, cross-country runners, professional athletes, and other occupations which require much physical activity, most men eat much too much. There is a tendency to blame outside factors and to give rather lame excuses for their excess weight. Many sedentary businessmen will often eat enough at lunch time to fortify someone engaged in strenuous physical work. Then by supper time, these same individuals will be ready for a "substantial dinner." Also, many of the restaurants encourage this overeating by serving too large portions.

One factor often ignored completely is the number of calories contained in alcoholic beverages. These can add up rapidly. One man who said he had only a "couple of beers a day" was required to forgo all alcohol because of a prostatitis. During the next ten days he lost twelve pounds without any other change in his diet.

Another man said, "All I had for lunch was a small steak, a few French fries, a cup of chowder, and a dish of ice cream." Of course all of these were loaded with cholesterol and calories.

There is one more tendency that should be mentioned. The heavy individual tends to remember the one meal where he cut down, even though it occurred during the previous week. He then asks, "Do you want to know what I had for breakfast this morning?" In contrast, the thin person remembers the one time he ate a big meal and says, "Oh, I always eat a lot."

Up until this point, we have discussed only the causes of obesity. What about the cures? While the causes of weighty problems are multiple, the solution is very simple, so simple it is usually overlooked completely. It consists of taking in only as much as is used. Sort of like filling the gas tank of your car. If you drive a lot, or drive a "gas guzzler" you will have to put more in the tank than if you drive an "economy" model. In either case, just don't overfill the tank.

"You Gotta Know the Territory"

Getting "from here to there" can present big problems, especially if you don't know the territory. Looked at in another way, it can also be very exciting and can present a chance to learn about others when asking them for directions.

The story is told of a traveling salesman who didn't know the territory. One day, while on a back country road, he took a wrong turn and ended up at an isolated farm house. The farmer happened to be sitting on the fence rail chewing a long piece of grass. When the salesman asked him how to get back to the main road, the farmer had trouble giving a good answer. Finally, the salesman said, "You don't seem to know much, do you?"

"Wah-ll, mabbe yur right, but at least I ain't lost."

A touring couple stopped in a small roadside village which consisted of a gas station, a grocery store, post office, and a small restaurant, all located on the one main street. The whole settlement was not much more than a wide spot on the highway. After getting some gas, plus some directions from one of the "locals," the woman tourist remarked, "I've often wondered what it would be like to live out in the countryside."

The "local" replied, "I wouldn't know. I've lived in this here city all of my life."

For many of us, when asking for directions from complete strangers, we have to accept what they say based largely on our faith in their honesty and their knowledge. The outward physical characteristics of the individual are very apparent: the gender, the approximate age, and the general appearance. What is unknown prior to the first questions asked is what goes on in their brain, or what are his or her primary interests? Once they begin to speak, several of their inner make ups begin to surface. It usually takes only a short time to get a fairly accurate assessment of the mental processes present. A word of caution is necessary before making a final conclusion about any one individual—it is wise to take into account the differences in the world's various cultures and national customs. These factors do have a marked effect on the response of the person being questioned. For example, those of some backgrounds are reticent; others, outgoing. Some are suspicious; others, trusting and naive. Some are sad, and others happy. There is a tendency for Italians to be emotional and warm hearted. The Scandinavians often seem outwardly cool and reserved. The English are for the most part prim and proper. The Irish appear to be at the ready for a laugh and a good joke.

The Scottish people, in spite of some popular misconceptions about their frugality, are often exactly the opposite. To illustrate, a few years ago while traveling in the British Isles, we had several examples of their generous characteristics. One day, Margaret asked a large, pleasant-looking constable, "Could you tell us how to get to the Sterling Castle?"

"Why I certainly can, lass." With this, he went out of his way to get us headed in the right direction. On another occasion when we stopped at a garage for guidance, the mechanic crawled out from under the car he was repairing and seemed only too happy to give us specific directions. Once, when we stopped a street vendor to buy a few postcards, the man not only furnished the stamps, but also insisted on putting them on the cards himself.

It should be mentioned it is often a dangerous practice to make too many generalizations about cultural or racial characteristics as there are bound to be many exceptions. However when discussing the differences found in individuals we can safely arrive at some fairly accurate conclusions. I will try to illustrate these truths and variations in the following paragraphs.

An average adult housewife, when asked for directions, will usually answer in somewhat this way: "Just go straight ahead until you see the first department store, turn right and drive past the large fruit stand, then make a left turn at the Jiffy Market."

Her husband will probably say, "Go to the hardware store, make a right, then straight ahead until you pass the ballfield, then left at the Texaco gas station."

Their ten-year-old son will answer as follows: "Go to the Toys R Us, turn right past the Candy Kitchen, then turn left at the Baskin Robbins."

His older brother's reply: "Just past the Sports Shop take a right, then a block past the gym make a left, then keep going until you see the girl's school."

The local minister's directions: "Keep going until you reach the Presbyterian Church, turn right and drive until you see the Catholic Church's steeple, then left and head for the Methodist Seminary."

The car buff will direct you as follows: "Turn right at the Ford agency, then left at the auto parts store, and then straight ahead until you pass the body repair shop."

The attorney will direct you past the county courthouse, to a block this side of the federal building, and then straight ahead until you reach the county jail.

Of course, the local doctor will guide you past the drug store, the first aid station, and the hospital.

Likewise, the farmer will send you by the feed store, the tractor sales agency, and the large open pasture.

Boston's winding streets can be confusing even to the natives. To a stranger, they present a nearly unsolvable maze. One of the briefest sets of directions was given by a big burly Boston policeman. When he was asked for directions to the airport, he looked at the questioner, listened to his western accent, and then said, "Follow me." By the time they had completed the complex maneuvers required and had arrived at the airport it was easy to understand why the policeman had not attempted to give verbal directions.

It has been said one of the characteristics of the male gender is his unwillingness to ask anyone for guidance, feeling that doing so reflects on his male prowess; he can find the right way by himself. Whether this is a true or false assessment is open to question.

However, one thing is certain. There does come a time when it is necessary for even the most stubborn person to consult with someone who is qualified to give the proper answers. Also, it is well to remember when we ask for or in turn are asked for information on how to get from "here to there," before giving an answer, the guiding one should harken to the song from the musical comedy *The Music Man* which says, "YOU GOTTA KNOW THE TERRITORY."

The Sampler

Sandy loved to take medicines, especially if they were free. He was a big husky Scotchman who could wrestle a bear without much effort. In spite of his apparent good health, he had a multitude of physical complaints for which he made frequent visits to the doctor. It became apparent early that he was not content with advice only and always expected a prescription of some tangible medication. During the majority of his examinations no medication was indicated. In fact on one occasion the doctor deliberately didn't give him anything to take at home. A short time later Sandy called to tell him he must have forgotten to write a prescription.

Because of this penchant, as well as because of Sandy's rather precarious financial condition, the doctor began to give him samples of various medications. In most instances no therapy was indicated so the doctor would give him a vitamin preparation. Sandy's favorite was a liquid vitamin B in a tasty wine. This was a somewhat innocuous mix which was not of much help, but certainly was not harmful.

On one of the visits the doctor was called to the telephone before he had a chance to give Sandy a sample. After the call he found Sandy had already left. Surprisingly there was no follow-up phone call from him about a sample.

When the doctor asked the next patient for a urine specimen he said, "I brought one from home in a vitamin B sample bottle and gave it to the office nurse." A search failed to find the specimen, so the patient left another.

A couple of weeks later, Sandy returned for a follow-up exam. As he was about to leave, the doctor handed him another sample of his favorite vitamin B preparation. This he refused saying, "I guess I won't need any more of that, doctor. The company must have changed their formula. The last bottle was sitting on the counter when you went to answer the phone so I took it. It didn't taste anything like the previous ones and was really salty."

The mystery of the missing specimen was solved. Also lost was some of Sandy's desire for free samples.

The Pot That Called the Kettle Black

"Did you notice the thumbs of that woman who was just in your office?"

"I guess I was so busy taking care of her other problems I didn't pay much attention to her thumbs. Was there something wrong with them?"

"They were so odd looking, especially at the ends."

The questioner was an attractive young woman, but her queries aroused my curiosity. As soon as I could gracefully do so and without being obvious, I glanced at her thumbs. Talk about odd looking! The end segments resembled ping-pong paddles. Each one was flat, broad, and extended laterally well beyond the rest of the digit. It was difficult for me to tell whether she was so used to them that normal-looking thumbs appeared odd to her or, more likely, she was so conscious and possibly ashamed of them that she downgraded these same parts in others.

As no one of us is perfect physically or mentally, and in many instances we are conscious of our own defects, we have a tendency to try to compensate for these deficiencies. One common mechanism is transference. In this process, we mentally move our real or imaginary problems to someone else. For example, a woman who had severe osteoporosis with a partial collapse of several of her vertebral bodies resulting in a markedly stooped posture, said, "Look at Mrs. So-and-So. Isn't her posture terrible?" In truth, while Mrs. So-and-So's posture wasn't good, it was better than that of the speaker.

In other situations, individuals who have a tendency to talk constantly become very impatient with others who don't allow them (the talkers) a chance to speak.

Impatience and intolerance are two of our most common defects. One judge has a plaque in front of him as he sits at his bench in court. This reads, GIVE ME TOLERANCE AND GIVE ME PATIENCE BUT MAKE IT FAST. Still another man said, "There are two things I can't stand. One is waiting in line at the grocery check stand. The other, impatient people."

Many of our imperfections are not of our own doing and cannot be helped. These, in turn, require understanding by us and tolerance of the same problems when they exist in others. The defects often call for compensatory behavior by us in order to make the best of adverse situations. There are two possible approaches, namely advance or retreat. It is interesting to note that approximately one-half of our medical school class was composed of men and women who had experienced physical problems themselves or in one of their family members. One student who had lost one of his children to an illness changed from his previous legal career in order to study medicine so he could help to prevent a similar situation in some other family.

Compensatory mechanisms often have a humorous side. Have you ever noticed how many men who have become prematurely partially bald tend to let what little hair does remain on top to grow inordinately long? Sometimes they even wear what's left in a pony tail, or they may grow long sideburns, beards, or moustaches.

We all, either consciously or otherwise, make some adjustments in our habits and life styles. Often, small men drive large cars, and occasionally large men drive small ones. Short men tend to stand as tall as possible, while very tall men often stoop over, perhaps to try to appear shorter or maybe to hear better what the shorter ones are saying.

Overcompensation is common when a person lacks complete knowledge about a product or subject. Someone once said that one road to success as a sales person is to be somewhat ignorant of all the facts, but to have an enthusiastic approach. It is not to be assumed this lack implies a low IQ. In fact, the individuals may be quite knowledgeable in some entirely different field. Their positive attitude allows them to speak without any doubts or hesitation with authority about the merits of the subject or product in question, be it alfalfa tablets, medical treatments, or a particular make of automobile. Conversely, if he or she happens to be in opposition to some belief or product, the exact opposite is true, and in their minds leaves no doubt about the deleterious effects of the subject at hand, such as table salt, sunshine, sugar, or any one of a number of other products.

On the flip side, very often the person who has made an in-depth study of a product or subject may have found that some doubts regarding its efficiency or its harmful effects may have surfaced. He or she may then become cautious and have some reasonable hesitancy about his conclusions. This, in turn, may inhibit him from making any dogmatic statements until all the evidence is complied, proven beyond a doubt, and then duplicated at a later time. This, of course, is the basis for all true scientific research.

Speaking of research, there are two types: the one where the data dictates the final conclusions; the other, where the researcher has a preconceived idea and then tries to prove this by his experiments. Obviously, the former is the true one. The real scientist is never afraid to say, "I don't know."

Let us return to the original theme of this missive which is the differences that exist in the physical, mental, and the spiritual make up of each of us from our fellow man. One of the keys to understanding and solving the problems which may arise because of these differences is to develop a tolerance for the other person's beliefs and actions; to give him or her the benefit of the doubt when a controversy arises. Don't be like the lady with the odd-looking thumbs or like the proverbial, insensitive POT THAT CALLED THE KETTLE BLACK.

Retrospective Vision

If I had only sold my buggy whip company stock when it was at its peak and then bought some shares in Microsoft when those two young whippersnappers started their company, I'd be in good shape financially today. If I had had enough sense to practice the piano when I was young, I'd now be able to play. If I had looked twice at the crossroads, I wouldn't be lying here in this hospital bed strung up and hanging like a butcher shop turkey. Of course, I'm like most everyone else whose retrospective vision is always 20/20. It is easy from our present position in time to see what and how we should have acted in bygone days. It's like the ninety-five-year-old man who said, "If I had known I was going to live this long, I would have taken better care of myself."

Nineteen ninety-five was the fiftieth anniversary of the first use of the A-bomb and we, as a country, are in the throes of retrospection and self-flagellation over its use. At this time, there are certain groups clamoring about the inhumanity of its use at Hiroshima and Nagasaki. As terrible as the bomb was in its destructive power, and as well meaning as these groups might happen to be, it is doubtful the personnel of the groups contains many of the American armed forces veterans who were scheduled to be in the Japanese homeland invading waves.

One of the cries of today's protestors is so many innocent civilians were the victims. As horrible as this was, we don't hear them cry about the fact more innocent civilians were killed in the taking of Okinawa than were killed at Hiroshima. It's just that in the latter instance, the casualties occurred in such a sudden and spectacular manner. When considered realistically, all war is horrible and no one, civilian or military, is exempt from harm.

These same retrospective protestors also seem to conveniently forget about the vast number of casualties which would have occurred on both the American and Japanese sides of the armed forces, as well as the civilians lost if an invasion of the Japanese Islands had taken place. Also forgotten is the A-bomb's shock effect. Its devastation was so great and so sudden even the most rabid Japanese war lord knew the "jig was up" and it was time to quit.

Forgotten too are what would have happened to all of us had we lost World War II. As one so aptly said, "If it were not for all the many millions who sacrificed and fought the Axis, we would all now be eating sauerkraut with chopsticks."

To a lesser extent, the retrospectors use the internment of the Japanese in the United States at the beginning of World War II as an example of man's inhumanity to man. While it is true there were many injustices performed in that relocation procedure, most of the present criticism seems to originate from the "Johnny come lately" group who were not present at that time. They were not there and didn't experience the anxieties and tensions of those days. From their present position today it is easy to look back and say how it should have been done. In other words, their retrospective vision is 20/20.

They didn't experience the fear of impending invasion of our mainland. Rumors abounded the Japanese troops had landed in Alaska and were headed for the lower forty-eight states. The protestors were not aware of the presence of spies in our cities. They didn't know about those who took pictures of our coastal port facilities and those who sent secret radio messages of our troop and ship movements.

Who of us at that time was all knowing and could decide who of the locals were loyal citizens and who were enemies? One man's photography hobby served as a cover for his spying on our military and naval activities. Actually he was a high-ranking Japanese naval officer but appeared to be just an average American until shortly before the Pearl Harbor bombing when he disappeared from our local scene and returned to Japan. It is now easy to identify those who were loyal and who were not.

And so before we criticize the actions of those who have made important decisions in the past, let us review our own actions. Did we always do exactly the right thing, say the right words, and always make the correct turn in our many journeys through life?

Let us learn not only from our own, but also from other's mistakes and be more tolerant in our retrospective vision.

Life's Phases and Ages

A famous man was once asked what he would choose to be if he were given the chance to live his life over again. His answer: "A perpetual baby. Who else gets such care and privileges and has such a complete lack of responsibility?"

While said in jest, there is an element of truth and reason in his answer. However to be completely true, the infant would have to be able to choose the proper parents, the quality of care, food, and surroundings.

At one time or another, many of us have had the desire to return to an earlier age or to have the chance to live over some previous phase of our life. We commonly hear the statement, "If I could do it again, I would be an engineer, lawyer, musician, or I would do it in such and such a manner." This statement would then be followed by an explanation as to why these same objectives were not achieved on the first trip through life.

This type of retrospective and wishful thinking brings up some interesting questions. Would we really live our lives differently if we had a second chance? In a different vein, what is the most desirable age? Is there such a thing as the best time of life?

While a good case can be made for each different phase of life, no one time is exclusively good nor, on the other hand, entirely bad. The individuals who wish to return to their younger years, either as a child, teenager, or young adult are deluding themselves. One of the characteristics of the mind is its ability to suppress the negative and the unpleasant. This is a protective mechanism. It not only makes possible the emphasis of the positive and best features of the past, but also deemphasizes the negative and the unpleasant experiences.

The man who said he wanted to be a permanent baby was overemphasizing what he pictured as the happy gurgling experiences of infancy; the periods without responsibilities, work load, stress, or even ambition. Those who desire to return to the "teens" or "twenties" tend to remember the carefree happy times, the nearly unlimited energy, and the voracious appetites, in many cases without any concurrent weight gain. These stages were, for the most part, wonderful years but did have a few problems which have now been forgotten.

Mother's "home cooking" and the "old swimming hole" are good examples of recalling the good. While Mother's cooking was undoubtedly good, much of its aura originated in the healthy appetite of the growing, very active body of the young child. The old swimming hole, if viewed again, would look rather small, be quite cold, and perhaps even a bit muddy. Certainly not to be compared with the warm, sparkling, clear, modern swimming pool of today.

A young army bride, after her wedding, was following her husband as he was moved from one post to another during World War II. The farther she got from her small hometown on the Kansas plains, the more glamorous it became in her mind. She kept telling her husband about all its desirable features. Finally the chance to revisit this so remembered "Utopia" came. Once there, the realities of the small village were somewhat of a shock to the young lady. So much so she rarely mentioned the area again.

In the marital field, it has been said if one loses a spouse and is contemplating remarrying, it is better to marry a divorcee than a widow as in the latter case, there are many hazards. Once, during a church service, the minister asked the congregation, "If there is anyone in the sanctuary who has never committed a sin, please stand." When one lone man rose from his pew, the minister asked, "Do you mean to imply that you have never sinned or made a grievous mistake?"

"Oh, no sir. I've done my share of both. I'm simply here in place of my wife's long since departed first husband."

Often adults say, "I wish I could play the piano well." Sometimes they will turn to their parents and accusingly remark, "You should have made me practice." They try to shift the blame and to overlook the long hours required at the keyboard, when in reality during those same hours they would have preferred being at the shopping mall, or out in the sunshine playing baseball with their pals. From their present position, their retrospective 20/20 vision is completely accurate.

Early adulthood and middle age are not only periods of accomplishment, but also are periods of much joy. Raising a family has many rewards and pleasures. Any problems which do arise are more than compensated for by the positives of seeing the children develop into well-adjusted adults.

Later middle age and old age, while dreaded beforehand by some, do have many compensations. Ideally, with true maturity comes a peace of mind and a sense of tranquility often lacking in the earlier years. Certain physical assets, such as youthful beauty, may change and fade. However the accompanying decreased visual acuity makes these changes less apparent. The aching joints in the morning help to make them appreciate any that don't ache in the afternoon. The loss of physical prowess is somewhat compensated for by a change in the mental attitude regarding the goals. Winning becomes secondary to the pleasures of the game.

As free time becomes more available in the later years, many of our desires and hobbies previously neglected because of the rush of life may become feasible. Those who really want to play the piano, paint a picture, or write a book may now begin.

And so when all the various aspects of the different phases of life are considered, it seems there is one simple answer to leading a full and productive life. In the final analysis there is no one period which has all the advantages and none of the disadvantages. We should all be thankful for the chance to go through life the first time and to enjoy and utilize each age to its fullest. It might be wise, in times of difficulty, to adopt a modified Pollyanna approach for these parts of the trip.